The Social Circulation of Poetry in the Mid-Northern Song

SUNY series in
Chinese Philosophy and Culture

Edited by Roger T. Ames

The Social Circulation of Poetry in the Mid-Northern Song

Emotional Energy and Literati Self-Cultivation

Colin S. C. Hawes

State University of New York Press

Published by
State University of New York Press, Albany

For information, address State University of New York Press,
194 Washington Avenue, Suite 305, Albany, NY 12210-2365

Production by Judith Block
Marketing by Anne M. Valentine

Library of Congress Cataloging-in-Publication Data

Hawes, Colin S. C.

The social circulation of poetry in the mid-Northern Song : emotional energy and literati self-cultivation / Colin S. C. Hawes.

p. cm.

Includes bibliographical references and index.

ISBN 0-7914-6471-7 (alk. paper)—0-7914-6472-5 (pbk. : alk. paper)

1. Chinese poetry—Song dynasty, 960–1279—History and criticism. 2. Social interaction—Poetry. 3. Friendship—Poetry. I. Title.

PL2323.H39 2005
895.1′1093552—dc22

2004018835

10 9 8 7 6 5 4 3 2 1

To Shuyu,
M. and D.

Contents

Acknowledgments

My fascination with Chinese literature and culture began over twenty years ago, leafing through translations of Chinese poems and religious and philosophical texts by Arthur Waley, A. C. Graham, and other early and great sinologists. My first serious studies took place at Durham University in England, and I am especially grateful to Don Starr, Keith Pratt, Vicky Chu, and Caroline Mason for helping me set out on the long road of learning Chinese. Two years in Wuhan, China, followed, where I particularly appreciated Classical Chinese tutorials with Professor Dai Zijie, a teacher and calligrapher of the old school. I began copying down and commenting on Classical Chinese poems in Wuhan to improve my handwriting, and continued the habit during five years of graduate study at the University of British Columbia. There, Jerry Schmidt greatly inspired me with his enthusiasm for Song poetry, and I suddenly discovered that Chinese poems could be witty and humorous as well as profound, beautiful, and refined. At UBC, Michael Duke and Dan Overmyer honed my research skills and broadened my knowledge of traditional and contemporary Chinese culture. I began writing this book after crossing the Rockies to teach at the University of Alberta, and I am grateful to Eva Neumaier and Kenneth Norrie for strongly supporting my research and approving several research grants that enabled me to collect essential materials in China. I also benefited from the constant assistance of librarians at UBC and Alberta, especially Louis Chor and Yim Tse. And over the last three years, I received valuable input and suggestions for developing my ideas and improving my writing style from a number of scholars, including

James Hargett, Alice Cheang, Stephen Owen, Patricia Ebrey, William H. Nienhauser, Jonathan Chaves, Joanna Handlin Smith, Han Jingqun, and Alfreda Murck, not to mention the anonymous expert readers of SUNY Press. Without their collective help, this book would be sorely lacking in footnotes and far less scholarly in tone. Chapter Two first appeared in an article, "Meaning Beyond Words: Games and Poems in the Northern Song," *Harvard Journal of Asiatic Studies* 60.2 (Dec. 2000): 355–83, and is reprinted here with permission of the editors. Finally, on a more personal note, I wish to thank my parents for giving moral and sometimes material support throughout my lengthy and doubtless often mystifying educational quest. But my deepest gratitude is to my wife Shuyu, who has shared with me all the joys and troubles of life and work over the past decade, and more recently the challenges and pleasures of raising our son Owen. If anyone deserves a book dedication and plenty of other more valuable gifts, it is she.

Introduction: Poetry and Energy Circulation

This study had its germination in a curious fact. Reading through the titles in virtually any Song poet's collected works, one cannot help noticing the vast numbers of compositions directly addressed to other people. To provide some representative statistics, 867 poems (*shi*) survive in the collected works of Ouyang Xiu (1007–1072), the renowned Song statesman and writer. Among these, the titles of 557 clearly state they are addressed to, or exchanged with, a friend or acquaintance; in other words, almost two thirds of his poems. And this is a conservative estimate. The proportion rises to about three quarters if we also include poems that reveal their social function in the main body of the work, and poems Ouyang mentions in his letters as having been sent to friends.[1] As for Ouyang's contemporary, Mei Yaochen (1002–1060), the proportions are even higher, especially for his mature works. Taking all the poems in the standard modern edition of Mei's works into account, over twenty-four hundred of his approximately twenty-nine hundred poems, or 83 percent, are directly addressed to other people in their titles. Counting only the 586 poems that survive from the last four years of Mei's life, 564 or over 96 percent, are addressed directly to other people.[2]

Among the collections of other major Northern Song poets, the proportion of poems addressed to friends and acquaintances remains similarly high, whether we examine Ouyang's and Mei's contemporaries, such as Su Shunqin (1008–1048), or more famous poets of the succeeding generation, such as Su Shi (1037–1101) and Huang Tingjian (1045–1105).

Beside the two most common genres in these collections: poems to see off a friend, and poems matching the rhymes of a friend's work, numerous other poetic exchanges appear. There are poems to express gratitude for gifts, commemorate banquets and tea ceremonies, console bereaved friends, to give advice and moral instruction to students, to communicate with friends and family when living apart, and to criticize government policies—the list of social functions goes on and on.

Previous scholars note, in passing, the social nature of Northern Song poetry—and Chinese poetry as a whole—with its huge number of exchanged poems and occasional verses. However, most dismiss such social poetry as trivial unless it contains direct or disguised sociopolitical criticism. Moreover, scholars generally focus on the style and content of the poems rather than their functions, preferring serious poetry that deals with issues of clear public importance or momentous personal crises, and neglecting poems that seem to deal merely with trivial topics in a humorous manner.[3]

Such a focus on poetic content can lead to a distorted view of the achievements of Northern Song poetry. After putting aside the more lighthearted, occasional poetry of the period, many modern scholars conclude that Song poetry is generally dry and hard—in other words, plain in style and discursive in content, with few redeeming aesthetic features.[4] Certainly, the diction of most Northern Song poets is plain when compared with Tang poets like Du Fu (712–772) and Li Shangyin (c. 812–c. 858), yet they more than make up for this plainness with their wit, humor, caricature, structural ingenuity, and other aesthetic attractions.[5] However, in order to spot these features, one must include a broader range of poems than those that deal simply with politics and the suffering of the common people, or anguished reflections on exile to remote corners of the empire.

More significantly, dismissing the great majority of Northern Song poems as occasional verse begs the question as to why so few poems actually dealt with serious social and political issues. Answering this question is especially important in the case of Song poets, because many claim that writing should promote the Moral Way (*dao*) of Confucius. Yet the content of their poetry is often flippant and amoral. Scholars deal with this apparent contradiction in one of two ways. Some argue that Song literati are hypocritical, promoting strict Confucian values in their public prose, yet indulging in unrestrained and licentious behavior in private, a lifestyle that is reflected in their poetry.[6] Alternatively, others argue that Song literati considered poetry to be less effective than prose for expressing their deepest thoughts about society and politics. Hence, apart from a few poems in which they experiment with social and political criticism, they composed the rest of their poetry purely for entertainment and to fulfill polite social obligations. Therefore, it is no surprise that their poetry deals with trivial issues, and we should not expect too much from it in terms of literary value.[7]

In this study, the paradox is resolved in a different way. I will argue that, unlike some of their later critics, Mid-Northern Song poets saw no contradiction between composing and exchanging humorous poetry on minor topics and promoting Confucian morality. Ouyang Xiu, for instance, drew a direct parallel between some of his own and his contemporaries' most lighthearted, witty compositions and the canonical Confucian text, the *Classic of Poetry*. Ouyang even declares that Superior People (*jun zi*) should compose poems with crude, base, or comical subject matter, as long as there is a justifiable reason for doing so.[8]

I argue that the main justification for writing poems in this period was not so much to spread Confucian moral principles in their content, as to develop and sustain human relationships through the regular exchange of poems with friends and acquaintances. Thus, as long as their poem exchanges fostered harmonious social interaction—in itself a central Confucian virtue—Northern Song poets saw no reason to preach narrowly about social or political issues in their poems. In fact, since their poetry writing was frequently a group activity that occurred at informal gatherings and parties, witty and humorous verse was more appropriate for keeping the peace at such occasions than controversial political critique or fervent social activism.

In order to support this argument about the social nature of poetry, I focus on the functions of poems in Northern Song society rather than simply on their content, although once the function is clarified, one can often appreciate the content more deeply. I do not rashly attempt to cover the whole Northern Song period, but concentrate on the *shi* poetry of two major figures from the Mid-Northern Song, Ouyang Xiu and Mei Yaochen, who are generally considered the first poets to develop a distinctive Song style.[9]

Unlike poets of the succeeding generation, the poetry of Ouyang and Mei does not receive much attention from scholars beyond a handful of often translated pieces. Virtually nothing has been written on the poetry of Mei Yaochen in English since Chaves' groundbreaking study in 1976. Ronald Egan's book on Ouyang Xiu devotes only one chapter to *shi* poetry.[10] As a result, Western readers may be unaware of the important influence of these two poets on the development of a distinctive and entertaining Northern Song poetic style. More importantly, due to the different selection criteria of previous scholars, readers may have missed out on the chance to read many of these poets' most humorous and skillfully structured works. My conclusions also shed new light on the poetry of subsequent generations, especially the circle surrounding Su Shi and Huang Tingjian, albeit with some contrasts.

A common theme that runs throughout this study is that Mid-Northern Song literati used poetry primarily as a means of circulating positive emotional energy. We see this clearly in claims that writing poetry could restore balance to one's emotions, and even cure physical ailments through the release of tension or energy (*qi*) that had become blocked within one's mind and body. Yet, the circulation of emotional energy occurs not only within the individual but between different people as well. So in other chapters this organic metaphor is extended beyond the confines of the individual poet's mind-body. In a strictly regulated and hierarchical society like traditional China, poetry was a crucial vehicle enabling both friends and strangers to express their feelings and intentions to one another, thereby circulating their emotional energy whilst remaining within the bounds of propriety. Hence, just as poetry benefits the mental and physical health of individuals by allowing them to release pent-up emotional tension, so in theory, it benefits the health of society by encouraging harmonious interaction between members of different social groups.

Northern Song poets like Ouyang Xiu and Mei Yaochen saw this positive circulation of emotional energy in society as the most important function of poetry—one which coincided with their Confucian values and simultaneously allowed them to compose witty and entertaining verse. Whether the prevalence of poetic exchanges indeed led to social harmony or added to the rampant political factionalism of the later Northern Song period is an interesting, perhaps unanswerable, question.

This book is structured around six major functions of Mid-Northern Song poetry. In the first chapter, I challenge the idea that a central aim of Song poets was political and social criticism. I argue that modern Chinese scholars in particular overemphasize this function in Northern Song poetry, especially with regard to the overt content of the poems. Certainly there are some famous poems by Mei Yaochen in which he openly expresses sympathy for the starving and the oppressed, and criticizes harsh government policies. Likewise, both Mei and Ouyang occasionally wrote verse that indirectly satirized corrupt and greedy Imperial officials. However, such works make up only a small minority of these and other Song writers' extant poems and their influence on government policy would have been negligible. Instead, these so-called political poems actually functioned as a vehicle for poets to release personal frustrations and share them with trusted friends in a relatively harmless manner. This may explain why comments on poetry by Northern Song literati of Ouyang Xiu's generation rarely mention politics but constantly talk of using poetry to release emotional tension.

At the same time, though most Northern Song poetry is not politically or even socially engaged in its content, the group nature of poetic composition frequently provoked political consequences, not least because the well-known Northern Song poets were virtually all government officials. Poets tended to socialize and exchange poems with friends who shared their political views; they often gathered for banquets at which poetry competitions were the main form of entertainment. Even when they were exiled to the provinces they continued to send poems to their friends in the capital. Such close relationships among these poet-politicians naturally aroused suspicion in their opponents and the Northern Song saw a dramatic rise in the number of writers punished for exchanging subversive poetry even when their work displayed no overt political content. Nevertheless, the desperate and largely unsuccessful attempt of accusers to dig out poetic material that compromised political enemies supports, rather than disproves, my claim that Mid-Northern Song poetry was largely apolitical.

The second chapter, "Poetry as a Game", acts as a counterweight to the seriousness of the first chapter by examining the lighthearted poetic games played in the Northern Song. Poetic games, or contests, have a long history in China, dating back at least to the Six Dynasties period (222–589), but it was only during the Northern Song that writers began to preserve game poems in significant numbers. Chapter 2 introduces the main types of poetic games played by the circle of writers around Ouyang Xiu. These include three basic categories: games with rhyme (especially taking the rhyme-words of other poems and creating a new poem with them); games with meter; and games forbidding or controlling the use of certain images. I explain why poetic games became so popular during the Northern Song period, and more importantly, why the participants were so keen to preserve their game poems alongside more serious compositions.

Ouyang Xiu and Mei Yaochen saw themselves as the true heirs of ancient Chinese literary culture as exemplified by the Confucian Classics, including the *Classic of Poetry*, and various cultural heroes of the past. They used poetic games to promote the aesthetic values of spontaneity, wit, and plain diction that they associated with the best ancient writers and to encourage poetic composition as a group activity, an entertaining way to bring like-minded people together in harmony.

Of course, poetic games were not the only kind of social poetry. The third chapter, "Poetry and Relationship Building", examines other ways in which poems brought people together, or kept them in touch when they were living in distant places. These included: sending poems to rich and famous officials as a means of displaying one's talent and requesting employment; encouraging exiled or struggling colleagues; consoling friends who had suffered personal tragedies; mediating conflicts and settling family feuds; congratulating friends for receiving promotions, bearing children, and other happy occurrences; seeing off friends and acquaintances setting out on a journey; and finally, composing elegies to commemorate recently deceased friends.

I conclude the chapter by suggesting reasons why Northern Song writers considered poetry more suitable than prose for building friendships and alliances, a fact that is closely tied up with the informal and social nature of poetic composition. They were able to express private, often lighthearted, sentiments in their poetry that would have been quite inappropriate in most prose genres of the period.[11]

The fourth chapter, "Poetry as Therapy", turns to a very interesting but seriously neglected topic: the relationship between Northern Song poetic composition and health. First, I explain the close connection between traditional Chinese ideas of sickness and health (especially emotional health), and artistic production. Next, I provide evidence from Northern Song poets to demonstrate that they treated artistic activities, including poetic composition, as potentially beneficial to their emotional and physical health.

At least since the Han dynasty, Chinese medical theory had viewed all illnesses as resulting from an imbalance of vital energy (*qi*) circulating around the body. Frequently, this imbalance was caused by the emotional stress of dealing with difficult situations and people in society. Mid-Northern Song poets claimed poetry could re-balance emotions and prevent or cure illness by providing a constructive outlet for expressing intense feelings; by regulating emotions through the rhythmic recitation of metrical verses; and by releasing pent-up emotional energy through the physical gestures of writing out poems with a calligraphic brush.

Ouyang Xiu, in particular, was convinced of the therapeutic nature of artistic activity, and he composed several poems and prose pieces discussing the emotional and physical benefits of writing poetry. He especially emphasised the need to exchange poetry with friends going through stressful situations. He would often send poems to exiled or struggling colleagues and demand a response, knowing that the social obligation to write might help them to release negative emotions and prevent them from succumbing to depression and sickness.

It is here we see the clearest disjuncture between the content of exchanged poetry, which was often trivial and humorous, and its function, which could not be more serious, namely, helping to preserve the health of one's friends.

Chapter 5, "Poems Promoting Ancient Culture", extends the energy metaphor to encompass Northern Song poets' relationship with the past. It deals with two kinds of poems, both of which reveal the close bond Northern Song literati shared with their favored literary and historical predecessors, whom they tended to lump together as ancients even when they lived as recently as the Tang dynasty (618–907).

First, they composed numerous poems responding to, imitating, or matching the rhymes of ancient poets. Second, they frequently wrote poems on ancient objects, such as bronze vessels, weapons, and other archaeological finds. Though neither of these categories was new, the Northern Song period saw a sudden increase in the numbers of such poems in comparison with previous periods. Through them, Northern Song poets were able to visualize and evoke the untrammeled, heroic ancient culture they admired so much and bring it back to life. At the same time, lurking beneath the surface of their preoccupation with the ancient was a sense of impending mortality. Northern Song literati were particularly anxious to collect cultural objects and preserve writing from the past because it embodied a mysterious power of survival. They hoped that, by taking such antiques as the subject matter of their verses and imitating the style of worthy past poets, the vital energy contained in these ancient cultural objects would be transferred to their own lives and writings. Poetry on ancient topics thus became a channel through which vital emotional energy from the past could be circulated in the present and, ultimately, transmitted to readers in the future, long after the poet's death.

A similar concern with imbibing vital energy and transmitting it through poetry reappears in the final chapter, "Poetry as Humanization of Nature", which deals primarily with poetry on natural objects. My argument has two main strands that correspond to the two major ways in which Mid-Northern Song poets treated the natural world. First, these poets occasionally view cosmic disorders and aberrations—such as floods, earthquakes, and droughts—as signs that human society was irredeemably corrupt, or that those in charge of government were seriously neglecting their duties. As they grew older, however, they increasingly express the idea that the natural world as a whole was not necessarily on the side of good government or human virtue. Nature could in fact be ruthless, killing off innocent people and allowing the corrupt to survive and prosper. If they themselves wished to survive, they had to find a way to compete with the transformations of nature and to avoid the destructive aspects of natural forces while benefiting from their creative, vital side. Thus, they sought out exceptional objects within the natural world: plants that flourished when everything else decayed; exotic creatures or fruit that stood out in an unfamiliar environment; or refined objects like tea, which flourished ahead of other spring plants and imbued the drinker with creative, if sometimes overpowerful, energy.

Poetry is the vehicle that allowed them to celebrate these unusual, even trivial, natural objects, and draw parallels with their own exceptional talents and personalities. Poetry also embodied some of the vitality of natural objects with its various linguistic, aural, and formal effects. Long after the objects had disappeared, poetry continues to evoke the positive feelings the poets associated with these objects. Even more crucially, poetry preserves for future generations a vital record of the poets enjoying these objects with their like-minded friends and sharing their witty, entertaining impressions of them.

My aim is not to provide a comprehensive survey of all the varying styles and genres of Northern Song poetry but rather to stimulate discussion and view the poetry from a fresh perspective.

My interpretation of Mid-Northern Song poetry may seem idiosyncratic to some readers, but it is supported by numerous published comments of the period, and even more important, by the poems themselves.

The great majority of poems discussed have not been translated before, and unless otherwise indicated, all translations are my own. In some cases, I benefit from the work of previous translators, especially Chaves and Egan, while modifying their versions in the interests of stylistic unity. I attempt to give an impression of the meter of the original poems by translating each Chinese syllable with one English stress grouping. Generally, I have not adopted English rhymes, as this disrupts the original word order too much. However, where it is necessary to underscore a point, I rhyme the translation, for instance, in demonstrating Ouyang Xiu's attempt at ugly rhymes in chapter 6.

Though my conclusions differ in places from those of Chaves and Egan, I obviously could not have completed this study without the foundation they and other Western scholars have laid. I am also greatly indebted to a number of contemporary Chinese scholars, notably Zhu Dongrun, for his dated edition of Mei Yaochen's complete poetry; Chen Xin and Du Weimo, for their excellent selected anthology of Ouyang Xiu's poems and prose; and Wang Shuizhao, for several detailed papers on the Ouyang Xiu / Mei Yaochen circle.[12] However, only I bear responsibility for my interpretations and any errors that have crept in.

CHAPTER ONE

Poetry as Political and Social Criticism

Virtually all Chinese studies of Song literary theory—even those that allow for a number of competing theories—focus on two key terms: *wen* (Writing), and *dao* (the Way). Any divergences between theories stem from the different weight they attribute to Writing, including prose and poetry, in helping people to follow the correct Way. Certain groups of literati in the Northern Song, for instance Ouyang Xiu and his circle, claim that learning to write well is fundamental to following the Way. Others, most notably the *Daoxue* (Learning of the Way) group headed by Cheng Yi (1033–1107), and culminating with Zhu Xi (1130–1200) in the southern Song, were suspicious of Writing, seeing it as potentially distracting to the inner self-cultivation required of those who follow the Way.[1]

Whatever the differences between these thinkers, none question the basic premise that following the Way should be the main aim of peoples' lives. Yet what constituted this mysterious Way? Again, most mainstream Song thinkers agreed that the essence of the Way was expressed in the canonical texts of Confucianism, though they frequently differed in their interpretations of these texts. Most would have accepted the basic premises, namely, that the Confucian Way posited a moral order in the universe and, by extension, among human beings in society. This moral order required that people accept their place within the familial and social hierarchy and behave in a respectful and courteous manner towards each other, based on the exhaustive rules of propriety found in the Classics. Writing, as a vehicle for the Way, should promote correct social behavior and criticize abuses and corruption among scholar-officials who served in the government. It should also reflect the feelings and describe the plight of the common people, so that those in power could adjust their policies for the peoples' benefit.[2]

Northern Song poets were well aware of the social and political functions of writing, and occasionally their poetry reflects these ideas in a very direct manner. Nevertheless, to focus solely on poetry whose content deals directly with social and political issues, means neglecting the majority of their works. Even if we include poems that refer to sociopolitical topics indirectly or allegorically (a rather fluid and slippery category), there are still numerous excellent compositions that focus entirely on more personal issues and apolitical content. Rather than assuming only a handful of Northern Song poems actually fulfilled the requirement of making literature a vehicle for the Way, I will argue that the Northern Song poets' definition of following the Way was less tied up with the content of their poetry than most later critics have assumed. Instead, the crucial factor for these poets was to keep the writing of poetry as a social activity: a vehicle for exchanging views, bringing people together in a harmonious manner, and allowing them to release emotional tension in a constructive way.

POETRY AND THE WAY: A BROADER VIEW

Evidence that direct political and social criticism was not the most important function of poetry in the Northern Song comes first of all from the small numbers of poems on such topics. Zhu Dongrun, in the preface to his edition of Mei Yaochen's collected poetry, estimates that only about thirty or forty of Mei's 2900-plus poems can be counted among his best works—by which he means that they directly reflect the hardships of the common people and criticize the harsh Song government. These include Mei's famous "Words of a Farmer," "The Poor Girl of Ru Riverbank" and the like.[3] Zhu criticizes Mei for composing hundreds of poems on what he considers trivial topics and for wasting his time exchanging and matching empty verses with his numerous literati friends. On many occasions, Mei seems to treat poetic composition as little more than an entertaining word game, neglecting its sociopolitical function altogether.[4] If Zhu had evaluated the poetry of Ouyang Xiu and most other Northern Song poets, he would have found a similarly small proportion of poems showing sustained concern for the common people or directly attacking corruption in the government.[5]

Zhu's explanation for this imbalance is that even the greatest poets, such as Du Fu (712–772), composed large numbers of mediocre works, and we should not expect Mei and his contemporaries to be any different. Hence we should judge them by their best works alone, while pointing out their limitations.[6] Yet given the extreme statistics, it is more logical to conclude that these Northern Song poets saw direct political or social criticism as only one, and not the central, function of poetry. Furthermore, if we examine their own statements about poetry, we find that these writers considered even the most lighthearted of their poems to be consistent with making literature a vehicle for the Way. They were neither halfhearted nor hypocritical in combining their literary theories with their poetic practice.

Among Northern Song literati, Ouyang Xiu made some of the clearest statements about the functions of poetry (*shi*). One of his best known comments comes in a grave inscription for Mei Yaochen. He sums up Mei's reasons for composing so many poems:[7]

> Shengyu's character was kind, generous, joyful, and easygoing. He never caused offence to others. When he was poor and miserable, or moved by righteous indignation so that he had something to curse, mock, laugh at, or ridicule, he would always express it in poems. But he used this to find happiness, not to settle grievances. One could say that he was a Superior Person (*jun zi*).

It is significant that in this passage Ouyang describes how Mei released his pent-up emotions or energy in poetry to find happiness, but does not mention anything about the concerns of the common people or criticizing corrupt officials. An earlier sentence from the same text claims that even the lowest members of society knew about Mei's poetry, but this demonstrates Mei's fame rather than his social conscience: "Even reckless and ignorant fellows, who could not even understand the meaning of poems, would still say, 'Everyone in the world considers these valuable. If I can get one, I can use it to make myself look important!'"[8] The impression one receives is that for Mei, writing poetry was primarily a means of expressing or releasing his inner feelings—both joyful and sad—and sharing them with his friends and acquaintances.

Other comments on poetry by Ouyang Xiu provide a similar picture. His famous *Remarks on Poetry* (*Shihua*) are almost exclusively concerned with stylistic points—rhyme, imagery, diction and the like—or with recording memorable anecdotes about minor poets, and few of the poems he chooses as examples betray any concern with pressing social issues.[9] Elsewhere, when he does make a direct parallel between the poetry of his contemporaries and the canonical Confucian text, the *Classic of Poetry*, it is to support a quite unexpected, but in the light of his poetic theory, entirely characteristic, contention:[10]

> Now the Superior Person (*jun zi*), in broadly adopting things from others, should not neglect even the comical or the crude and base. All the more so in poetry! There is nothing that cannot be found among the three hundred poems of ancient times [i.e., the *Classic of Poetry*]. Yet they are free without being abandoned, joyful without being decadent, and ultimately they return to correctness. This is the reason they are considered so highly.

In other words, portraying "the comical or the crude and base" is just as acceptable in poetry as engaging in political or social criticism, and by extension, can accord just as closely with the Confucian Way. A similar idea appears in the passage on Mei Yaochen quoted above: Mei was a "Superior Person" because he was able to express his strong feelings, including laughter and mockery, in poetry.

Faced with the fact that much of Northern Song poetry does not deal with pressing social or political issues—that instead, it often focuses on humorous and trivial subject matter—some scholars conclude that poetry was simply not as important as prose for writers of this period. They claim that writers expressed serious political and social concerns in prose—especially official memorials, commentaries on the *Classics*, and historical treatises—whereas poetry simply became a diversion, a form of entertainment.[11]

To a certain extent, this view is accurate. The majority of Song literati were government officials; none considered themselves to be professional poets. Since poetic composition, like playing musical instruments or practicing calligraphy, was therefore a form of relaxation to while away their leisure time, it is more surprising that these writers did occasionally compose serious politically engaged verse than that much of their poetry focused on more personal emotions.

But did this make poetry less important to these writers than prose? As I demonstrate, poetry fulfilled a number of essential social and private functions during the Northern Song—just as it did in other periods of Chinese history. Rather than concluding that Song literati considered prose more important than poetry, they used these different forms of writing for contrasting, but equally significant, social purposes. Hence, comparing their lighthearted verses to the *Classic of Poetry*, as Ouyang did, was not an empty verbal gesture.

INDIRECT POLITICAL AND SOCIAL CRITICISM: A CHIMERA?

For the circle of Northern Song poets around Ouyang Xiu and Mei Yaochen, overtly sociopolitical poetry made up only a small proportion of their oeuvre, and was not their central focus when composing poems. But poetry does not always express its meaning directly, and many scholars of Chinese poetry claim to spot hidden political messages in works that appear innocuous and apolitical. Could it be that, even though these poets did not often deal openly with sensitive political issues, much of their poetry was in fact covert commentary on politics, including regular hidden attacks on their opponents in the government?

The obvious objection to this approach is that many Northern Song poets fearlessly and openly expressed their political views when they felt the need—in government memorials, prose discourses, and in some of their poems. There was little reason to hide those same views in other poems. Indeed, this search for hidden political messages is fraught with difficulties. To illustrate these difficulties, I examine poems that critics have often interpreted politically or that appear to contain allegorical elements. In the process, I suggest an alternative way of approaching such poems that accords more closely with the functions of poetry that the writers themselves espoused.

Let us begin with one of Mei Yaochen's most famous poems, on a blowfish or, as he calls it, a river-pig fish:[12]

During a Party at Fan Raozhou's, a Guest Talks About Eating the River-Pig Fish [1038]

On spring islets the reed sprouts grow,
On spring banks the willow catkins fly,
At this time the river-pig
Is treasured more than all other fish.
Its appearance is certainly weird,

And its poison extremely deadly;
When angry, its belly swells like a swine,
Furious eyes glaring like a frog of Wu.[13]
If you make a mistake when cooking
It will slice up your throat like Moye's sword.[14]
Since it can destroy your life in a trice,
Why even bother taking a bite?
With these arguments I challenged some Southerners,
But united as one, they wouldn't stop praising it,
They all claimed its flavor was incomparably fine,
None of them mentioned that it kills folk like flies.
Nothing that I said would make them relent,
Sighing, I could only remind myself:
When Tuizhi arrived in [southern] Chaoyang,
He worried about eating a caged snake,
But after Zihou lived in Liuzhou [for a while],
He was perfectly willing to consume a toad![15]
Yet even if these two creatures were abhorrent
They would not make you fear for your life,
They could never be compared to this so-called delicacy,
Which hides within it unending disaster.
"With great beauty, trouble will also appear":[16]
This indeed is a praiseworthy saying.

Many traditional and modern Chinese commentators interpret this poem as a work of indirect political or social criticism. Jonathan Chaves gives an excellent summary of these interpretations, showing how none bear really close scrutiny.[17] For example, he cites the argument of James T. C. Liu, that the river-pig fish poem composed at a drinking party held by former central government minister Fan Zhongyan was Mei's veiled criticism of his host for becoming too involved in factional politics at court. Liu's interpretation is part of a broader argument that Mei gradually grew more and more critical of Fan's extreme factionalism, and eventually broke off relations with him in the 1040s.[18]

It is true that Fan and several of his supporters, including Ouyang Xiu, were southerners, and had been exiled to the provinces two years earlier (1036) for their outspoken criticism of the chief councilor Lü Yijian. Over the next few years they would continue to alienate conservatives in the government, suffering further periods of exile in the mid-1040s.[19] Yet it is highly unlikely that Mei would have set out to criticize Fan in this particular poem, even indirectly, while he was his guest. The only real support for this argument comes from the southern Song philosopher Zhu Xi, who frequently made clear his dislike for Mei Yaochen's poetry and what he considered the loose morals of the Ouyang Xiu circle. He unleashed the following diatribe against the river-pig fish poem (in Chaves' translation):[20]

> Many of Shengyu's poems are not good. Take, for example, his poem on the river-pig fish. At that time, all the gentlemen said it was outstanding, but in my opinion that poem is like going into a man's house and cursing him to his face, just like throwing off one's clothes, going into a man's house and cursing his grandfather, cursing his father. From first to last, it is utterly lacking in deep and detached thought.

The violence of Zhu Xi's reaction suggests he has misunderstood the context in which Mei composed the poem. He assumes the host, Fan Zhongyan, had offered river-pig fish to his guests at the party, and that Mei was accusing Fan of trying to poison him with it, or at the very least, of providing an unsavory dish which he cannot imagine eating. This would certainly have been extremely offensive and un-Confucian, as Zhu claims, not only to Fan himself but even to his ancestors! But the unusual wording of the poem's title makes it clear that river-pig fish was not on the menu at Fan's party; one of the guests simply raised the subject of this strange creature during conversation—presumably describing to a fascinated audience the potentially fatal consequences of eating the fish when it was not properly prepared—and Mei composed a spontaneous poem recounting the ensuing lively debate on the merits of the fish.

If Mei was not insulting Fan directly as a host, was he still indirectly criticizing Fan for becoming too involved in factional struggles at Court? This might still be considered rude behavior from a guest, if not quite as heinous as Zhu Xi claimed. Several pieces of evidence challenge this interpretation of the poem. First, Ouyang Xiu, a strong political ally of Fan Zhongyan and one of Mei's closest friends, wrote comments about this poem on at least two separate occasions. Yet nowhere does he mention that the poem caused offence to anyone. On the contrary, he expresses unbounded admiration for the poem's craftsmanship and wit, which lifted his spirits whenever he read it. The following remarks are representative:[21]

> Mei Shengyu once composed a poem on the river-pig fish at a party given by Fan Zhongyan . . . Shengyu constantly worked hard at composing poetry, aiming for a relaxed yet profound, ancient, and bland [style]. Consequently, his structures and ideas are very carefully thought out. This poem was composed in the midst of eating and drinking, but the force of his brush is strong and rich. Though he completed it in just a few moments, in the end it turned out to be one of his outstanding works.
>
> . . . Whenever my body feels unhealthy, I recite [this poem] several times through, and immediately I feel fine. I have also copied it out several times to present to people as an unusual gift.

A poem criticizing Fan Zhongyan, and by extension, disagreeing with all southerners like Ouyang Xiu, who supported Fan's faction, would surely not make Ouyang feel so wonderful every time he read it. There must be some other more convincing interpretation to explain the poem's appeal. Traditional Chinese commentaries on the poem do not help much since they are mainly concerned with a minor textual point, first raised by Ouyang Xiu, about exactly when the river-pig fish swims upriver.[22] But taking our cue from Ouyang's earlier comment that Mei composed poetry to overcome negative feelings and find happiness—not to settle grievances—we could posit the following explanation of the river-pig poem.

Even if we allow that the poem may have political implications, there is no reason to treat it as Mei's attack on the political tastes of southerners like Ouyang and Fan. After all, Mei himself was from Anhui province on the south banks of the Yangtze River, a region where the river-pig fish thrived and was annually harvested.[23] One cannot therefore equate the critical narrator of his poem with Mei himself, since Mei too belonged firmly in the group of southerners.

At the same time, we can easily take the poem as Mei's reminder, both to himself and his southern colleagues, of the dangers of a political career. The rewards of attaining a high government post may be great, just as the flavor of river-pig is incomparably fine, but one small mistake can lead to disaster. And as with fish poisoning, a political disaster may not even be one's own fault, but the fault of somebody working behind the scenes. Composed at a time when several of Mei's friends were exiled to the provinces—due to events that I discuss further in the final section of this chapter—such an outpouring of emotion against the fatal attractions of the river-pig fish would have struck a chord with their own painful experiences. Reading the poem, they would certainly have admired and empathized with Mei's ability to express their shared pent-up frustrations in a spontaneously composed verse on a trivial topic.

Mei is careful not to restrict the poem to a single political interpretation. The poem may also refer to other areas of life in which beauty or sensual attractions can lead the unwary into disaster. Or it could simply be a sharp observation on the unthinking way in which people follow fashions or local customs even when it does them no good at all. Such themes are common in many later poems by Mei and Ouyang. Part of the poem's success is surely in leaving readers to draw their own conclusions and apply its method of emotional release to their own personal setbacks.

We should not overlook the tone of the poem, which is both satirical and humorous. It is a classic example of the caricatured reasoning of Northern Song: using the rhetorical appeals and diction of serious intellectual debate to discuss a strange and intrinsically comical object.[24] The effect is so incongruous—a group of cultured southerners vehemently standing up for this poisonous, swine-bellied fish with its furious glaring eyes—that most readers of the time would surely have doubled up with laughter. This is a major reason for Ouyang Xiu's enthusiastic recommendation of the poem's ability to make one feel better: it transforms negative emotions caused by political enemies, traitorous friends, or faithless lovers, into laughter.

Another example of a poem that seems, on the surface, to involve sociopolitical criticism is Ouyang Xiu's "Hating Mosquitoes," which dates from 1046, during his second period of exile.[25] Both Ouyang and Mei Yaochen had previously composed poems about mosquitoes in 1034, and these early works were barely disguised attacks on corrupt and cruel government officials. Mei's poem, for instance, contains the lines: "Would that in the homes [of the rich], / The mosquitoes flaunted their lance-like beaks! / Instead they frequent the poor and humble, / With no compassion for their gauntness, / Suckers sharp, they race to the attack; / Drinking blood, they seek self-increase."[26] Though he does not specify exactly whom the mosquitoes represent, Mei makes no secret that their victims are the poor and humble. There is little doubt that he is attacking greedy, tax-collecting officials, who harass the unprotected poor but leave the rich in peace.[27]

Yet turning to Ouyang Xiu's later poem, we find it much harder to reduce the interpretation to a simple political allegory. This is partly due to the inherent humor of Ouyang's self-caricature, as he vainly attempts to swat these pesky critters. But it is also because, despite his references to bad government allowing evil to arise, the mosquitoes are only attacking him, not some unfortunate and oppressed mass of poor people. At most, we can conclude that the poem expresses Ouyang's personal frustration with the petty forces of evil that disrupt his life, and in writing it he transforms that frustration into laughter.

Hating Mosquitoes [1046][28]

The ten thousand species are crowded together,
And among them some are decidedly hateful;
The mosquito is truly one of the tiniest:
Not worth leaving its traces on one's paper.[29]
The universe is broad and enormously capacious,
Containing and nourishing both good and evil,
In the desolate days before the ancient kings and emperors
People and beasts lived in each others' filth,
But Yu made a tripod that captured evil spirits,
The dragons fled far away to hide in the depths;
The Duke of Zhou expelled all surviving wild creatures,
And humankind reclaimed the lands and rivers.[30]
Since then, thousands of years passed away,
And Heaven and Earth grew peaceful and quiet,
One could say great disorders disappeared from sight,
And no-one paid attention to the tiny and slight:
To the flies, gadflies, fleas, lice, and nits,
Locusts, scorpions, vipers, cobras, and pythons.
And you [mosquitoes] belong to this group too,
With your bodies as small as grains of millet,
But even though you're tiny, you swarm in huge numbers,
And your small size means it's hard to avoid your poison,
I once heard that up in Gaoyou Prefecture,
A fierce tiger died from your cruel humiliation,
And how miserable any girl who exposes her veins:
Avenging your ancient grudge, you exact severe punishment![31]
The wetland regions especially suit your kind,
Pity the people in such remote frontiers!
At morning repasts, they lower their screen curtains,
At summer's height, their cattle stay deep in the mud.

I have come to govern this distant hill country
Where the land is extremely low and damp,
With few official duties, I lazily do what I choose,
It is sleep that really suits my inclinations,
But I hate that you come in such great swarms:
I'm tired of you swooping over my pillow and sleeping mat!
Smoking the eaves, I suffer from fumes and dust,
Scorching the walls, I'm exhausted lifting my candle.
By ruined city walls you assemble on plants and trees,
The air grows dry and the blazing heat rises,
Xihe drives forward the chariot of the sun,
But reaching the noon hour, it seems the wheels stop turning.
When finally a breeze blows and evening cool comes,
It feels like an amnesty: prisoners released from their shackles,
I sweep the courtyard, open to the sky,
Then sit in the moonlight in the shade of fine trees:
Why do you *insist* on choosing this moment
To make me endure such constant harassment?
Furling your wings, waiting for day to darken,
Gradually you emerge from ceilings and walls,
You fill up the sky, sweep over like a curtain,
Gather in crevices, so numerous you'd fill cupped hands,
Crowding round my body, you besiege and defeat me,
Clamoring in my ears, you wail for the deceased,
Fiercely you charge: ready to unleash your crossbows,
Cruelly you strike: sharper than flying arrows,
My hands and feet are powerless to save me,
You soon take control of both front and behind,[32]
Tired of fanning and swatting my dinner tray,
I force my stiff servant to rouse from his slumbers,
Vainly he exhausts the hundred strategies
Then sinks back down and closes his eyes in defeat.[33]
I am certainly powerless to struggle any longer,
And you are truly too cruel and ruthless!
Who can explain the laws that creatures follow?
Don't they just obstruct us in all we do?
As for the Chuyu, Phoenix, and Kirin,[34]
No-one has glimpsed them for thousands of years,
I long for them now, but cannot hope to see them,
There's nothing to drive the evil ones away.

The traditional aim of the poetry of social and political criticism in China was to persuade the Emperor and his officials to govern more justly by describing to them how the common people were suffering under their present inefficient and corrupt system. In theory, the Emperor would be moved to compassion by reading versified accounts of ordinary peoples' lives, and would initiate sweeping political reforms.[35]

Some Northern Song poems could conceivably have had such an effect—assuming that the Emperor had read them—for example, Mei Yaochen's "Poor Girl of Ru Riverbank," which shows the hardships caused by the forcible enlisting of commoners to serve in military campaigns on China's borders.[36] Even Mei's "Swarming Mosquitoes" might have acted in a similar way, encouraging political leaders to look into the injustices perpetuated by an inefficient tax system. But what about Ouyang's "Hateful Mosquitoes"? What audience is he aiming to reach with this comical, mock-heroic battle between himself and a mass of evil little creatures? It is highly unlikely central government leaders would read such a poem and be moved by it to reform their policies, since the only real victim here is Ouyang himself. He shows no concern for the common people. Likewise, it is not clear what kind of social evil the mosquitoes represent. A crude allegorical reading of the poem suggests the mosquitoes refer to ordinary people and minor officers in this backward region, who constantly bother their local governor Ouyang Xiu with all their problems, preventing him from getting any sleep! Then again, the mosquitoes could be Ouyang's many petty-minded opponents in the central government, who gathered in swarms to falsely accuse him and his fellow reformers of illegal acts, resulting in his exile the previous year (1045). Alternatively, Ouyang could be expressing a broader view that the natural world contains just as many destructive forces as human society. Such a reading would harmonize best with his concluding questions: "Who can explain the laws that creatures follow?/Don't they just obstruct us in all we do?" (lines 65–66).[37]

Whatever interpretation one chooses, and whether or not the poem is related to the political events of the time, the crucial point is that Ouyang uses poetry to release his personal frustrations, taking a difficult and uncomfortable situation and making it into the stuff of caricature and comedy. Like most of his other compositions, the poem is for himself and for circulation among his friends; it is not written for some amorphous mass of common people, or as a kind of versified policy statement directed towards a righteous ruler.[38]

There are numerous other poems by Ouyang and Mei, especially from the 1040s and 1050s, which at first appear to fit the indirect political and social criticism model, but on closer examination turn out to be more personal in scope. I will save detailed discussion of these poems, and their various nonpolitical functions, for the rest of this book, but will provide one further example here to bolster the argument.[39]

In Ouyang Xiu's "Answering the Poem 'Heavy Rain' Sent to Me by Mei Shengyu," dated 1057, one might expect the topic, a flood, to inspire an effusion of sympathy for the suffering common people.[40] And certainly Ouyang's lines referring to "people below on the Earth . . . / Wallowing about in the midst of mud and mire . . . / No different from ducks or common swine" (lines 19–22), and his mention of the Sage Emperor Yao, if taken out of context, might lead some readers to assume that the poem is in the social criticism mold. Nevertheless, Ouyang spends most of the poem expressing concern for himself rather than for ordinary people. In the process, he creates another vivid caricature of his own misfortunes, similar to his mosquito poem, which can only be offset by the consolation of receiving a poem from his friend Mei Yaochen:

> Evening clouds roll over like a mountain avalanche,
> Night rain pours down like a burst pipe overflowing.
> For a moment, I see the dark blue sky,
> Flaming brightly, the toad-moon rises,
> Then suddenly the Spirit of Yin strengthens,
> On all four sides it gathers momentum.
> Wild thunder roars through obscure blackness,
> Startling lightning illuminates fierce monsters![41]
> They go on the prowl, waking dragons from hibernation,
> Descending, they strike the tombstones and the graves.
> Every time the thunder sounds its rumbling cartwheels,
> The rain correspondingly adjusts its pace.
> It seems that the downpour will never cease,
> But finally the storm retreats, silent and exhausted.
> Only a thousand-foot rainbow remains suspended,
> Violet and azure, stretching across the emptiness.
> In a matter of moments, a hundred changes of aspect:
> Who rolls up and unfolds this darkness and light?
> And do they know of the people below on the Earth,
> The watery downpour flooding their sleeves and hems?
> Wallowing about in the midst of mud and mire,
> They seem no different from ducks or common swine!
> Alas for me! Just come to the capital city,
> With hardly a mean hut to shelter my body.
> In the leisure district I'm renting an ancient hovel,

Crude and mean, it's hidden among back alleys.
The gushing from the neighbours pours into our ditches and drains,
The flow from the street surges over our courtyard.
Going out of the gate, I'm shocked by vast floods,
But if I stay behind closed doors, I fear being drowned.
The walls are full of holes opening out in all directions,
It's fortunate my family has no valuable possessions!
Toads croak beneath the kitchen stove,
My old wife can only snivel and sob.
At the nine city gates they've run out of firewood,
We're about to smash our cart for the morning cooking-fire,
Weighed down and under water, I worry about survival:
How can I focus on my writings and books?
Now I understand that when Emperor Yao was alive,
People started to fear they would turn into fish![42]
But Master Mei remembered me in times of trouble,
He sent me a poem and sympathised with my plight.
He consoled me with this latest composition:
Brightly shining, as pure as jasper and jade.
My official duties are few, and my abilities are meager,
I'm ashamed I've done little to pay back the State.
My life will soon reach its final destination,
Why do I not retire to rivers and lakes?
Since anyway I dwell in a traveler's rest,
There's no point delaying my departure plans!

Ouyang gives a remarkably vivid portrayal of the storm and its aftermath, focusing particularly on his own plight. Yet even though everything he describes is plausible, even realistic, the combined effect of his series of images is incongruous and humorous. As in his mosquito poem, he makes himself out to be a hapless and rather ridiculous victim, quite unable to deal with the misfortunes that the world throws at him. The fact that Ouyang was by 1057 an eminent central government official in Kaifeng, the Northern Song capital, on the verge of becoming the city's mayor the following year should remind us not to take the description of his crude and mean home too seriously.[43]

However, Ouyang has two motives for emphasizing the utter desperation of his situation, as he makes clear in lines 41 to 50. First, he wishes to show that Mei Yaochen's poetry, arriving in the midst of hopelessness, is an enormous consolation: "He consoled me with this latest composition,/ Brightly shining, as pure as jasper and jade" (lines 43–44). Mei's poem improves his mood and inspires him to write this poetic response, in which he transforms an ugly situation into something he can laugh about. Secondly, the major disruption caused by this single shower of rain reminds Ouyang of the need to enjoy life while he has the opportunity. Earlier in the poem, he remarks that "in a matter of moments, a hundred changes of aspect [occur]" (line 17). By the poem's conclusion he realizes that he too is changing quickly—"my life will soon reach its final destination" (line 47)—and he should not waste his life in a job that contributes nothing to society, especially since he must live in such a run-down hovel. "Why do I not retire to rivers and lakes?" he concludes (line 48). In reality Ouyang did not retire from office for another decade or so, but writing the poem in response to Mei Yaochen allowed him to imagine wandering off into serene reclusion, and doubtless gave him a temporary distraction from his present difficulties.

I have shown that Ouyang Xiu and Mei Yaochen did compose a small number of poems directly concerned with the plight of the common people or the need for political reform. They show no reluctance about criticizing the government quite openly in their poetry (and in Ouyang's case even more so in prose works), when they see the need. However, the majority of their poems do not deal directly with political issues. Even those that seem to lend themselves to allegorical interpretations rarely fit the traditional mold of disguised political and social criticism. Rather they express the poets' frustration with the personal difficulties they must face as individuals, and allow them to channel that frustration safely into a creative endeavor, improving their mood and empathizing with their friends in the process.

Of course, even if the content of such poems is not directly concerned with current political struggles, it is true that occasionally political enemies made use of a poet's works to slander him. In part, this was because virtually all Northern Song poets were first and foremost government officials. Moreover, they constantly exchanged their poems with like-minded friends and acquaintances, who were generally also government officials. Therefore, it is hardly surprising that at times of political crisis their enemies suspected them of seditious tendencies and hidden factional alliances, and sought evidence of this in their poetry.

Following is a discussion of this misuse of poetry by political opponents, focusing specifically on the 1040s, and arguing that it challenges, rather than supports, the view of Mid-Northern Song poetry as primarily political in content.

POETRY AS EVIDENCE OF POLITICAL WRONGDOING

As James T. C. Liu and others have noted, the period from the mid-1030s until the end of the Northern Song in 1126 was one of increasingly bitter factionalism in Chinese politics.[44] During the decade from 1035 to 1045, Ouyang Xiu and Mei Yaochen were part of a loose-knit group of reformers led by Fan Zhongyan, who called for a tougher policy to combat the incursions of foreign tribes in the north and west, and for an end to corrupt government practices. The members of this group, who include Yin Shu (1001–1046), Shi Jie (1005–1045), Fu Bi (1004–1083), and Han Qi (1008–1075), frequently met to exchange ideas and poems, and when most were exiled to the provinces in 1036 due to their numerous memorials attacking chief councilor Lü Yijian, they continued to send supportive poems to each other. By the early 1040s, as the members of the group gradually returned to the central government, their poetry exchanges continued unabated. Although some of their poems were overtly political—for instance, in a 1041 poem, Ouyang Xiu declared that unseasonably warm winter weather was due to "Treacherous generals not being killed, demeaning the country's punishments" and upsetting the normal progress of the seasons[45]—much was simply polite and conventional expression of mutual admiration or consolation in times of difficulty.

The very closeness of the social bonds between these like-minded scholar officials—as evidenced by their frequent poetic exchanges—worried and irritated the more conservative groups in the central government, especially when Emperor Renzong decided in 1043 to place Fan Zhongyan and Han Qi in charge of executing their proposed policy changes—the so-called Qingli Reforms.[46]

The opposing faction, led by the censor Wang Gongchen (1013–1086), found the uncompromising and overbearing attitude of the reformers insufferable. Nevertheless, conservatives could not directly attack these imperially sponsored reforms, because they did not wish to appear as supporters of corruption and capitulation to foreign invaders. Instead, they sought to discredit reformers by digging out evidence of their subversive intentions and disrespectful attitude towards the Emperor. To make a convincing case, they had to prove, firstly, that the reformers were actually a faction—in other words, a group of officials who had secretly agreed to collaborate in order to promote their own political agenda—and secondly, that this Qingli reform faction was seeking to wrest control of the government from the Emperor. To fulfil both these purposes, the conservatives made use of the poetry of their opponents, cunningly interwoven with other examples of what they claimed were the reformers' corrupt and subversive practices, to produce a web of circumstantial evidence sufficient to raise the Emperor's suspicions.

For instance, in 1044 a palace eunuch reminded Emperor Renzong of a poem series entitled "Four Worthies and One Villain" by Cai Xiang (1012–1067), written eight years earlier (1036) to protest against the first exile of Fan Zhongyan and three of Cai's friends, Ouyang Xiu, Yin Shu, and Yu Jing (1000–1064).[47] Cai compared the young reformers with ancient worthies bravely willing to take an independent stand against shameless accusers. Since Cai had lumped these four people together as early as 1036, the censor argued, it was obvious that their faction already existed for many years and was now in a position to do some real damage to the government. Other accusations followed, some based on forged letters in the reformers' names, designed to prove their disloyalty towards the Emperor.[48]

Though not completely persuaded by these charges, Renzong sent the leading reformers on temporary missions outside the capital while considering his options. Then, in the winter of 1044, some of the younger supporters of Fan Zhongyan, led by Ouyang Xiu's close friend Su Shunqin (1008–1048), held a banquet at which they entertained themselves in traditional literati fashion by drinking wine and composing poems spontaneously. Unfortunately, word leaked out to Wang Gongchen that one of these wine-inspired poems contained lines insulting to the Emperor. According to the Qing scholar Pan Yongyin, the verse in question was by one Wang Yirou, a friend of Su's, and included the following declaration: "I wish to recline on the North Star, ordering the Lord of Heaven [or Emperor] to support me / The Duke of Zhou and Confucius I will drive forth as slaves."[49] Added to this impertinence was evidence that the party-goers had funded their banquet by selling old paper money belonging to the government, a practice which, even though common among Northern Song officials, was technically illegal.[50] When Renzong banished all those who had attended the party, Fan Zhongyan realized that he too was under attack and offered his resignation as councilor. However, after discovering that

Fan was not really sincere about resigning, the Emperor exiled him to the provinces as well. Fan never returned to the central government.[51]

In this way, the conservatives cleverly manipulated their opponents' poetry to buttress their accusations and bring down many of the reformers, and by 1045 they had succeeded in having all the Qingli Reforms reversed. However, Ouyang Xiu had thus far escaped punishment and remained influential as a censor in the central government, a thorn in the flesh of his conservative enemies. Since there was no longer a reform faction left to which they could accuse Ouyang of belonging, they resorted instead to a personal attack on his moral behavior, accusing him of a criminal offence so that he would be forced from his position. Once again, they made use of poetry as evidence for their case: some of the erotic song lyrics (*ci*) that Ouyang had written in his youth, spiced up with more scurrilous forgeries added for good measure.[52] They were also able to persuade the stepdaughter of Ouyang's sister, who happened to be in the capital jail at the time on an unrelated adultery charge, to accuse Ouyang of forcing her into a sexual relationship when she was a young girl staying at his house. Even though the girl was not his blood relative, such a relationship was considered to be incestuous in the Northern Song.[53] This accusation was made slightly more plausible by the content of Ouyang's song lyrics, which included lines like the following (in Egan's translation):[54]

> Young, a golden sparrow pin in her hair buns,
> She practices drawing eyebrows and dabs her face with rouge.
> No matter how often implored, how much loved
> All she understands is how to laugh.
> In a well-fitting dance dress
> She runs to the elegant banquet-mats, displaying her charm.
> Master Liu is filled with the love of flowers
> But for this one he's come a little early.

Fortunately, the judge in Ouyang's case realized the accusations by this stepniece were slanderous, and dismissed the so-called evidence from Ouyang's lyrics, calling them typical examples of the genre unrelated to the case at hand.[55] Yet, under pressure to find Ouyang guilty of something, he sentenced him on a separate charge of tax evasion. As a result, Ouyang was exiled to become governor of the remote region of Chuzhou (in present Anhui province).[56] Despite the fact that the poetic evidence did not prove as damning as Ouyang's enemies had hoped, when combined with the accusations of incest it seriously stained his reputation and ultimately led to further personal attacks in the 1060s.[57]

What does this whole episode tell us about the relationship between poetry and politics in the Mid-Northern Song? Certainly it reveals that writing poetry could be dangerous, especially if one was a central government official. But whether or not any particular poem would land its writer and his friends in trouble was quite unpredictable, and often bore no relation to the writer's original reason for composing the poem. Obviously Cai Xiang was taking a clear and uncompromising political stand when he wrote "Four Worthies and One Villain," and it is no surprise that the poem series resurfaced to haunt the reformers eight years later. But Wang Yirou was surely not consciously aiming to offend the Emperor when he composed his drunken couplet at Su Shunqin's party, and Ouyang Xiu could have had no inkling that his youthful romantic song lyrics would later be used to corroborate slanderous charges of incest against him and force him into exile. In both Wang's and Ouyang's cases, although their poems were personal, their opponents treated anything that they wrote, no matter what the original context, as politically significant simply because they were government officials. And poetry was a particularly useful weapon for their accusers, both because they could easily misinterpret it and because poetry supposedly expressed the poet's true private feelings, or intent (*zhi*), as opposed to his deceptively decent public persona.[58]

On the other hand, poetry itself was not sufficient to condemn any of the reformers. Poets like Ouyang and Mei circulated scathing verse criticisms of Song military policy in the early 1040s without adverse consequences. It was only when their words were accompanied by illegal acts—selling off government property, or seducing a stepniece—that judges took them seriously, and even then, the poetic evidence might be discounted, as in Ouyang's case. Indeed, the overall impression one receives from this episode is that poetry was not a catalyst for these political events at all, but was simply dragged in haphazardly to provide an extra layer of circumstantial evidence after the conservative faction had decided to ruin the reformers.

Ironically, because the reformers, like most of their Northern Song contemporaries, treated poetry writing not primarily as a political activity but as a means of releasing and sharing their personal feelings, it is more likely their poems, rather than their more public prose works, contained indiscreet remarks enemies could use against them.

Finally, we should remember that political enemies do not make the best literary critics. Clearly, in the case of Wang Yirou and Ouyang Xiu, their poems were misinterpreted. We cannot rely on this political misuse of poetry to prove that Northern Song poets themselves treated poetry as a political weapon. It would be more realistic to base our conclusions on the evidence of their own poetic theories, which virtually ignore the political function of poetry, and of the large numbers of poems that they composed on nonpolitical topics. In some ways, therefore, Zhu Dongrun's criticism of Mei Yaochen is a fair one. He claims that, later in his life, Mei spent too much time exchanging poems on trivial topics with his friends, and virtually transformed poetry writing into a kind of word game. This is an admission that for Mei, political comment was neither the only nor the main function of his poetry. But Zhu's view is based on the assumption that political or social criticism should be the primary aim of poets—the Way of Poetry, in traditional terms—and that poetry neglecting this aim is worthless in terms of its value for society. In the following chapters, I will demonstrate that in fact poetry fulfilled a number of other valuable social and personal functions in the Northern Song, and that poets themselves subscribed to a much broader definition of the Way of Poetry—perhaps even the Confucian moral Way itself—than most modern scholars have assumed. In short, the main purpose of poetry for Northern Song poets was to promote social cohesion through the *activity* of poetic exchanges, not through the content of the poems as such, a purpose that even the most trivial and lighthearted subject matter could fulfil in the right circumstances.[59]

CHAPTER TWO

Poetry as a Game

Both Chinese and Western studies tend to overlook the importance of the playful aspects of Northern Song poetry. Although there were periods in the late-Ming and Qing dynasties when critics attempted to revive its reputation, the typical account of Northern Song poetic style as rational, discursive, and plain prevailed until very recently.[1] This characterization—prevalent as early as Yan Yu's *Canglang shihua*—is at best a half-truth, neglecting many aspects of Northern Song poetry that make it literature rather than mere rhymed philosophizing, namely, its wit, humor, ingenious structuring, and what I have termed "caricatured reasoning."[2]

Scholars often seem uncomfortable with the idea that some of the greatest and most soberly moralistic statesmen and ancient-prose writers—Ouyang Xiu and Wang Anshi (1021–1086), for instance—should have expended so much creative energy on seemingly trivial poetic subject matter, literary games, and ridiculous self-caricatures. Unlike the writers themselves, who were quite happy to publish the entertaining fruits of their leisure alongside more serious literary and philosophical undertakings, scholars censure them for their frequent lapses of taste, or they focus only on poems whose rational, plain appearance outweighs their entertainment value. The remarks of Zhu Dongrun concerning the poetry of Mei Yaochen are representative of this tendency:[3]

> From the beginning of the Song period, more and more answering poems and rhyme-matching poems were written. The effect of this was to push compositions on personal topics strongly in the direction of word games. This was a bad practice! . . . When we see that among [Mei] Yaochen's poems there are some compositions full of noble ideas and significance, but many more compositions that are insignificant or do not rise above the level of word games, how should we evaluate him? . . . The only standard we should use to measure a poet's greatness should be that of his best compositions.

According to Zhu, Mei's best compositions were his plain and serious poems of social criticism.[4] Yet were his poetic word games as worthless as Zhu implies? Despite their trivial contents, did they not in fact serve a very useful social function? Before dismissing such poems out of hand, we should first examine them in the light of Northern Song statements on the purposes of poetry. Indeed, these game poems may turn out to be even more representative of Northern Song poets' aesthetic and cultural concerns than their serious, overtly political verse.

Over the last decade, some Chinese scholars have revised their negative views of Northern Song poetic games and wordplay. Wang Shuizhao, for instance, in a paper originally published in 1979, condemned Northern Song poets for being no better than bandits and thieves, stealing their poetic lines and ideas from earlier poets. Wang chose to ignore the witty ways in which these poets often transformed their models, creating new and original works of art.[5] By the mid-1990s, however, encouraged by the more open political and literary environment in China, Wang was able to draw the following more balanced conclusion:[6]

> [Practices such as] rhyme-matching doubtless had some negative effects on the creative art of poetry. Nevertheless, the competitive spirit and craftsmanship that they fostered helped to stimulate poets' vitality and exercise their minds, and encouraged them to enjoy the refined pleasures of life. Honing and improving their basic creative techniques through such tests of ingenuity could also result in a whole new artistic style.

In this chapter, I incorporate and expand on recent scholars' positive evaluations of the less serious side of Mid-Northern Song poetry. Specifically, I discuss poems by Ouyang Xiu and Mei Yaochen that were obviously produced from literary games with rhyme, imagery, and meter. By literary games I mean contests among two or more participants in which the object was to produce a poem based on specified rules. These contests usually took place at a social gathering where food and wine were consumed and an atmosphere of levity prevailed. These games, far from being strange anomalies in the otherwise serious oeuvre of Northern Song literati, helped to promote one of their central aesthetic, and by extension political, ideals: the revival of ancient style in both prose and verse. And just as important, as Wang Shuizhao noted, poetic games helped bring educated people together to participate in civilized, playfully competitive, activities. Though their content was often trivial, the poems produced from such games reveal behind their wit and wordplay the broader and weightier aim of encouraging social cohesion.

Though certainly not the first Chinese poets to engage in ludic pursuits, Ouyang Xiu, Mei Yaochen, and their colleagues were tireless refiners of inherited literary games and imaginative inventors of new ones. And unlike most previous poets, they left numerous poetic records of game playing scattered among their collected works. Using these records, I will address the questions of why literary games became so popular in the Northern Song; what broader social roles they might have served; and how they may have influenced the development of poetry and aesthetics during the Northern Song period.[7]

ANYTHING YOU CAN DO: GAMES WITH RHYME

A number of poems in Ouyang Xiu's and Mei Yaochen's collections bear titles that indicate the poem originated in a rhyme game, such as: "On *Ren* festival we gathered at Constellation Hall, drew lots for rhymes, and I received the character *feng*" (*Renri Juxingtang yanji tanyun de feng zi*).[8] The participants would look up the randomly selected character—in this case, *feng*—in a rhyming dictionary such as the *Guangyun*, find other words in the same rhyming category, and spontaneously compose a poem using as many of those rhyme words as possible.[9] Presumably the content of the poem would be wittily related to the particular social occasion. The poem on the *Ren* festival, for instance, includes the lines:[10]

Look at me: I'm really crude and shallow
This crowd of heroes futilely places me on a pedestal;

> But to receive anything at all [from them] is already an honor,
> So even if it's too much, can I refuse such "abundance" [*feng*]!

The wit of the poem lies in the double function of the word *feng*. If we read the fourth line literally, Ouyang seems grateful to his friends: he appreciates their "abundance" (*feng*) of generosity in allowing such an untalented fellow as himself to join their poetic gathering. However, behind the surface politeness we can sense Ouyang's resentment, albeit tongue-in-cheek, that he must produce a poem on demand. Hence, the final line could instead be translated more literally: "I cannot refuse [this difficult challenge of rhyming with] *feng*."

This kind of rhyming game sets up a test of ingenuity, a competitive challenge, in which the victor is not so much the profound or refined artist as the quick-thinking, clever, and spontaneous wit. Another point to note is that if one were to read the poem without the clue provided by the title, one would almost certainly miss the game-like quality of the poem, and take it for a simple expression of Ouyang Xiu's self-deprecating modesty. In other words, these writers are anxious to let us know that this is a game.

Random selection of rhyme categories was one of many rhyming games, and certainly not the most common, judging from the poems that survive. It was more popular for poets to compete at creating a verse using rhyme words or rhyme categories supplied by a well-known previous poet. This kind of game added a dimension to the random selection of rhymes. It enabled the participants not only to compete against their fellow literati at a social gathering but also to seek to match or even outdo the compositions of famous writers of the past.

Several variations on this rhyme game appear in Ouyang Xiu and Mei Yaochen's collections. There are poems emulating the skill of mid-Tang writers—especially Han Yu (768–824)—at using particular rhyme categories for expressive effects.[11] Another variation was a game known as matching rhymes (*ci yun* or *yi yun*). Here the poet used not just the same rhyme category of a previous poem but exactly the same rhyme words in the same sequence. The object was to come up with a composition quite different from the model—a fresh mood, or even an opposite conclusion—despite being restricted to the same rhymed endings.

When they matched rhymes, poets obviously delighted in rhyme words with double meanings, especially if they allowed for an incongruous contrast with the original poem. A poem by Ouyang Xiu and its matching composition by Mei Yaochen will illustrate this point. According to the title, Ouyang's poem was written to respond to an earlier work by Mei. In the translation, I have put the matched rhyme words in bold type:

Answering Shengyu's "Don't Drink Wine" [1057][12]

You say, "Don't drink wine!"
I say, "Don't write **poems**!"
Flowers bloom, leaves fall, insects and birds grow **forlorn**,
All four seasons the hundred creatures disturb my **cogitation**,
Mornings I chant, shaking my head; evenings I knit my **brows**,
"Carving liver and sculpting kidneys," I keep hearing [Han] Tui**zhi**,[13]
And with those words, that old man even **contradicted** himself!
Can this compare with drinking wine and losing all **awareness**?
From ancient times, even abstainers have not escaped mortality,
There were some that performed good deeds, but they too could not **delay** it.
You may offer yourself to the world with sagely and worthy behavior,
Or compose essays and writings to be **passed down** through the millennia,
But the rest of the time, get plastered on a goblet of fine wine,
And the strife of ten thousand concerns will become completely calm.[14]
"Rotting innards," "pickled meat": the theories of both these schools
Are just so much pedantic tattle: **base** in the extreme![15]
There's little to choose between long life and premature mortality,
Since even the span of a hundred years is really not much **time**.
So just continue drinking wine,
And don't write any **poems**:
You ought to pay heed to my advice, so you won't seem like a **fool**!

Matching the Rhymes of Yongshu's Irregular Meter Poem Urging Me to Drink Wine and Not Compose Poetry [1057][16]

In my life there is little I crave,
My only desires: wine and **poems**,

A single day without these two, and my heart grows quite **forlorn**;
4 Lasting name or noble status: these I never **long for**,
My jars are empty, my cooking pots cold, but I do not hang my **head**;
My wife and young ones freeze and go hungry: they often rage about **that**,
Yet once I begin to chant and get drunk, I **turn away** from the world,
8 No longer do ten thousand affairs cause me any **concern**.
For meetings with the high and mighty, everyone else departs early,
But as I grow old I've grown lazier: I don't arrive till **late**,
The sun towers high: like a weary servant, my face becomes dejected,
12 Especially riding my skinny horse, its two ears **drooping down**.
I cannot stand such trouble and suffering; no longer enjoy going out,
Only in writing, now and again, can I still manage to perform;
Yet all my friends still fear that I'll exhaust my stores of wisdom,
16 They urge me to drink and be merry, to stop **looking down** at myself!
Thanks again for giving your advice,
It's just that **when** you corrected me,
You loved **poetry** alone,
20 But you said that *I* was the **fool**![17]

The rhyme scheme is irregular: a partial *Boliangti*.[18] Lines two to eight rhyme on every line; from lines ten to eighteen the rhyme relaxes to alternate lines; and the final two lines again share the same rhyme words. Mei matches Ouyang's rhymes almost completely. Only in line fourteen does he choose not to use the same rhyme word as Ouyang.

Looking at the rhyme words shared by the two poems, it is clear that Mei plays with variant meanings of the same character. For instance, the *zhi* in Han Yu's style name Tuizhi in Ouyang's poem (line 6) becomes the object pronoun *zhi* (that; it) in Mei's work. And *chui*, which means lasting or to be passed down in Ouyang's poem (line 12) takes on the more literal meaning of drooping in Mei's poem, in the process replacing Ouyang's heroic sentiments ("essays and writings . . . passed down through the generations") with a pathetic self-caricature of himself as a cantankerous old man on his skinny, droopy-eared horse.

Although the two writers use the same rhymes and a similar method of argumentation—the caricatured reasoning typical of the Northern Song—they manage to draw opposite conclusions: Ouyang wrote a poem to persuade Mei that writing poems will only bring trouble, and Mei responds by declaring that writing poems (and getting drunk while doing so) is the only way he can escape his troubles.

A further variation on rhyme games promoted by Ouyang, Mei, and their acquaintances involved writing a whole series of poems with matching rhyme words. The model setting the rhyme could be one's own poem or that of a fellow poet; the challenge was to produce as many different compositions as possible without duplicating the content of earlier poems in the series. If a group of poets was involved, one of them would compose a model, and the others would all compete to match its rhymes two or three times. Either the winner or losers would then presumably be forced to drain a goblet of wine.[19]

Writers of Ouyang and Mei's generation tended to restrict exact rhyme matching to their contemporaries' works. Later generations greatly extended the game, frequently matching the rhymes of famous past writers too. The best known example, of course, was Su Shi's almost obsessive project to match the complete poems of his illustrious predecessor Tao Qian (c. 365–c. 427). By this stage, rhyme matching had developed from a lighthearted game into a fulfledged poetic technique used to express a broad range of human emotions.[20]

A slightly different kind of rhyming game involved a pair or group of poets composing linked verses (*lian ju*): the first player would write, say, three lines of a poem, and the others would take turns to complete the second—or overhanging—couplet, then add another line of their own to continue the game. Various combinations of poem and line length were possible, although normally, Song linked verses preserved the same rhyme category throughout the poem. The challenge was to maintain a consistent style, even though several writers were participating in the composition. There was also the test of continuing the narrative line when the preceding player had willfully sent it in a quite unexpected direction. Ouyang Xiu's friend Su Shunqin (1008–1048) and his brother Su Shunyuan (1006–1054) were probably the most enthusiastic practitioners of linked verse in the Northern Song, and numerous examples survive in Su Shunqin's collected works.[21]

Few of these rhyming games were actually invented by Ouyang Xiu or his contemporaries—in fact, examples appear in the collections of mid-Tang poets like Han Yu and Meng Jiao (linked verses), and Bai Juyi and Yuan Zhen (rhyme matching).[22] One could also argue that prototypes of these literary games appeared even earlier, in the Wei-Jin and Six Dynasties period (220–589), as illustrated by anecdotes in the *Shishuo xinyu* (*A New Account of Tales of the World*) and poems of the period matching the style of earlier poets.[23] Nevertheless, the sheer number of such games in Northern Song poetry collections, especially when augmented by other kinds of literary diversions, provide ample evidence that game playing was particularly common among the literati during this period.

Whether or not Northern Song poets actually indulged in literary games more than their predecessors, they placed a higher value on recording and preserving the poems such games inspired. Doubtless, this is because these rhyming games related to their broader stylistic and cultural concerns. There are three features of these games, in particular, that poets of the period found especially captivating, features that recur in other kinds of literary games involving meter and imagery.

The first noteworthy characteristic of Northern Song rhyming games is that the great majority were composed in ancient style verse forms—long, often rambling, poems with plain diction, few parallel couplets, and little description of natural scenes. A second feature is the spontaneous and competitive nature of these games, which produces poems that are witty, humorous, and loosely argumentative rather than dense, emotional, and highly crafted. A third feature is the random quality of rhymes—since there is usually no semantic relation between words that rhyme—which results in incongruous, even awkward, transitions and juxtapositions within poems, as the writer strives to include as many rhymes as possible to win the competition while still retaining a modicum of sense.[24]

These three features are central to Northern Song literati conceptions of ancient writing style; they are not simply aberrations confined to poetry produced from literary games. On the contrary, literary games were an ingenious method of promoting ancient style through an enjoyable and fashionable pastime.[25]

THE LONG AND THE SHORT OF IT: GAMES WITH METER

In games involving poetic meter, the same three characteristics emerge. Even though the majority of poems composed in the

Song adopted five or seven syllable meters, whose regularity allowed little leeway for ludic variation, Ouyang Xiu, and to a lesser extent Mei Yaochen and Su Shunqin, engaged in two kinds of games using irregular meters.

The first kind involved creating an unusual metrical scheme as the basis for filling in the blanks. An example is the peculiar composition entitled "Chant of the Drunken Old Man" (Zuiweng yin). According to a colophon by Ouyang Xiu, he and Mei Yaochen composed it together in 1056.[26] However, the text does not appear in Ouyang's collected works but survives only in one edition of Mei's poetry. It gives a whimsical portrait of Ouyang's famous alter ego:[27]

The Old Man comes,
The Old Man comes,
The Old Man comes riding his horse.
How can one describe his drunkenness?
Beneath the forest and the spring
The sun sets in gloomy mist, the valley darkens,
Sounds of hooves echo through the rural plains.
The moon appears from the East and shines upon him,
He clutches its brightness but can never fill his hands!
The wine wears off, but before he sobers up
Again he grabs the jade wine-jar
And pours it down his throat—
This is
The Old Man's drunkenness!
Alpine flowers dazzle oh,
Alpine trees tower high oh,
The Old Man is plastered oh.
Birds call to the right oh,
Beasts cry to the left oh,
The Old Man is unsteady oh.
Insects and cicadas chirp oh,
Stony spring-waters gurgle oh,
The Old Man is sozzled oh.[28]

This chant is playful in tone; note the various colloquial expressions for drunkenness in lines 15–23, mixed with folksy natural description. A note to the title makes it clear that this is as much a game as a literary work: "In this zither tune, the [line lengths] increase from two to seven syllables and then decrease [back to two]."[29] This kind of meter is not based on an existing zither tune, but is Ouyang and Mei's own creation. Although there are earlier examples where meters gradually expand from one to seven or more syllables, I have not come across any previous poem whose meter then shrinks back to two syllables.[30] Doubtless the unsteady arrival and departure of their drunken subject inspired the poets to invent a new game.

Most Chinese *shi* poetry adopted regular five or seven syllable meters, so no other examples of this game of fitting words to a tricky, preset irregular meter survive among Ouyang and Mei's *shi*. However, the game closely resembles the technique of song lyric (*ci*) composition, which also involved filling (*tian*) words into a preset meter based on an existing tune, and often included lines of irregular length. The mood of lyrics was normally melancholy, but Northern Song poets such as Ouyang Xiu and Su Shi made the genre a vehicle for wit and humor as well.[31]

Moreover, according to many anecdotes of the period, even apparently serious lyrics were often the result of competitive games. To give just one example from the collection entitled *Qianshi sizhi* (*Master Qian's Private Records*) attributed to Qian Mian (late Northern Song): the young Ouyang Xiu arrived at an official banquet late, disheveled and accompanied by a courtesan. The courtesan's excuse for their tardiness was that she had been looking for a lost hairpin. Ouyang's boss, Qian Weiyan (973–1034) wanted to punish the courtesan, but agreed to pardon her if Ouyang would spontaneously compose a lyric containing the word hairpin. Ouyang acquitted himself brilliantly—without hesitation he created a lyric in two stanzas, using a highly irregular 7-6-7-4-5 meter. Amidst applause from the assembled guests, Qian ordered the concubine to reward him with a cup of wine.[32] Although such anecdotes may contain spurious information, they at least demonstrate that the Northern Song penchant for game playing occasionally extended to lyric composition as well, a fact that is not always clear from the content of the lyrics themselves.[33]

The second kind of game that Northern Song poets played with meter was varying individual line lengths in ancient-style poems to produce specific expressive effects—what we might more accurately term a playful technique rather than a full-fledged game. Ouyang Xiu was especially keen on this device. For example, in his poem "Picture of a Climbing Cart", the first few lines describe a tired traveler on a rickety cart, painfully negotiating rocky mountain roads. The meter is a correspondingly uneven 4-4-7:[34]

Pale mountains, crag on crag,
Jumbled stones, pile on pile;

Mountain rocks are sharp and jagged; the cart goes bumpety bump.
淺山嶙嶙，亂石疊疊，山石磽聱車碌碌。

The asymmetrical placing of the three binomes (*linlin* 嶙嶙, *diedie* 疊疊, and *lulu* 碌碌) at the end of each line heightens the uneven effect, so that readers can almost hear the old cart lurching from side to side as it rolls up the road.

Ouyang delighted in creating such vivid metrical effects to emphasize his point. In the last line of his poem "Lu Mountain High!" for instance, he exclaims: "Alas, I would like to express myself, but where can I find a mighty brush standing as high as a flagpole?" (嗟我欲說安得巨筆如長杠). The word, translated "high", is actually *chang* 長 (literally: long), and it is no coincidence that this line of 11 syllables is the longest in the poem—almost as long as the brush Ouyang is looking for.[35]

Ouyang similarly uses line length to make a point in his "Song on a Stone Screen of Scholar Wu," which describes the immense efforts expended by supernatural spirits to carve out a stone screen with a beautiful natural grain pattern.[36] The lines stretch out, as if embodying the painful and extended struggle: "Gods grieved and ghosts wept, night and day unable to take their rest; / Otherwise, could they achieve what cunning craftsmen and skillful hands—wearying their spirits, exhausting their thoughts—could not attain: / Visible yet almost invisible, faintly rising tendrils of mist?" (神愁鬼泣晝夜不得閑，不然安得巧工妙手憊精竭思不可到，若無若有縹緲生雲煙。)[37]

Su Shi, who was not normally given to such irregularity in his meters, produced a similar effect in a poem on the same topic as Ouyang's. He claims that the pattern on the stone screen resembled a small yet ancient pine tree, therefore he stretches out the line to embody the tree's great longevity:

Who was it gave you this stone wind screen?
On it are the finest, wispiest traces of watery ink.
He did not paint towering forests or enormous trees,
But only the solitary pine that lives for ten thousand years without
growing old on the snowy peaks of Emei's western range!
(何人遺公石屏風，上有水墨希微蹤，不畫長林與巨植，獨畫峨嵋山西雲嶺上萬歲不老之孤松。)[38]

These literary games with meter frequently generated poems that have a rough and uneven feel. Yet in many of these poems the irregularity is quite appropriate for their subjects—jagged mountains, strange shaped stones, wizened trees. What may have begun as a game or playful technique ultimately produced an innovative and artistically convincing aesthetic effect: a *haofang* (untrammeled) topic treated in a suitably untrammeled, expansive form. Hence, with their lighthearted games, Northern Song literati found an excuse for experimenting with new poetic techniques or for reviving unfashionable old ones. They could claim to be merely playing, when in fact they were still seriously engaged in transforming the writing style of their time.[39]

As the following group of games based on imagery will indicate, for at least some Northern Song poets, the central aim of these apparently trivial exercises was to throw off the frothy accretions of the Chinese poetic tradition, and to return to the simpler, more direct, and human poetic language and sociable poetic practices of the ancients.

PLAYING WITH ABSENCE: IMAGERY GAMES

In 1050, Ouyang Xiu composed a poem entitled "Snow":[40]

> The forces of *yang* are still weak, spring buds just breaking through,
> When the parting guest *yin* uses its strength to elbow its way back in.
> The morning chill is biting, and none can oppose the wind,
> Evening snow, in bits and pieces, stops then falls once again.
> Driven at a gallop, clouds in the wind are pale and vague at first,
> Dazzling, sparkling, mountains and rivers begin to reveal their forms;
> Their bright radiance charms in the rising sun's reflection,
> But warm air will soon make the melting moisture glisten.
> The fair lady in her lofty hall rises startled in the morning,
> A hidden recluse, through open windows, hears it falling in the silence.
> Before the wine-shop a path has formed; bottles and wine jars pile high,
> Hunters ride out seeking footprints, and bag a fox or raccoon dog.
> Tracks swept by dragons and snakes come to a halt, then continue,
> Gnashing tigers, formed from snowballs, bare their teeth and claws.
> We all look forward to harvest-time: we'll gorge ourselves with barley,

Why should we pity the hungry birds within the empty forest?
On Sandy Dyke at morning celebrations, one loses his ivory seal,
In rural fields, singing as she walks, another has her straw sandals buried.
I know well that whenever it snows, ten thousand people rejoice,
Yet look at me, not allowed to drink: what can bring me happiness?
Suddenly I see Heaven and Earth cleared of atmospheric dust,
It makes my insides feel that they've been washed utterly clean,
I escape and leave behind stale words—laugh at their dusty confusion,
Search and explore ten thousand phenomena, gazing at boundless infinity.
Even if Ying[zhou] is a backward place, there are plenty of literary types,
One by one they wield huge brushes as if brandishing spears or halberds.
But had I not helped them get this [pastime] going in the beginning,
Our frozen mouths would have no excuse for opening up and grinning!

This work is entertaining, especially with its vivid sketches of children's snow sculptures (line 14), and peoples' joyful reactions to the sudden whiteness of the landscape (lines 11–12, 17–19). But toward the end of the poem, Ouyang digresses. He talks of "escaping and leaving behind stale words," and "laughing at their dusty confusion" (line 23). He claims to have invented some pastime to share with his friends in Yingzhou, a pastime that will give them joy in the freezing winter weather (lines 27–28). To explain this sudden transition, we need the help of Ouyang's preface, which states: "I requested that words such as jade, the moon, pear and apricot [blossoms], silk, catkins, white, dancing, geese, cranes, and silver should not be used [in our poems on snow]."[41] In other words, all images typically associated with snow in the Chinese poetic tradition were forbidden.

References to similar games avoiding certain images appear elsewhere in Northern Song texts. In his *Remarks on Poetry*, Ouyang Xiu relates an anecdote about the Nine Monks—Buddhist poets of the early Northern Song. A local good-for-nothing named Xu Dong wished to show these monks lacked creativity and imagination. So he invited them all together and asked them each to write a poem avoiding references to "mountains, water, wind, clouds, bamboo, rocks, flowers, plants, snow, frost, stars, the moon, birds, and the like." At this, the Nine Monks all put away their writing brushes.[42] Since these topics and their associated images are the staples of the Chinese poetic tradition, it is hardly surprising the monk poets failed to rise to this challenge.

Another, less tightly structured example appears in a poem preface by Mei Yaochen. In 1055, Ouyang Xiu wrote a verse about his pet white rabbit and requested that his friends match his rhymes.[43] When he received their responses, writes Mei, Ouyang "said that all our compositions used Chang'e and the Moon Palace to explain [the creature's origins], whereas he really hoped we would each write another poem with a different context. In this way, we might rise above the common herd."[44] Ouyang, in his own subsequent poems on the rabbit, overturned the traditional habit of associating whiteness with the moon, cold, snow, and the force of *yin*: he pointed out that his other pet, a white parrot, was much more at home in the fiery latitudes of the tropics, where seas boil over and the force of *yang* reigns supreme.[45]

These episodes show that Ouyang and his circle were preoccupied with creating new images, breaking free from the platitudes of their contemporaries, and setting up a method (or game) to encourage experimentation. Nevertheless, their stated aim in doing this was not to be innovative, but to emulate the directness of ancient writers. In a well-known eulogy to Mei Yaochen's poetic style, Ouyang's choice of epithets illustrates this point:

> His recent poems are especially *ancient* and tough:
> I chew, but they're extremely hard to swallow;
> It's just like when I try to eat olives:
> Their true flavor only deepens over time.
> . . . Mei is poor, and I alone understand him:
> *Ancient* goods are hard to sell at present.[46]

Of course, by promoting the ancient, these writers were also seeking, in Ouyang Xiu's words, to "rise above the common herd": to distinguish themselves from competitors of their own generation by identifying themselves with the vitality of brilliant and humane scholars of the past. And in the Northern Song context, claiming to be ancient often went hand in hand with both literary innovation and playfulness.

JOYS OF THE ANCIENTS

The literary games played by Northern Song poets are too numerous to discuss comprehensively here. Besides the more structured games with rhyme, imagery, and meter already mentioned, the poets engaged in numerous other playful literary practices that added wit and lightheartedness to their poems. For example, Northern Song literati were fond of creating eccentric personae—Ouyang's Drunken Old Man (*Zuiweng*); Mei Yaochen's Poet Elder (*Shilao*); Su Shi's Recluse of East Slope (*Dongpo jushi*), among others—to serve as semicomical protagonists in their poems. They also delighted in challenging each other to write on unusual and slightly ridiculous topics, such as lice, mosquitoes, and other insects, bulgy-headed fish, a plate of clams, a wine cup shaped like a parrot, and so on.[47] And they liberally used incongruous juxtapositions and humorous hyperbole in their poems.[48]

The purpose here is not to survey these games exhaustively but to view them in the broader context of the functions of poetry in the Northern Song period. One could dismiss the poems resulting from these games as mere entertainment, and focus instead on more serious poetry of the period dealing with issues of obvious social concern. Yet such an approach is one-sided. It ignores the complexities of Northern Song poetic style and, more crucial, overlooks the fact that the writers themselves frequently justified their game-playing inclinations in published prefaces.

One revealing preface dates from the very beginning of Mei Yaochen and Ouyang Xiu's official careers. Both men served in the entourage of Qian Weiyan, the cultivated governor of Luoyang during the early 1030s. On an outing with friends to a nearby temple they created a game in which each participant composed five quatrains with rhymes based on the words of famous phrases of poetry.[49] Ouyang Xiu, for instance, picked the line, "On the pavilion mound, the leaves fall from the trees" (*ting gao mu ye xia* 亭皋木葉下), and his first poem, based on the rhyme *ting* 亭, translates:[50]

Above the stream, again we recline on the rocks,
Happily we grow drunk and then sober up together;
Sunset clouds linger on the mountains, not yet gathered in,
But the moon [reflected] in the pool comes soaring high above them
(*tingting* 亭亭).

Ouyang reduplicates *ting* (pavilion), the first of the rhyme words in the source line, to produce his matching word *tingting* (soaring).

After the game, Mei Yaochen composed his preface, describing the occasion and explaining why they decided to preserve their poems:[51]

> When I was about to return north to Heyang, my friend Ouyang Yongshu and two or three other gentlemen prepared wine and dishes, selected a historical site, and arranged for us to spend the whole day enjoying ourselves to the full as a means of bidding farewell to me. So we found Puming Temple and strained our wine in the bamboo grove there. Old and young sat in a circle, and we dispensed with the polite rituals of offering and passing around [the wine], yet superiors did not lose any dignity, and inferiors did not cause disorder. We whistled and sang harmoniously, and attained a state of transcendent freedom.
>
> When we had drunk our fill of wine, Yongshu said: "Our joy today is certainly no less than that of the ancients: far from the dusty world we have found a beautiful site where we can open our mouths and express our true feelings. But, though we have attained such [joy], we have not yet set it down in writing." He told us to take paper, write out some famous poetic phrases of the past worthies, and place them by our seats.[52] Each of us would then select one phrase and make a rhyme from every character to record the beauties of this gathering.
>
> Someone said: 'Yongshu is correct. If we do not do this, people of future times will think we are merely madmen who guzzle meat and wine!'
>
> In a short while, everyone presented his poem, and then we retrieved our wine cups, got completely drunk, and departed. The following day [Ouyang] delivered the collection of poems, and asked me to compose an account of all that had happened.

By borrowing lines from famous poets as the basis for verses celebrating their present joy—a joy no less than that of the ancients—these young Song officials raised their poetic game and farewell picnic to the status of a civilized cultural event, just as significant as any gathering of worthies in the past. In this connection, one might note the conscious echoing by Mei Yaochen of Wang Xizhi's (c. 321–c. 379) much more famous, and by Song times certainly ancient, "Preface to the Orchid Pavilion Collection" which described a similar gathering of literati playing poetic games.[53]

In addition, these poets desired to preserve this event for the future, to describe it in words so that later generations would know their transcendent happiness and outstanding talent and realize that they were not a crude, hedonistic bunch of wine and meat-guzzling madmen. In short, they wished to define themselves as literati, to create a recognizable cultural group with its own civilized, free, and relaxed ethos inspired by the ancients. Part of that ethos was the ability to compose poetry spontaneously—to excel at literary games.

Despite its subtle allusions and exalted mood, Mei's preface also has a touching and down-to-earth honesty, especially in the verbatim record of his friends' comments. He is quite comfortable revealing their youthful pretensions and implicitly mocking their self-image of sophistication. The reader is left with an incongruous, yet convincing, portrait—a complex of high literary ideals, ancient aspirations, ambition, playfulness, and earthy friendship—stylistically similar to the poems we have discussed.

A similar picture appears in an account (quoted briefly in the previous chapter), which Ouyang Xiu wrote some twenty-five years later when he was reaching the peak of his political and literary powers.[54] Once again we see a gathering of literati. Mei Yaochen was present, along with a new group of like-minded colleagues. Locked in the Ministry of Rites, grading the *jinshi* exams of 1057, they passed their evenings exchanging poems and playing literary games. Later Ouyang, the chief examiner and presumably chief gamester, brought out a collection of these poems with his own preface. He justified their joking and playfulness by comparing their poems to the ancient *Shijing* (*Classic of Poetry*). Indeed, he declared, the Superior Person (*junzi*) should draw inspiration from all aspects of life, including even the base, crude, and comical—especially when composing poetry.[55]

Toward the end of his life, in 1071, Ouyang once more recalled this episode in glowing terms:[56]

> The six of us were delighted to find ourselves together, and spent every day in each others' company creating long compositions with perilous rhymes, taking turns to treat every genre. The writing clerks wearied of copying them down, and the servants had to dash back and forth [taking poems between the examiners]. With humor and joking, expressing ourselves in satirical vein, we kept responding to each other, constantly breaking out into laughter. I'd say it was the

most memorable event of that whole period: nothing like it had ever happened before!

Like Mei, but perhaps more tongue-in-cheek, Ouyang attempted to raise a series of parties and poetic games to the status of a defining cultural moment—what he called the most memorable event of that whole period—and he claimed the participants were Superior Persons. In other words, they were living completely in accordance with Confucian ideals. Like Mei, Ouyang published these poems with an accompanying preface, preserving the event for future generations.

In traditional accounts of Song poetry, Ouyang and Mei Yaochen's serious ancient-style verse normally opposes the flowery, ornamented, and empty regulated verse of the so-called Xikun School as represented by the early eleventh-century collection entitled *Xikun chouchang ji*. Both Chinese and Western scholars often claim that Ouyang and Mei's group attacked the Xikun poets for ignoring the socio-critical function of poetry.[57] While the style of Ouyang and Mei's mature poetry is generally much plainer that of the Xikun contributors, they share several attributes, most notably an appreciation of the multiple meanings of words, an enthusiasm for creating witty poetic allusions, and a desire to be seen as part of a cultivated group of literati. Doubtless, this is the reason Ouyang Xiu praised a number of the Xikun poets highly in his *Remarks on Poetry*.[58] Indeed, Ouyang's and Mei's first employer, Qian Weiyan, was one of the main contributors to the *Xikun chouchang ji*, and was apparently a keen literary gamester himself.[59]

Clearly, Mid Northern Song poets believed that their poetic games had a useful social function in the sense that the game could not be isolated from the solidarity and companionship of the participants. In organizing such games, the group's members demonstrated to outsiders that they were relaxed, witty, and appreciative of life's pleasures—especially wine and exotic foods—while being literate and erudite, worthy transmitters of the Chinese cultural tradition. Hence, the important aspect of these game-poems was not so much the superior quality, attractiveness, or seriousness of the finished products; rather, it was that they were produced by a civilized group of literati, humane scholars who were bound by sincere friendship and mutual respect, and who did not seek to profit at the expense of others. They were what Ouyang Xiu, in his famous prose piece On Factions, termed a faction of Superior Persons rather than of petty people (*xiaoren*).[60] The test for the former was whether its members could manage to stay together, following the same path (*dao*) and basing their association not on profit or material benefit but on the Confucian virtues of sincerity, trustworthiness, and righteousness. By contrast, factions of petty people would soon fall apart due to mutual conflict and betrayal. What better way to display the disinterested nature of one's alliances than by playing literary games (and letting everyone know that one is doing so)?

There were, of course, political ramifications that arose from this alliance building function of poetic games. For instance, Ouyang Xiu just happened to compose linked verses with his main political ally Fan Zhongyan (989–1052) in 1043, around the same time that he was writing "On Factions." By doing so, he doubtless hoped to prove the natural closeness of their friendship and, by implication, their suitability for working together to overcome corruption in the government. One of these linked verses, entitled "Swords," begins with Fan's blunt couplet, "The sages produced spiritual weapons, / With which they settled the troubles of the Empire." A later couplet by Ouyang then declares: "Ghosts and ghouls disappear without a trace, / Factions of sycophants quake with abject terror!"[61]

In this respect, the extreme reaction of their conservative opponents to the poems of Ouyang and Fan Zhongyan's supporters, discussed in the previous chapter, becomes more understandable. Suspicious of all this camaraderie, they were convinced that even the most lighthearted literary games played by politicians were much less disinterested than they appeared.[62]

At the same time, however, most of these games were not played during times of political crisis like the mid-1040s, when suspicions of factionalism ran rife. In general, they would have served a much more personal function for the participants, spurring them on to greater creativity, helping them transcend difficult circumstances through flights of fancy, and preserving a record of memorable friendships. Mei Yaochen and Ouyang Xiu, for instance, sustained a remarkable poetic partnership over some thirty years. Whenever they met, they would play their games with meter, imagery, rhyme, and personae; and even when posted to different places, they would match each other's rhymes from a distance. In terms of their literary merits alone, some of the poems resulting from their exchanges may not seem worth preserving, but to ignore them is to miss the profound value that these poems had as reminders of friendship. Ouyang Xiu expressed the point most clearly and movingly toward the end of his life, when justifying his preservation of the slightly ridiculous "Chant of the Drunken Old Man": "[In 1056] I composed this poem with Shengyu. Five years later Shengyu died. It is now fifteen years since we composed the poem, and ten years since Shengyu passed away. Reading his words now, I immediately begin to weep. This is why I am mounting it on a scroll and keeping it."[63]

CHAPTER THREE

Poetry and Relationship Building

In the previous chapter, we saw that Northern Song literati regularly met with friends and acquaintances to play poetic games, using these games as a way to cement their relationships and express their shared outlook on life. In this chapter, I examine numerous other ways in which Northern Song writers used and exchanged poetry to build and sustain their social relationships, and to create alliances for both practical and personal reasons. In the process, I demonstrate further that for Mid-Northern Song poets, the Confucian Way was revealed not so much in the content of their compositions—which could vary from the sublime to the ridiculous—but rather in the social harmony that resulted from the activity of writing and exchanging poetry with others.

POETRY AND LOVE? A BRIEF DIGRESSION

In the introduction to his *Annotated Selection of Song Poetry* (*Song shi xuan zhu*), Qian Zhongshu noted that poets of the Song period rarely wrote about romantic love, unlike their Late Tang and Six Dynasties predecessors.[1] This generalization is accurate in the sense that, when dealing with human relationships, Northern Song poets focused most of their attention on friendship and brotherly affection rather than romance. Yet before going on to discuss the various functions of Mid-Northern Song poems dealing with such orthodox Confucian relationships, we should note two major qualifications to Qian's claim.

First, many of the better-known Song poets, such as Ouyang Xiu, Su Shi, and Huang Tingjian, did not confine their poetic talents to the *shi* forms, but also produced significant numbers of *ci* (song lyrics), whose frequent topic was erotically charged, often illicit, romantic love. Even some of the greatest statesmen of the Northern Song, including Fan Zhongyan and Yan Shu (991–1055), though not known for their talents in the *shi* forms, left some outstanding examples of love lyrics in the *ci* form.[2]

Some later commentators have attempted to interpret the romantic sentiments of these *ci* as disguised political comment—since they do not seem to fit with the Confucian family values trumpeted by cultural leaders like Ouyang Xiu and Fan Zhongyan.[3] As with indirect political critique in their *shi* poems, it is quite possible that Northern Song poets occasionally used their lyrics on lover's betrayals and secret assignations as a vehicle for expressing emotional frustration with corrupt government practices. But even if we allow for this extra level of interpretation with some lyrics, it is impossible to ignore the overwhelming evidence that many Northern Song literati spent their leisure time socializing with young female entertainers. Indeed, it is very likely that they composed most of their love lyrics spontaneously at parties, intending these entertainers to sing them, and possibly hoping to initiate a more intimate relationship with an entertainer who had caught their fancy.[4] Thus, rather than concluding that romantic love was not a major concern of Song poets, it would be more accurate to say that during the Northern Song the song lyric became the main vehicle for expressing romantic sentiments, whereas *shi* poetry generally dealt with more orthodox relationships, especially friendship.

However, the second qualification to this general statement is that most Northern Song poets were not ashamed of describing romantic moments spent with female entertainers in their *shi* poetry either, even though this was not usually their main focus. As part of their detailed depiction of everyday life, they occasionally included expressions of admiration for a friend's recently purchased female entertainer, praise for the singing girls in a local tavern, or other candid references to illicit sensual pleasures. For instance, in an early poem from 1034, Ouyang Xiu, then a twenty-seven-year-old married government official, described an enjoyable excursion with friends to view the local mountain scenery. He then continued with the following suggestive passage about the meal and entertainments they shared on their return to town that evening:[5]

. . . We returned to sit before wine cups and plates.
Flying Jasper was only just eighteen,
Seductive and delightful, with her hair in double plaits;
4 She warmed the cold bamboo [flute] with her phoenix beak,
With silver plectrum, she tuned the goose-gut strings,
And after she improvised her White Clouds Melody,
She offered around the golden boat [of wine].
8 The pearl blinds were rolled up to reveal the bright moon,
The night air was just like springtime mist;
Dappled candlelight played over her powdered complexion,
Reddened by wine, lotuses bloomed on her face.
12 In the eastern hall, the pomegranate blossoms were fine,
She adorned them in patterns to brighten her skirted waist,
She inserted a flower into her cloud-styled locks,
Then spread her sleeping mat in the green shade;
16 But before our joys had reached their apogee
Our drunken singing turned to sighs . . .[6]

Though the amount of detail Ouyang provides here is quite unusual for a *shi* poem, there are passing references to entertainers throughout the collections of most Northern Song poets, and they are not confined to poems of their youth. At fifty-seven years old, for instance, Mei Yaochen persuaded the reluctant Ouyang Xiu to go home in the rain after an enjoyable party by tempting him with a caricatured vision of the pleasures awaiting him:[7]

. . . You are complaining that the way back is dark,
But your neighing horse can find its way home,
And in your house are eight or nine entertainers,
4 Their silky black hair arranged in raven style,
They have crimson lips and white jade skin,
And they've only just reached the melon-splitting age.[8]
For several days we've endured pouring rains,
8 Fish and prawns are now leaping up the streets,
But you can lock your doors and drink unstrained wine,
Then tie a swing to the forked branch of a tree,
And when all those girls have finished their playing,
12 They'll serenade their master with songs and laughter,
This is the time when you should be drinking your fill:
Such joyful pleasures will not last for ever! . . .

A final example in this vein reveals that while Northern Song literati considered the enjoyment and even purchase of female entertainers to be perfectly acceptable, it was important that these young girls be treated humanely. In 1059, Ouyang and Mei visited a friend, Yang Bao, and listened to his recently purchased entertainer play the *pipa*. Though the two visitors greatly admired her playing, they were both shocked that Yang fed and clothed her so poorly. In their poems recording this occasion, they criticized Yang for focusing so much on aesthetic enjoyment and so little on basic humanity. Ouyang wrote:[9]

> The sound of the low strings lingers; the high strings hurry on,
> Sweetness, only ten years old, performs the "Woodpecker" tune.
> The woodpecker doesn't try to peck at newly-sprouting twigs,
> It only pecks the gnarled and jagged trunk of a withered tree . . .
> . . . The sweet child is still small but her fingers pluck quite firmly,
> The administrator's hall is cold, and the strings clearly resound.
> The dense timbre and urgent pulse overwhelm all the guests,
> As a toast to her I'll drink dry a golden goblet of wine!
> Master Yang loves elegance: his heart isn't vulgar at all,
> But his University post is low, and he sups on coarse husked grains.
> Sweetness wears a skirt made from two plain widths of cloth,
> On a wooden bed with only three legs, she sits and plays her tunes.
> Yet rare books and ancient paintings he buys at any price,
> He stores them in brocade bags, and mounts them on jade rollers.
> Opening his pictures and closing his volumes, sometimes he feels weary,
> He lies down and listens to the *pipa*, contemplating his chambers.
> When guests come he calls the girl quickly to comb and wash,
> Her forehead is filled with flowery ornaments, stuck with yellow chrysanthemums.
> Although her appearance is lovely, and her eyes and brows are graceful,
> Can she hide the prolonged hunger that shrivels her head and neck? . . .

Though in his title he claims to be writing in jest, Ouyang strongly censures Yang's willingness to expend great amounts of cash on the purchase and mounting of "rare books and ancient paintings" (line 13) while forgetting to provide the basic necessities for the young entertainers in his household. In other words, Mid-Northern Song poets apparently saw nothing shameful in visiting courtesans or keeping young girls to satisfy their emotional and physical needs, as long as they looked after them humanely and, presumably, did not indulge themselves to the extent of neglecting their public duties.[10]

Northern Song poets also saw no contradiction in using their poetry both to praise female entertainers and to express affection for their wives, although they tended to address the latter in a less suggestive manner than the former. Ouyang Xiu, for instance, facing the likelihood of a second exile in 1045, composed a touching verse letter to his wife, apologizing for his rash political behavior and expressing gratitude for her loyal support in the past. He wrote, in part:[11]

> . . . I once scuttled off to the Man of Jing, exiled,
> They forced me to flee as if lashing a whip.[12]
> Over mountains and streams, miasmal fog was dense,
> Through rivers and seas, the gales blew the waves.
> Constantly beside me, you shared all my suffering,
> Through demotion and loss, we disappeared together.
> Escaping with our lives, we were out of peoples' sight,
> Already exiled, who could envy us now?
> Amidst alpine flowers and wild grasses,
> I grew drunk, and you plucked your zither.
> We knew only contentment in our poverty,
> And paid no heed to the racing months and years.

Likewise, Mei Yaochen, after the sudden death of his first wife in 1044, poured out his grief in numerous poems over the next decade, recalling in detail the happy times they had spent together. Though not the first Chinese poet to compose a series of poems mourning a wife, Mei extended the unflinching vivid descriptive style characteristic of the Northern Song into this area of private grief and marital love, giving a much more convincing expression of his emotions than his Tang predecessors.[13]

As we have seen, mid-Northern Song poets did not entirely neglect romance, love, and matrimonial affection in their poetry. Yet the great majority of references to such topics in their *shi* poems are in works addressed to friends and acquaintances rather than to the purported objects of their affection. In other words, though a poem takes romantic love as a topic, in most cases its function was to maintain or build social ties with a friend or acquaintance. For instance, this function is obvious in Mei Yaochen's playful entreaty to Ouyang Xiu to return home to his female entertainers, a poem Mei composed at the end of a pleasant evening drinking together. Alternatively, such poems function as direct, if lighthearted, criticisms of acquaintances who had overstepped the bounds of human decency, as in the case of Ouyang's and Mei's poems censuring Yang Bao for treating his pipa-playing girl so meanly.

POETRY AND FRIENDSHIP

As noted in the introduction to this study, exchanges of poetry in Northern Song China were sometimes accompanied by exchanges of gifts and were central to the circulation of emotional energy between educated people. Poetry acted as a vital channel for initiating and sustaining close relationships with people in positions of power, forming mutually beneficial alliances and support groups with those of one's own social status, or even doing favors to those at lower levels on the social hierarchy.

Since maintaining relationships was probably the most important function of poetry during this period, literally thousands of poems exchanged among friends survive—too many to cover comprehensively here. To show the various ways in which such poems functioned, in this chapter I will select some representative examples from the works of Mei Yaochen and Ouyang Xiu arranged under three basic categories: poetry written, (1): to initiate relationships or overcome social barriers; (2): to sustain and deepen existing relationships; and (3): to bid farewell to friends departing on journeys and to commemorate the dead, in other words, poetry of separation. From these examples, we discern the sometimes awkward combination of practical and spiritual functions that poetry exchanges served in Northern Song. We conclude by explaining why poetry was more suitable than other forms of writing for circulating emotional energy within the rarefied social environment inhabited by Song literati.

INITIATING RELATIONSHIPS: POETRY AS ICEBREAKER

The official biographies of famous Chinese writers commonly contain passages that reveal the precocious literary talent of the subject at a very early age. Many accounts describe the visit of a distinguished scholar or established society figure at which the young child prodigy amazes the visitor with a brilliant spontaneous poetic composition. The visitor then makes predictions about the auspicious future awaiting the child if he continues to work hard and watch his behavior. Ouyang Fa, the son of Ouyang Xiu, recorded one such encounter in his biographical account of his father:[14]

> When my father [Ouyang Xiu] was three years old, his father died and the family was left poor and without resources. My grandmother taught him to recognize characters by writing them on the ground with a stick. She also made him recite the essays of the ancients and learn how to compose poems . . . The diction of the poetry and rhapsodies that he composed when he was still a child was already like that of an adult. When the regional head of the military affairs department read them, he said to my grandmother: "Madam, you need not be concerned that your family is poor and your children still young. This boy is outstanding. Not only will he improve the station of your family; in time, he will certainly also make a name for himself in the world."

Even if we allow that biographers embellished their accounts to exaggerate the brilliance of their famous subjects, it is clear educated parents in traditional China trained their children to compose poetry extemporaneously at an early age so they could impress potential patrons. Certainly, children also learned prose composition and memorized the Confucian classics, but unlike these activities, poetry writing was an integral element of the social gatherings attended by literati. Therefore, an acceptable way for a child to make a good impression on a prominent scholar without risking an embarrassing rejection by directly asking for patronage was for his parents to introduce him at such a social gathering, and prod him to recite a well-turned poetic couplet or quatrain on demand.[15]

Thus, Chinese children would early on have realized the practical social benefits of learning to compose poetry. Their initial aim, of course, was not to seek fame as poets, but to find an influential scholar who would train them to pass the civil service examinations and introduce them into society, after which they could seek a high-ranking position in the government. Ouyang Xiu expressed this practical aim in a poem contrasting his enjoyment of book reading in old age with the much more materialistic outlook of his childhood:[16]

. . . I think of the past, when I first followed a teacher,
Studying hard, I hoped for official appointment,
I did not dare pursue fame and reputation:
All I expected was to escape poverty and baseness,
"Forgetting to eat," day would approach evening,
"Burning firewood," night encroached on the dawn;[17]
I expected that after attaining my ambition,
I'd be able to destroy my brushes and ink-stone;
And to make up a little for my times of hardship
I'd concentrate only on sleeping and eating! . . .

During the Northern Song period, civil service examinations, in which composing poetry was a major element, became the most important means of selecting future government officials, unlike the Tang period when the selection process was more informal and slanted in favor of the sons of established aristocratic families.[18] Yet simply passing the examinations did not guarantee one a good position in the government. Therefore, in order to seek their support and recommendation, most successful candidates would aim to become proteges of their examiners—invariably powerful scholar-officials—even though in most cases they had received no previous instruction from them and perhaps had never met them. To accomplish this, candidates had to impress examiners with their social graces and cultivated behavior. This was in addition to the intellectual ability they had already demonstrated in the examination. Exchanging poems at social gatherings was an excellent and socially acceptable means of initiating these new relationships. The most gifted young scholars managed to flatter their new patrons indirectly in their poems, while maintaining the polite convention that this was simply a relaxing and civilized meeting of friends with no materialistic purpose.

For instance, Su Shi composed two poems in 1059 that address his examiner, Ouyang Xiu, in the titles. In the first poem, matching a composition by his younger brother, Su Shi imitated Ouyang's game poem "Snow," with its playful prohibition of stereotypical images associated with snow. As he notes in his long title: "Encountering Snow on the River, I Imitated the Ouyang Form, Restricting Myself by Not Making Comparisons to Salt, Jade, Cranes, Egrets, Willow Catkins, Butterflies, Flying, and Dancing, and Also Not Using Words Like Dazzling, White, Pure, and Silken—Matching the Rhymes of Ziyou [i.e., Su Zhe, 1039–1110]."[19] In the second poem, Su describes a pavilion erected by Ouyang in Yiling, his place of exile during the late 1030s, and includes several lines praising Ouyang's righteousness and literary talent, for example:[20]

> Though Yiling may be a small settlement,
> It held sway in ancient times over Jing and Wu;
> These days the center of power has shifted North,
> Its heroes of yore have long passed away;
> Who could have guessed that a literary giant
> Would journey here, exiled from the distant emperor's capital?

Though Su composed these particular poems while travelling to the capital with his brother, not at a social gathering with Ouyang, the content leaves little doubt that he intended to present them to Ouyang. Through these imitations and compliments, Su made it clear that he considered Ouyang to be the cultural leader and master poet of his generation, but he also implies that he had the talent to match Ouyang's poems line for line—possibly even to surpass him. And faced with such literary brilliance, combined with the requisite social graces and formal examination credentials, Ouyang was delighted to recommend Su for high government position, and aid his meteoric rise to prominence in the Northern Song.[21]

Unfortunately, Su Shi later neglected the importance of flattering his superiors with poetry. He composed a number of poems during the 1070s strongly criticizing the protégés of Wang Anshi, who had gained control of the central government, and their New Policies. As a result, Su barely escaped execution in 1079. This episode is a negative example highlighting the necessity of using poetry to initiate and develop social relationships with superiors, because offending them could have disastrous consequences.[22]

Apart from poem exchanges in which students attempt to develop relations with a teacher or famous scholar, there are numerous examples of poems written by teachers that enthusiastically praise the talents of a favorite student. For example, in 1049, Ouyang Xiu composed poems praising in the highest terms two students whom he had tutored, Jiao Qianzhi and Xu Wudang:[23]

> . . . Since I discovered these two students,
> It's as if I have found a pair of dazzling jades . . .
> . . . Master Xu is pure and transparent: a white jade disc,
> Master Jiao is bright and glowing: ice in a cold spring;
> Your clear lights shine forth, each reflecting the other,

In the middle of summer you drive away the oppressive heat . . .
. . . Your heads are clear, your eyesight good, and you still have strength in your legs,
8 I envy your ambitious vitality, poised to soar into the sky,
With your hearts and minds developing, already so refined,
You are destined to achieve greatness in your future careers.

Although it is not known how much direct influence these flattering poems had on students' searches for official positions, it is certain that, coming from a powerful and respected scholar and circulating among his elite acquaintances, they would have enhanced the students' reputations and opened doors for them in much the same way as a reference letter from a renowned scholar today. For instance, Xu Wudang, having passed the civil service examinations, very soon received an official position in Mianchi (present Henan province) in 1054. Not content with his previous accolades, Ouyang sent him off with another highly complimentary poem, doubtless designed to impress Xu's new colleagues and subordinates with his high-powered connections, and cow them into submission:[24]

I envy you for being so young and just setting out on the right path,
You are like the sun beginning to rise over the fabled Fusang tree,
You made your name in examination halls; you've proved that you are outstanding,
4 If any great scholars were alive today, they'd certainly welcome your visit.[25]
Emerging from my door, I see you off as a friend and a family member,
I'm no different from a hedge sparrow looking up at the cloud-winged roc.[26]
I sigh that my brush and ink-stone have been idle for such a long time,
8 I'm grateful that you have inspired me to compose these stanzas and phrases.

Because of the obvious practical benefits that could come from such poetic relationships, even those who had few illusions about passing the civil service examinations would often take their versified doggerel and visit a well-known poet-official in the hope of receiving a responding poem. They would be able to use this evidence of a personal relationship with an influential patron to impress gullible acquaintances and, possibly, to protect them from harassment by their immediate superiors. This must be the reason that Ouyang Xiu, describing Mei Yaochen's fame as a poet, noted:[27]

> Even reckless and ignorant people who couldn't understand the meaning of [Mei's] poems would still say, "Everyone in the world considers these valuable. If I get one, I can use it to make myself look important." Consequently, those who sought [poems] would crowd round his door every day, and as a result Shengyu's poetry circulated all over the empire.

Among Mei's surviving works are many poems in which he evaluates volumes of poetry sent to him by aspiring young writers.[28] Presumably, these writers would mine Mei's response for complimentary comments which they could use to promote themselves in literati society, just as publishers today use the praise of famous reviewers to promote their latest writers.

Unlike the exchanges between successful students and their examiners or teachers, in which the expressions of mutual admiration were often sincere, this use of poetry to pretend to a nonexistent friendship with a superior was often shamelessly manipulative and materialistic. Indeed, some social climbing experts attempted to claim poetic friendships without even obtaining evidence in the form of poems. In an episode mentioned earlier in a different context, one Li Ding, a minor central government official, attempted to gain admittance to a fashionable banquet held by Su Shunqin, Wang Yirou, and several other young supporters of the Qingli reformers. Rather than impressing the banquet organizers with his own poetic talents, he merely claimed that his uncle, Yan Shu, then chief councilor, was a great admirer of the poetry of Mei Yaochen, someone whom Li knew to be allied with the reformers. In other words, Li was borrowing someone else's poetic relationship for his own ends. On this occasion, however, his ruse did not succeed, and full of resentment at being rejected, he accused the banqueters of various illegal acts, including slandering the Emperor in verse, which led to them all being exiled.[29]

We can draw two conclusions from such examples. First, although the Li Ding episode was perhaps extreme, Ouyang's reference to streams of visitors besieging Mei Yaochen for poems despite his low official status suggests that the exploitation of poetic exchanges for materialistic ends was quite a common practice in

Northern Song China. Second, even when poets felt such visitors lacked talent and were simply taking advantage of them, it was not a good idea to offend them, especially in the faction-ridden environment of the mid-eleventh century. As Su Shunqin and friends discovered, a refusal to welcome strangers and engage in poetic exchanges with them could, depending on the timing of the snub, turn out to be as dangerous as directly insulting the Emperor. This helps to explain the large numbers of perfunctory and polite regulated verses addressed to obscure people in the collections of every well-known Song poet. The consequences of not responding to strangers' requests for poetry could be more troublesome than simply dashing off four rhyming couplets with a well phrased, personalized title.

BREAKING DOWN SOCIAL BARRIERS

Composing and exchanging poetry was not only a useful way to get to know one's social superiors and promote inferiors but it could also help to overcome other kinds of social barriers between strangers. For example, both Ouyang and Mei frequently express their distaste for the doctrines and way of life of Buddhist and Daoist monks, seeing their rejection of family responsibilities and government service as antisocial and contrary to Confucian morality. Yet they shared with the more cultivated monks a love of poetic composition and an appreciation for natural scenery, refined zither music, and tea drinking. They were happy to exchange poetry with monks on such topics and lightheartedly respond to monks' invitations to leave the dusty world with counterpersuasions urging them to return to official life. Thus, poetry enabled these educated cultural and religious leaders to coexist in a harmonious and cordial way, despite their differences of opinion on proper social behavior.[30]

Moreover, during periods of exile and personal suffering, or when they were aging and yearning to retire, Northern Song literati were often tempted by the ideal of escaping the burdens and miseries of the dusty world and finding contentment in the simple life of a recluse. Rather than actually abandoning their social responsibilities, however, they found temporary psychological escape by writing poems to Buddhist or Daoist adepts. The following poem by Ouyang Xiu to a Daoist musician, dating from his second exile, is typical:

First of Two Poems Presented to "Master of Spontaneous Action" Li, Practitioner of the Way [1047][31]

The three-foot zither of Spontaneous Action, Practitioner of the Way,
Encompasses all the eternal tones surviving from ancient times.
The tones evoke pouring waters running over stones,
4 He pours them out unceasingly, drawing from deep sources.
Although the plucking is in the fingers, the sound is in the mind,
I do not use my ears to listen: instead I use my heart.
Since heart and mind are both engaged, I forget my bodily form,
8 I'm unaware of miserable clouds overshadowing the sun of Heaven and Earth.

Neither Ouyang nor Mei voluntarily gave up their official positions until they became physically incapable of serving due to illness and old age. They presented an idealized view of the religious life—remarkably similar to the civilized and cultured lifestyle that they adopted in their own leisure time—in order to distract themselves from present problems and evoke a mood of transcendence in their mind. However, despite their lack of real engagement with Buddhist and Daoist ideas, the literati of Ouyang and Mei's generation paved the way for a profound dialogue between scholar-officials and religious leaders later in the Northern Song. The most famous poets of the next generation, such as Su Shi and Huang Tingjian, not only exchanged poetry with Buddhist and Daoist masters but also experimented with many of their meditation techniques and spiritual exercises. They made it more acceptable for literati to become lay followers of orthodox religions without having to relinquish their official positions or leave their families.[32] In a sense, therefore, the communication that poetry exchanges allowed between cultural leaders of different beliefs in the first half of the eleventh century led to a more serious exchange of ideas and sharing of experiences. In turn, this led ultimately to a kind of religious synthesis in the late Northern Song.[33]

Poetry could also help to overcome social barriers caused by political differences, and their resultant family feuds. One particularly successful example involved Ouyang Xiu. In his youth, Ouyang was recklessly outspoken.[34] During the late 1030s and early 1040s, while serving in the capital, Kaifeng, he became frustrated with the corrupt and inefficient behavior of many high-ranking government ministers. He considered Lü Yijian, then chief councilor, to be the worst of the pack, and after Lü's resignation in 1043, sent up a memorial in his capacity as censor urging the Emperor never to employ Lü again, and attacking his family in the following scathing manner:[35]

> [When Lü was in power] he acted as a tyrant both within the Court and outside; everyone feared him but no one dared censure him. So when he became ill, the whole Empire rejoiced together that a treacherous and evil person, so difficult to remove, had for now been deposed by Heaven . . . But I still worry that he will . . . seek your gracious favors for his sons and younger brothers . . . And since now in our border regions we face so many problems, and those officials who worked so hard outside the capital have never been granted accelerated promotion, how can such a treacherous, evil, and hugely venomous family, with its block-headed sons and younger brothers greedy for bribes, be granted endless favors?

With such an attitude, it is hardly surprising Ouyang was soon exiled, in 1045, after alienating Lü's conservative supporters who were still influential in the government. Six years after presenting this memorial, Ouyang was still languishing in the provinces. Recently appointed as governor of Yingzhou (present Anhui province), he discovered that one of his subordinates happened to be Lü Gongzhu, the son of Lü Yijian. Instead of seeking a pretext for dismissing Lü, the now slightly mellowed Ouyang went out of his way to develop good relations with him, sending him a number of poems inviting him to drinking parties. In one of these poems, entitled "Offered in Answer to the Composition the Grand Tutor and Magistrate [Lü Gongzhu] Gave Me Entitled 'Declining to Drink,'" Ouyang overcomes Lü's reluctance to make up with him in the following persuasive way:[36]

> If you don't enjoy yourself when you can
> Your youthful face will soon become haggard,
> Time gallops past like a racing steed,
> And when it is gone, you cannot catch it up.
> If you don't make the effort to drink today,
> Later, even if you regret it, there's nothing you can do.
> . . . I have long heard about West Lake,
> Now I see it surpasses its fame,
> Lotuses drift about, reds mixed with greens,
> Mandarin ducks swim through rippling waters,

In all four seasons flowers and bamboos grow,
Food and wine appear whenever I desire them.
Even better if I can share them with worthy people,
Wafting the fragrance of orchid and angelica.[37]
My excellent wine is cold and flavourful,
The sounds of clear songs gently linger,
Guests on all sides are already tipsy,
How could you alone hesitate to drink? . . .

Several later poems that Ouyang exchanged with Lü make it clear that they subsequently had regular friendly social contact during their shared postings in Yingzhou. Clearly Ouyang was anxious to put aside his past conflict with the Lü family, and made use of poetry exchanges as a tool for reconciliation.[38]

In these situations, where a social, religious, or political barrier existed between individuals, poetry was especially useful as an ice-breaker because it highlighted the shared cultural background and interests that most educated people of the time, whatever their ostensible beliefs, held in common. Also, by reading a poem the recipient could gain a clearer idea of the sender's talents, tastes and intentions than by simply looking at a name card. Finally, the indirectness of poetry exchanges meant that a skilled writer could use them, as Ouyang did in addressing Lü Gongzhu, to express his feelings and sound out a potential acquaintance's attitude, without either side losing face if a closer relationship was not possible at the time.

CELEBRATING AND SUSTAINING EXISTING RELATIONSHIPS

Poetry was not merely useful for initiating relationships with strangers or overcoming social barriers. Among those already acquainted, continued poetry exchanges were an important and entertaining way of cementing their friendships. And when friends were separated and posted to distant parts of the Empire, poems were essential for sustaining the relationship. By composing and circulating their latest poems, distant friends could express strong emotions that might seem out of place, even rude, in a letter, while keeping each other up-to-date on their news. In this connection, it is interesting to note the frequency with which Ouyang refers to receiving Mei Yaochen's poems in his letters, and the relatively formal brevity of the letters compared to the lengthy and frank poems that they exchanged at a distance.[39]

Exchanges of poetry between separated friends have a therapeutic effect. In particular, they draw lonely and bitter exiles back into a mutually supportive community, allowing them to release pent-up emotions safely, and possibly helping them to ward off what today we would term stress-related illnesses. This is the subject of the following chapter. Here, I focus on another major function of these poetry exchanges, the celebration and idealization of friendships in print. The heightening of emotions and concentration of description that occur in poetry could transform an ordinary gathering of friends into a transcendent, larger-than-life encounter, making those who participated feel that their lives were remarkably exciting. Even more crucial, the poetic record would remain for years to come as evidence of their urbane, witty, and socially cohesive behavior.

Some examples from the 1030s, during and after the period when Ouyang, Mei and a number of other scholars served under Qian Weiyan, the governor of Luoyang, illustrate how Northern Song literati used poetry to sustain, celebrate, and immortalize their friendships. Ouyang described the members of this group in verse very early on—in fact, his earliest dated compositions are seven poems, each depicting one of his colleagues.[40] He concludes with a poetic self-portrait, in which he questions whether he is worthy or talented enough to belong to such a group, since he already views his new friends as dazzling cultural luminaries:[41]

> By nature I am lazy and unrestrained,
> And thus, as an official, I am also dissolute.
> Don't I resemble a leather sack
> Laid on a cart and moved about by the cart wheels?
> The fashionable gents didn't cast a glance towards me,
> Left in solitude, I had no-one to talk to.
> But thankfully some of the young blades of Luoyang
> Allow me daily to aspire to their heights.
> I drink in their virtues, "intoxicated by fine wine,"
> Wafting fragrance, they "adorn me with spring orchids."[42]
> Frequently, when finished with our military missives,
> We compose poems and drink wine, enjoying ourselves to the full.

While Ouyang humorously exaggerates both his own incompetence and the outstanding talents of his friends, he leaves the reader in no doubt that this is a special group of people whose activities deserve recording in verse.

Soon afterwards, this group of young officials began to call themselves the Eight Elders of Luoyang, perhaps echoing the group of famous Jin dynasty literati known as the Seven Worthies of the Bamboo Grove.[43] Besides working together, they would also take trips to admire the local scenery, arrange banquets and drinking parties, and share their writings with each other. They commemorated most of these activities in poem exchanges, in which they constantly depicted themselves as vigorous and outstanding, if slightly eccentric and comical geniuses. They celebrated the transcendent joys of their friendship, yet without losing sight of the individual oddities and foibles that revealed their earthy humanity. In a poem from 1034, for instance, Ouyang includes the following series of couplets, each a thumbnail sketch recalling one of his friends:[44]

> Xishen liked to write in a wind and bone style,
> And distanced himself from the dusty world.[45]
> Shilu had a reliable heart,
> He nobly conversed on [Fu] Xi and [Xian] Yuan.[46]
> Zijian seemed to be slow of speech,
> But when he recited the *Documents*, a thousand words poured out at once.
> Yanguo loved to pour back the wine,
> After one hundred cups, his face was still not flushed.
> Jidao focused on freedom and transcendence,
> Unfettered in character, just like Xie An.[47]
> Zicong played the military attache,
> Constantly riding off to hunt for tigers.
> Ziye was actually a balding old man,
> To tease him, we sometimes removed his hat!
> Cigong's talent was wide-ranging and rare,
> His writing brush flew like a galloping warrior.
> Shengyu was skilled at chanting his poems,
> Joking, we called him the Immortal of Lang.[48]
> And my sobriquet was Precocious Elder,
> But when drunk, I became more like Zhang [Xu's] wild script![49]

Though several of these friends later became famous as writers or statesmen, they were all still minor provincial officials in the early 1030s. In fact, some of the group remained obscure and undistinguished for the rest of their careers. Yet it is interesting how at this early stage Ouyang is already seeking to make them larger than life by celebrating their accomplishments in verse and comparing many of them to ancient sages and worthies. He uses poetry to give their everyday lives and friendships meaning by placing them in a larger historical context.

This desire to be seen as part of a long line of talented and civilized scholar-officials emerges even more clearly in Mei Yaochen's description of the farewell party held for him in 1032, before his transfer from Luoyang to Heyang, translated in the conclusion to the previous chapter. Sharing poetry at that party was the means by which these friends demonstrated their affinity with the ancients and the joy their cultured fellowship brought them. It was also a way to preserve, for future generations, a record of their civilized and harmonious behavior.

Not long after Mei left Luoyang, Qian Weiyan was transferred away from Luoyang, and most of his employees also moved on to different posts. Ouyang Xiu, for instance, moved to Kaifeng in 1034 to work on the Imperial Library catalogue. The former colleagues sustained their friendships by regularly sending poems to each other, in which they recalled and further immortalized their happy exploits in Luoyang. In 1032, for example, Mei, Ouyang and Yang Yu had climbed Mount Song, one of the five sacred peaks of China. They composed numerous poems together during their trip, describing the impressive alpine scenery and their various adventures en route.[50] In 1034, Ouyang recalled this excursion with a poem sent to Mei:[51]

> . . . Suddenly we left for the summit of Song peak:
> Surrounded by green foliage we climbed to ten thousand feet,
> Through distant mists we looked down on the Three Rivers.
> Amid flowers and grass we spied gullies and caves,
> Between jagged rocks we found springs emerging from stones.
> You chanted poems, leaning back on a tree,
> I became drunk, and lay down to sleep on the clouds.
> Zicong said that the sun was so close,
> He thought he could pluck it from the sky with his hand!
> Together we wrote verses on the Stone of Three Drunkards,
> And left our couplets right beside the Terrace of Eight Immortals.
> But when we grew weary of wandering through streams and clouds
> We returned home to sit before winecups and plates . . .

This poem incongruously mixes transcendent aspirations—immortal terraces and cloud wandering—with down-to-earth humanity—such as Yang Yu's naive comments about the sun, and the travelers' youthful appetites upon their return home. The effect makes their friendship believable and realistic, yet larger-than-life and worthy of preserving for the enjoyment of future generations.[52]

The Luoyang period was not the only time Ouyang and Mei celebrated their friendships in verse, and the Luoyang compositions are representative of the way in which Northern Song literati used poetry as a relatively permanent record of their individual personalities and the memorable times they spent together. This record became particularly important as they grew older and were forced to live in distant places, and as their friends gradually passed away. In poetry, the vitality of their social relationships could remain and be revived even when those relationships no longer existed. Later in his life, Ouyang Xiu expressed this function of poetry movingly in the preface to poems he and five colleagues had composed and exchanged in 1057:[53]

> Alas! One could say that in will and spirit the six of us were then in our prime. But the strong, over time, weaken; the weak, over time, age. In our employment and reclusion, separation and coming together, there will be a great disparity between us. Nevertheless, these poems will be sufficient to revive past days once more, to let us shake hands and be filled with laughter and joy. And there are also some that will make one close the book with a sigh and burst into sobbing tears. Even so how can I withhold them for this reason alone?

POEMS OF SEPARATION AND ELEGIES

Apart from initiating and celebrating relationships with poetry, educated people of the Northern Song wrote and exchanged poems to commemorate all significant events in their own lives and those of their friends. On occasions when people today would send a greetings card—whether congratulatory or sympathetic—it was customary for Northern Song writers to present a personalized poem composed for the occasion. This is another reason why the titles of Song poems are often extremely detailed, giving both the poem's context and the names and official ranks of the recipients. There are large numbers of polite and conventional occasional verses in the collections of even famous Song poets. Many of these poems were preserved more to demonstrate the writers' wide-ranging social connections and concern for their fellow human beings than to reveal their literary talents. This is further evidence that Northern Song literati composed poetry primarily to foster relationships and circulate positive emotional energy, and only secondarily to reach anonymous readers beyond their immediate social circle. Of course, some writers were so talented that even their most polite social verse is entertaining, brilliantly crafted, and profound, appealing to readers far removed from its original context. Yet generally speaking, a poet of the Northern Song whose works did not appeal initially to his friends and acquaintances (whatever their possible value for anonymous readers or future generations), would have considered them a failure.

We conclude this chapter with two poetic subgenres that underscore the importance of poetry in smoothing the channels of social interaction. In parting poems, we see the clearest examples of poetic exchange as a means of circulating positive energy among friends and acquaintances. The enormous numbers of such poems that survive reveal, first, the frequency with which scholar-officials had to move to different posts (and, incidentally, to become acquainted with new colleagues through further poetry exchanges) and second, the strong social obligation on those who remained behind to compose poems to send off even people whom they did not know very well in order to avoid causing offence.

Prior to the Northern Song, the majority of parting poems had a sorrowful tone, often concluding with a reference to tears soaking the robes of the separating friends.[54] Such poems expressed the sense of loss felt by the poet and implied strong feelings of affection for the parting friend. They also tended to connect this sorrow with the transitory nature of all worldly pleasures—good friendships always end with premature separation, just as joy ends in sorrow, and life in death.

Many Northern Song parting poems include similar gloomy sentiments. However, the better known poets of the period realized tearfulness and self-pity were not necessarily the best attitudes to adopt when seeing off their friends. Though no theoretical statements survive on this point, their poetry clearly demonstrates they preferred to lift the spirits of parting friends, encouraging them with thoughts of the joys awaiting them at their destination, and reminding them they could continue to correspond. This optimistic attitude may be due to the relative stability of the Northern Song (especially during the eleventh century), and the increasing efficiency of communication between far-flung parts of the Empire.[55] It may have been because Northern Song poets realized that too much sorrow could overburden people and damage their health rather than console them. After all, the point of such poems was consolation, not desolation.[56]

Even in their regulated verses, which were generally more conventional than their ancient-style poetry, Northern Song poets displayed an upbeat attitude towards separation. For example, in 1059, Ouyang Xiu wrote a parting poem for Mei Zhi (995–1059), a close friend who had acted as one of the examiners during the 1057 civil service examination, and with whom Ouyang and Mei Yaochen had exchanged numerous poems:

Seeing Off Scholar Mei Gongyi [Zhi] to become Governor of Hangzhou[57]

The ten thousand households of the South East are prosperous and flourishing,
I'm envious that you'll have power and authority, yet still find time for relaxation.
Together with fishermen and woodcutters you'll enjoy the rivers and lakes,
4 Amid conversation and laughter you'll compose poems at banquets.
When days are warm, pear blossoms will urge you to drink fine wine,
In cold seasons, cassia seeds will drop in the empty mountains.
Postal deliveries will never stop, moving at the speed of flight,
8 So don't begrudge sending new poems regularly back and forth.

While it is true that Mei Zhi was being transferred to an important post in a beautiful and cosmopolitan region, a reader schooled on Tang poetry would normally expect some lines of the poem to mention the sadness of separation. Ouyang, however, focuses entirely on positive emotions, confident that Mei will enjoy his new position and keep in touch, frequently sending poems back to the capital. To prove that this optimistic outlook was not confined to parting poems for friends receiving promotions, here is an example by Mei Yaochen addressed to a young scholar returning home after failing the civil service examination:[58]

Has not the intention of the fisherman
Always been to catch the fish?
With a little bait and many fish biting,
His cast-out rod has never returned empty.
But those who are selected, priced at a hundred gold pieces,
Will surely be forced to pant for breath and flap their silvery tails.[59]
A parched pool is one thing that the ancients warned us to avoid,
Better just to incubate all those books in your belly.
The time will come when winds and storms will cause [the climate] to change,
And you will return on an [overflowing] Mengzhu Lake.[60]

Mei manages to sustain his curious fishing metaphor throughout the poem. The fish are presumably the examination candidates like Fang Yun, the bait is the promise of an official position, and the fisherman is the Emperor (by extension, the central government) looking for talented people to help govern the country. Mei consoles his young friend by asserting that the life of an official is not as comfortable as their salary ("a hundred gold pieces") makes it appear because the Emperor puts his officials under such pressure they "pant for breath and flap their silvery tails." Therefore, his friend should not to be too ambitious until he has built up a "Mengzhu Lake" of learning and experience to help him swim back to the capital and survive there. Alternatively, the "winds and storms" could refer to political reforms that will make the government a safer environment in which to serve.

In his quirky and indirect way, Mei writes a poem that gives the shamefaced and miserable scholar a morsel of hope for the future, when he returns to face his disappointed family and resume his studies.

Occasionally, poets felt inspired to go far beyond the call of polite social duty and produce a poetic tour de force to see off their friend in style. To receive such a poem must have been a great boost to the traveller, not least because the ancient style in which such bravura works were composed lent itself to hyperbole and exaggerated praise of the recipient. One outstanding example is Ouyang Xiu's mighty poem about Mount Lu. The full title reads: "Lu Mountain High! Written to See Off Liu Zhongyun as He Goes to Retire in the South."[61] In this poem, Ouyang claims the majestic landscape surrounding Mount Lu is the only place in the world outstanding enough for such a noble person as Liu to live in. Another fine example is Mei Yaochen's "Seeing Off Su Zimei," written at the time of Su Shunqin's exile in 1044. Mei borrows imagery from the "Summons to the Soul" section of the *Chuci* ("Elegies of Chu"), pretending to persuade Su's soul to return to the capital. In the process, he implies Su is a righteous official and brilliant poet like Qu Yuan, who is traditionally considered the author of many of the *Chuci* songs:[62]

Bravely you journey out to rivers and seas,
Winds and waves do not scare you in the slightest,
You only wish to seek out famous mountains,
Your single boat has no fixed destination.
But in the South are huge birds like owls,
On their faces are stone beaks sharp as swords.
Poisonous plants will beckon when they see you,
Squat foxes will grow angry just meeting your shadow.
Even in the near distance you'll feel bitterness of separation,
The further you go the thicker will the pestilent fog surround you.
And the Eastern region lies beside the ocean,
Where sea snakes and turtles are still more terrifying,
Creatures with strange shells are scattered about,
Molluscs and barnacles too numerous to count,
Their salty stink will destroy your teeth,
The moon and sun will soon be swallowed up,
And just like these two [Heavenly Bodies]
After you arrive there, you certainly won't last long![63]
Instead, you should return here to the North West,
To get drunk on wine and cook plump lamb,
In summer you won't tire of soy sauce and preserves,
In winter you won't tire of pheasant and rabbit;
Don't say this is just focusing on mouth and belly:
Since mouth and belly are what everyone cares for most!
Tiantai Mountain is certainly rare and enormous,
But its Stone Bridges are a dangerous climb,
And the peak of Mount Lu is the most difficult to reach:
You'll be gazing at its waterfall with a starving stomach!
Though such destinations may appear noble,
In actual fact, it's hard to admire them for long.
As you depart, you should listen to my words:
If you don't listen now, the truth will soon hit you.

Though Mei adopts a tone of mock terror at the horrible fate awaiting Su in the South, the poem is actually quite comical. After all, Su was heading for Suzhou, not a particularly wild or remote place by the Northern Song. Most of the threatening creatures and strange climatic phenomena that Mei warns him about are obviously mythical, posing no real danger to the eleventh-century traveller. In fact, the main reason Mei gives for Su to stay in the North is that he could continue to stuff himself with tasty and filling northern dishes, whereas southern food may not suit his palate, and he could end up looking at the strange southern scenery with an empty stomach. Of course, lurking beneath the surface of this poem is the fact that Su did not choose to take this sightseeing tour of the South for pleasure, but was being exiled there. By inventing his own slightly ridiculous version of Su's prospects on his travels, Mei intends to distract Su from the misery of exile and cheer his spirits as he leaves his friends in the capital. Thus, the poem fulfils a consoling function. Indeed, all these parting poems share a strong concern for the traveler's well-being as well as an intuitive realization that it is better to send someone off with encouragement and humor than with maudlin weeping and indulgent self-pity.

It is interesting to compare parting poems and poems addressed to friends generally with poetry of bereavement from the same period, specifically poems that mourn deceased friends and acquaintances. Since the addressee of the poem was no longer alive, we might expect such works to be more preoccupied with the poet's grief and much less concerned with the effect of the poem on the friend's feelings. To a certain extent, this is true. Tears flow freely in Northern Song poems of bereavement as the poet releases pent-up sorrow and finds a way to channel overwhelming, negative emotions in a constructive way. An example of this is Ouyang Xiu's lament for Mei Yaochen, composed after Mei's death in 1060. While the content of the poem focuses on Mei's talents, loyal friendship, and his inexplicably low official status (ending with Ouyang weeping at the funeral), the rhyme scheme (a *Boliangti*) gives a more profound sense of Ouyang's grief: by repeating the sound 'ou' at the end of every line, he sets up a kind of recurring moan like the wail of a mourner.[64] In addition, Ouyang's division of most of the poem into three-line stanzas, rather than the normal couplets or quatrains, adds a further off-balancing emotional edge to the poem.

Since rhyme is such a crucial feature of this poem, I have attempted to retain a similarly consistent rhyme in my translation, even when it results in some slightly odd English syntax:

Weeping for Shengyu[65]

I met the Poet Elder at the head of the Luo River long ago,
In a dark shirt on a white horse he crossed the Yi's tributary flow,
The rapids sounded in eight beats, echoing round the towers of stone;
At social gatherings the force of his words pierced the autumn glow,
He could drink down a hundred cups of wine in one go,
Drinking his fill, his thoughts became free, his speech still more mellow.
The Governor of Henan at that time was admired as a worthy fellow,
Daily his visiting carriages would be filled with Mei's and Zou's,[66]
I was the youngest [of this group], but my strength was starting to grow;
We threw bright pearls to each other, and precious jades to and fro,
Our poems complete, Xishen would chant them, holding a hand to his nose,[67]
And Shilu would lash out with sharp critiques like a spear-throwing foe;
Then thirty years passed in the moment it takes to raise an eyebrow,
Suddenly, nine out of ten companions had returned to their graves below,
Scattered and sparse, we who survived were beset with a hundred woes;
Late in life I climbed the jade steps, to attend the imperial throne,
But you, Poet Elder, ate pickled salty food, a miserable Academy Fellow.[68]
At times we were separated, other times together: couldn't predict how things would go,
[Our final meetings] were due to Heaven's favor, a matter beyond our control,
Our cheeks were pale, whiskers white, our teeth loose and wobbling so,
Yet even though you were older than me, you didn't seem to know,
We still managed to find some happiness, and steal some leisure too,
We paid no heed to the years speeding towards the end of our life's flow.
Whenever you took your brush to write, you shook [Heaven] and all below,

But after the noon hour, in your cooking pots there wasn't any rice to show;[69]
The good times quickly passed, and in coming to you they were slow,
Hidden in a box, your jade was ignored like a broken tile or a stone;
28 The Ancients considered promoting worthies an outstanding thing to do,
In this I've fulfilled my duty: I need not feel shame before you,
Yet fate is incomprehensible, its patterns no one can know,
Your dazzling name and reputation remain buried and undisclosed.
32 Fluttering, a plain silk banner, over your departing funeral boat,
I see you off, and like streams in flood, my gushing tears overflow.

While such poems certainly expressed grief, they also allowed the poet a final opportunity to celebrate the friend's talents and personal attributes. The gradual loss of friends made these poets realize their exchanged poetry was the only record of their relationship that survived and would continue to survive. Thus, in their poems of bereavement, they added a summation of their friendship with the deceased, and constantly reminded themselves of the vitality of their poetry and the need to preserve it. In the above work, Ouyang wrote that Mei's poems "shook [Heaven] and all below". In another poem, mourning Mei and Su Shunqin, he declares:

Only the writings they left behind still dazzle like the stars and sun,
Their energy skims over mountain peaks, constant in its stupendous power;
Since ancient times, both wise and ignorant have come to their end,
Vivid and prominent, all that is left is a name for future generations.[70]

And in an elegy for another friend, Shi Yannian (994–1041), Ouyang is quite rhapsodic about the strange vigor of poetry, and emphasizes that poems should be treasured even if the poet himself was careless about preserving them:[71]

. . . You composed poems numbering in the hundreds!
Brocades and lace linking jaspers and jades,
Time and again you came up with perilous phrases,
4 Extraordinary, the way you mixed crude with refined.
Exhausting the rare, you caused clouds and mists to swirl,

Searching for the strange, you made dragons and sea-snakes coil,[72]
Completing your poems, you would copy them yourself,
With brushstrokes like those of the master calligraphers,[73]
Then discard them at once, with nary a further thought,
So those that survive are few and far between,
But sometimes they fell into the hands of others
Who treasured them as if they were priceless pearls.
You also loved to write on the walls of peoples' homes,
Leaving rainbow dragons there to twist and unfurl,
In place after place the traces you left survive:
The ink remains damp and will never go dry . . .

Shi Yannian's poems were so full of vitality that when he wrote them on walls with his calligraphy brush, they twisted and uncoiled like dragons, and the ink never dried. These are suitably vivid metaphors for the power of poetry to bring the past to life even when the scenes and people it describes are long gone. It is significant that Northern Song poets used this power most frequently to sing of their social encounters and to immortalize their friendships.

We have seen various ways in which Northern Song writers used poetry to initiate or sustain relationships. Poetry acted as a channel for the educated elite to express and exchange feelings that might otherwise have had no socially acceptable outlet in such a hierarchical and regulated environment. This function of poetry is what I term the social circulation of emotional energy, or *qi*. In the following chapter, I develop the connection between poetry writing and the circulation of *qi* using theories of traditional Chinese medicine, especially as they relate to emotional health. Medical theory emphasizes maintaining balanced *qi* within the body and mind. Its underlying assumption is that harmful imbalances frequently had their source in the world, including the social world. Poetry was an essential tool for smoothing social relations and reducing the stresses of dealing with other people. It should be no surprise therefore, that some Northern Song literati believed writing and exchanging poetry could potentially benefit both their individual health and the health of society as a whole.

CHAPTER FOUR

Poetry as Therapy

In this chapter I discuss an important function of traditional Chinese poetry that literary critics generally neglect or touch on indirectly, perhaps because it straddles the boundary between literature and medicine. Northern Song poets sometimes describe the effects of poetic composition using terms we would normally associate with healing. Occasionally, they claim that writing poetry helped cure them from certain illnesses.

Therapy is the most suitable English word to describe this function of poetry because it encompasses both mental and physical aspects of healing, and emphasizes prevention as much as cure. However, this does not imply trained poetry or art therapists existed in traditional China, as they do in the West today.[1] Rather, belief in the ability of poetry to release harmful emotional tensions was an intuitive assumption accepted by many of the major Chinese writers of the Northern Song. Moreover, some writers, such as Ouyang Xiu, publicly declared that composing and exchanging poetry and practicing the related arts of calligraphy and music had helped them to recover from illnesses caused by depression. Some basic ideas from traditional Chinese medicine clarify and substantiate these claims. Central to this discussion is the term *qi* (vital energy; configurational energy) which, in the Chinese view, is a life-giving force that circulates within our bodies and throughout the universe.[2] Next, I give some examples in which Mid-Northern Song poets drew the connection between poetry or related arts and healing, followed by a broader discussion of the emotional release function of poetry in traditional Chinese literary criticism. Finally, I illustrate the kinds of poetic styles and themes that Northern Song writers considered most beneficial to their emotional and physical well-being, concluding with a case study of poetic therapy in action, involving exchanges between Ouyang Xiu, Mei Yaochen, and Su Shunqin.[3]

BALANCING EMOTIONS / HEALING THE BODY

A key idea in traditional Chinese medicine is that, in order to remain healthy, we must balance or regulate the circulation of *qi* around our bodies. *Qi*, in the Chinese view, is a life-giving force that circulates within our bodies and throughout the universe.[4] Besides regulating *qi* within our bodies, therefore, we must also learn to control our response to the energy flows that we encounter in the world outside our bodies.[5] A buildup of tension or an imbalance in one part of our body, whether due to internal or external factors, blocks the circulation of *qi* and illness follows unless we find some way to release the tension and correct the imbalance. According to the traditional view, our emotions and mental states are also inextricably linked to our physical health: each emotion—anger, sorrow, joy and so on—corresponds with one area of the body, and any extreme emotional shocks or outbursts likely result in sickness.[6] As with physical stress or tension, extremes of emotion are imbalances obstructing the regular circulation of *qi*. Hence, it is crucial to develop techniques for regulating our mental states and releasing emotional tension.[7] According to Nathan Sivin, some traditional Chinese doctors developed therapeutic techniques for treating illnesses caused by imbalanced emotions—what we might term stress-related illnesses. Sivin calls their approach emotional countertherapy, curing an emotional imbalance by encouraging a surfeit of the opposite emotion.[8]

While such therapeutic techniques may not have become part of the mainstream of traditional Chinese medicine, many Chinese literati viewed artistic practices, including music-playing, calligraphy, and composing and reciting poetry, as a form of preventive emotional regulation. In some cases, they claim artistic practices even helped cure them from illnesses. Indeed, there is a significant amount of anecdotal evidence, particularly from the Northern Song period onwards, that draws a link between artistic practices, regulation of emotions, and prevention of emotionally induced illnesses.

Ouyang Xiu, for example, was very much a believer in the connection between emotions and illness, and he gives a detailed account of the emotionally balancing and therapeutic effects of artistic practice—here referring to playing music—in his "Preface to See Off Yang Zhi":[9]

> Previously I had an illness caused by depression, and even though I took leave [from work] and lived at leisure, I could not regain my health. But soon afterwards, I began learning the zither (*qin*) with the help of a friend, Sun Daozi. He taught me several tunes in the *gong* mode, and after some time enjoying them I was no longer aware of any illness in my body. Now illness comes from too much worry, and even the most potent medicines that can attack the accumulations of illness are no match for the all-encompassing reach of sounds. So it is fitting that sounds can bring harmony to imbalances in the heart, and when the heart is balanced and what lacks harmony is harmonized, then one's illness will be forgotten . . .

Thus playing music, or more generally making harmonious sounds, balances the emotions, especially negative feelings of frustration and worry, allowing us to overcome the illnesses those emotions engender. It is significant that Ouyang composed this preface in 1047 during his exile to Chuzhou, following the disgrace of his trial in 1045 for sexual assault. It is very likely that the worries he claims were the cause of his illness stemmed from the stressful events leading up to this exile.[10]

Though Ouyang focused this preface on playing the zither, there is little doubt he saw a close relation between musical performance and poetic composition or recitation. For instance, in a discussion of Mei Yaochen's poetry, he made an extended comparison between poetry and music, including the statement:[11]

> Music is what communicates the harmony of Heaven and Earth; it comes in contact with people through their *qi*. Consequently, its fast and slow [rhythms] excite and move us, and can cause us to respond with our hearts; and our happiness or misery can be discerned in its sounds . . . Those who have attained [the harmony of Heaven and Earth today], even if they cannot respond to it with music, can still sing of it in their poetry . . . Is not poetry therefore a shoot that grows from music?[12]

Like music and poetry, calligraphy is an effective means of balancing emotions and overcoming stressful distractions. Frequently, calligraphy and poetic composition were combined in a single artistic act.[13] In his *Comments on Calligraphy*, Ouyang noted the mental and physical benefits that came from writing with a brush:[14]

> During the long summer days, all I desire is to find some activity in which I can lodge my mind to help me endure the heat of the day, and the only thing that does not wear me out is practicing calligraphy at my desk. When the brush goes flying along so that my hand cannot stop, then even if thunder and lightning tried to shock me, and rain and hailstones came pouring down, I would not bother to glance at them!

Mei Yaochen subsequently rewrote Ouyang's comments on the therapeutic benefits of calligraphy in a verse entitled "Answering Secretary Yongshu with Rhyming Words." After paraphrasing the above passage, Mei concluded with the following explanation:[15]

> The Grand Old Secretary Ouyang [Xiu]
> Was lately delighted to recover from an illness;
> Letting his brush fly, he penned these words,
> He claimed they could help him forget worries and sickness . . .
> . . . So I dressed them up into casual rhymes
> To assist him a little in their recitation.[16]

Both Ouyang and Mei frequently declare their own calligraphic talents are minimal. Yet they continued to practice calligraphy, copying out their own and others' poetry, not so much to produce great artworks as to receive the mental and physical benefits of the activity.[17] Likewise, though Ouyang Xiu's original words describe the therapeutic effects of calligraphic writing alone, the fact that Mei paraphrased them in rhyme for recitation suggests he considered composing and reciting poetic words just as effective for overcoming thoughts of illness as writing them with a brush.

Two more examples illustrate the beneficial effects of reciting poetry and its ability to release mental and physical tension. An anecdote about Mei Yaochen's exhilarating and visceral reaction to one of Ouyang Xiu's poems gives a vivid impression of how recitation might have been performed in the Northern Song:[18]

> One day, Guo Gongfu visited Mei Shengyu [Yaochen], who told him: "Recently I received a letter from Yongshu [Ouyang Xiu]; he has just written 'Lu Mountain High!' and is quite satisfied with it. I regret that I haven't seen this poem yet." Gongfu recited it for him. Shengyu beat the rhythm, sighing in appreciation, and said: "Even if I were to write poems for another thirty years, I couldn't manage to compose a single line like this." Gongfu recited it again, and they couldn't help becoming elated, so they laid out wine and recited it again. The wine went round several times, they both recited it several dozen times, then concluded the meeting without further conversation.

Finally, a comment by Ouyang Xiu praising Mei's river-pig fish poem makes a direct connection between reciting poetry and overcoming illnesses. Ouyang declared: "Whenever my body feels unhealthy, I recite [this poem] several times through, and immediately I feel fine."[19] Although Ouyang is rather vague about his malady—the term *ti zhong bu kang* could presumably refer to various kinds of uncomfortable physical state—he makes it very clear that reciting Mei's poem has an immediate beneficial effect on his condition.

POETRY AS EMOTIONAL RELEASE

Though traditional Chinese discussions of literary composition frequently refer to the energy that is embodied in a poem or prose work and emerges upon recitation as *qi*, they do not usually refer so directly to the healing powers of poetry in the way that Ouyang Xiu does.[20] The Tang writer Han Yu, for example, whose poetry and prose had a major influence on the Ouyang Xiu circle, wrote about *qi* in the following terms:[21]

> *Qi* is water and words are floating objects. When there is plenty of water, then both large and small objects will be lifted up to float on it. The way that *qi* relates to words is similar: when one's *qi* is abundant, then the various lengths of one's written lines and the various pitches of one's sounds will all be appropriate.

For Han Yu, *qi* was a kind of energy that originated in the writer's body and could be lodged in compositions. When these were recited, latent *qi* would manifest itself in vital rhythms and tonal variations and flow through the minds and bodies of the reader and listeners.

Focusing more specifically on Mid-Northern Song poetic criticism, we find that Ouyang Xiu, in his summation of the poetry of Mei Yaochen, drew a similar connection between poetic composition and the circulation of *qi*:[22]

> At the beginning [Mei] enjoyed composing in a pure, beautiful, free, even and bland style; but over time, [his poetry] gained clarity and depth, including works that were carefully structured to reveal his strange skill. Yet his *qi* was complete and his strength abundant, becoming even more lean as he grew older . . . When he was poor and miserable, or moved by righteous indignation . . . he would always release his emotions in poems. But he used [poetry] to find happiness, not to settle grievances.

Likewise, Su Shunqin, in a preface praising the poetry of his friend Shi Yannian [Manqing], drew together poetry, emotions, and the release of *qi*:[23]

> Composing poetry is closely tied up with people's lives. When people have within them the pent-up *qi* of joyful happiness or miserable depression, they must release it in words. Those with ability will transmit it through poetic meter and in this way it will circulate everywhere, spreading out and communing with ghosts and spirits!

While it is quite unusual in traditional Chinese poetic criticism to find the concept of literary *qi* directly related to emotional and physical healing, there are numerous passages stating that poetic composition could be used to release pent-up negative emotions. Even when such comments do not mention the word *qi*, they underline the point that regulating emotions was a major and necessary function of poetry. And as we have seen, according to Chinese medical theory, a balanced emotional state was considered essential to maintaining mental and physical health and preventing illness. Following are just a couple of representative examples, drawn from Northern Song texts, of the regulating or emotional release function of poetry. The first is by Huang Tingjian, from a comment written at the end of a friend's poem series:[24]

> Poetry comes from one's human emotions and one's nature: it should not be inspired by the struggles of powerful ministers at Court, the insults of bitter and resentful people on the street, or angry neighbours cursing each other. If one is sincere and respectful, living

according to the Dao, when one encounters misfortunes in one's career or situations that cause sadness or joy, but no friends or acquaintances are around to sympathise, one can transform emotions that one cannot endure into rhymed verses filled with laughter. In this way, one's heart will feel the freedom of release, and those who hear [the poems] will also be encouraged by them.

Another comment by the Late Southern Song writer Mou Xian (1227–1331) criticizes Tang poets like Du Fu for wallowing in their misery, which only made them feel worse, rather than writing poetry to transform their mood:[25]

> Wearing out their hearts with sadness in order to entertain their senses, they were like fat frying in a pan, really quite pathetic! But everyone still competed to emulate them, never stopping their tragic cries on every side, so that their complaints could never be supplanted by their joys!
>
> Master Yu Haowen made it his business to compose poems every day, and I assumed that he had also fallen victim to the bitter complaining of those people of the past. But he just smiled contentedly and said: "I do this to lighten my heart." When I read his scrolls, the excellent lines overflowed from the page. He did not aim for profundity or emotional intensity, . . . but reading them could still make one happy. Isn't this a perfectly good way to express one's feelings and nature?

In a recent study of Song poetics, the contemporary scholar Zhou Yukai formulates the term "self consolation" (*zishi*) to describe this emotion-balancing function of poetry.[26] Citing numerous examples from traditional collections of poetic anecdotes, he particularly emphasizes both the lighthearted aspects of Song poetry and the important psychological benefits of transforming negative emotions into witty verse, something that many Song poets excelled at:[27]

> Song writers' humorous poetry, including even works that one could call "word games," . . . all exercised this function. When the writers were smoothly progressing in their official careers, the humor and wit were a means of displaying their superior intelligence and breadth of learning, both to entertain themselves and give pleasure to others. But when they came up against obstacles and setbacks, the humor and wit could then become a kind of spiritual medicine to disperse their sadness and suffering and to soothe their heartache through self-caricature and laughter.

Zhou is perhaps using the term "spiritual medicine" (*lingyao*) in a figurative way here, but he makes it clear that many Song writers viewed poetic composition as an important method for overcoming emotional distress and maintaining psychological equilibrium in times of trouble.

THERAPY, STYLE, AND ANCIENT TRANSCENDENCE

Having established that Mid-Northern Song writers often used poetry to overcome negative emotions, and that on occasion they also claimed poetry could cure illnesses caused by emotional imbalances, we now analyse the specific poetic styles and subject matter that these writers considered particularly therapeutic. In the following sections, I select a number of poems that were either praised for their invigorating effects by Ouyang, Mei and their contemporaries, or contain references to the healing powers of poetry.

Dealing first with the question of style, I will translate a composition whose emotionally releasing effect was documented above. This was Ouyang Xiu's poem on Mount Lu, which Mei Yaochen and his friend found so exhilirating:

Lu Mountain High! Presented to Fellow Student Liu Zhongyun on his Retirement to Nankang [1051].[28]

Lu Mountain, oh so high! Several million feet—
Its base twists for several hundred miles,
It towers up, rising sheer and prominent, beside the Yangtze River.
The Yangtze River, flowing from the west, rushes past its foot,
Here it has formed Zuoli Lake, lifting its waves—
Flooding waves, huge breakers, night and day clashing and pounding together.
When clouds disperse and wind ceases, the mirror of water grows clear,
Mooring my boat I climb the bank and gaze at it from a distance—
Above, it scrapes the blue sky with its dark misty clouds,
Below, it crushes the huge vastness of the Deity of Earth.
Now I venture closer, to enter into its midst—
Climbing up to a rocky ledge, I glimpse the empty abyss:
A thousand peaks, ten thousand valleys, echo through pine and juniper.
From huge rocks overhanging the cliff a flying torrent gushes,

The sound of water, crashing and dashing, brings chaos to my ears:
Flying snow in the middle of summer, splashing the ledges of stone.
Constantly I encounter Immortal Elders and Sons of Sakyamuni[29]—
Once I despised them for following illusion and speaking words of nonsense;
Yet now I see crimson clouds and azure cliffs, far and near, reflecting their halls and pavilions,
Morning bells and evening drums sound deep and distant, with strings of flags and banners.
Secluded flowers and wild grasses: I do not know their names—
Blown in the wind, moistened by dew, their fragrance fills the canyon,
And sometimes pairs of white cranes arrive here on the wing.
Though secluded searching takes me far, I cannot reach the end,
Thus I intend to break from the world, and leave its confusion behind.
I envy you for purchasing land and building a home to grow old at its foot,
Transplanting rice shoots to fill your fields—
Fermenting wine to fill your vats.
You wish to have drifting alpine mists, and the warm azure of ten million forms
Constantly facing your terrace and windows, while you sit or recline.
Within your heart, many-faceted, there lies a priceless treasure,[30]
But the vulgar world cannot distinguish pure jade from colored stones.
Your name was listed as an officer for a period of twenty years,
In dark robes, hair growing white, still you were confined to an outpost.[31]
You wouldn't use base and servile means to seek favor and glory, fame and profit—
If it weren't that dark clouds and white rocks held such a profound attraction,
What reason could your towering spirit find to descend [to this world]?
How few men of strength and virtue there are to compare with you:
Alas, I would like to express myself, but where can I find a mighty brush standing as high as a flagpole!

The meter of this poem is irregular, loosely based on a seven-syllable line and with numerous longer lines that make the reciter breathe deeply and exhale thoroughly. The diction is quite loose and prosaic, especially the description of Liu Zhongyun in the second half, and, when combined with the irregular meter, gives the recitation a rough and simple feel. Some transitions within the poem are jerky and sudden, particularly the leap from Ouyang's imaginary journey through the mountain scenery to his summary of Liu's achievements and plans for retirement (lines 24–26).

As for the rhyme of the poem, it is what Ouyang elsewhere termed a difficult or narrow rhyme, in other words, a rhyme category with few homonyms, according to the categories in traditional Chinese rhyming dictionaries.[32] An approximate English equivalent might be composing a poem in which every other line had to rhyme with placebo or Bach. Since words that rhyme do not necessarily share similar meanings, the consequence of choosing a difficult rhyming category is to force the poet to jump from one topic to another in order to fit the content to the fixed rhyme words. An example of this is in the last line, in which Ouyang ingeniously manages to incorporate the rhyme word flagpole, though it has little to do with the mountain subject. This jumping about adds to the rough and unrefined feeling of the poem.

Another stylistic feature of the poem is Ouyang's use of humor. We see this in the ending, with its joke that one can only do justice to a larger-than-life personality like Liu if one has an enormous writing brush; also in the witty juxtaposition of Liu with Mount Lu (lines 34, 36), in which Ouyang implies that Liu's "dark robes and white hair" (*qing shan bai shou*) suit him especially well for retiring to the "dark clouds and white rocks" (*qing yun bai shi*) of the mountain.

As suggested in the chapter on poetic games, Mid-Northern Song poets saw this rough, jerky style laced with humor as typical of the Ancients, a reflection of their unrestrained and dynamic character. And they clearly believed that poetry written in such a style would produce beneficial effects when recited or copied with a brush—not just moral benefits, but emotional and physical benefits too. This is doubtless because Northern Song literati such as Ouyang Xiu shared the traditional Chinese idea that the Ancients had a monopoly on the essential wisdom necessary for living, including accepted theoretical principles on the causes of health and sickness.[33]

Admittedly, these ancient stylistic features do not appear in all Northern Song poems. Even poets like Ouyang and Mei, who advocated the ancient style most strongly, produced numerous conventional, smoothly crafted, recent-style regulated verses. But the kind of poetry they praised for its therapeutic qualities or powers of emotional release tends to exhibit one or more aspects of the ancient style.

THERAPEUTIC SUBJECTS

Turning to the content and mood of such therapeutic poetry, we can clearly see these poets choosing subjects that help them "transcend their sorrow", to use the concept coined by Yoshikawa Kojiro.[34] Likewise, their frequent use of wit, caricatured self-portraits and mock intellectual argument lightens the mood of poems that deal with gloomy subjects like sickness, suffering, and old age.[35]

We can divide the transcendent moods and subject matter of such poems into three broad and sometimes overlapping categories: dynamism, purity, and strangeness.

Dynamic subjects include mountains, such as Mount Lu and Mount Song; watery subjects, such as major rivers, the ocean, and storms, with their accompanying dragons; and great people or events of past ages, such as Emperor Yu, the semimythical ancient tamer of China's waterways. The following poem by Ouyang Xiu, on a sacrificial offering to a storm-dragon, is typical of these dynamic topics, and provides a watery counterpart to his poem on Mount Lu above:

Offering to the Dragon at Cypress Pool [1046][36]

I sigh at the wisdom of the dragon! Who can possibly grasp it?
Emerging and sinking, its transformations are truly abrupt and sudden.
The altar is level, the trees ancient; the Pool's waters blacken;
4 A dark shadow and muffled echoes: I doubt if it's there at all.
Clouds and mist on surrounding mountains suddenly merge in broad daylight,
With a flash it leaps up vertically, and seizes the empty sky.
Turtles and fish are carried in its wake, dropping down from the heights,
8 Thunder rumbles and lightning shoots: each drives the other on.
It brings down cliffs and overturns ravines just for its own amusement,

In no time ten-thousand creatures are completely soaked to the skin!
But blue skies then sweep across; a thousand miles grow calm,
All I see is green countryside, wiped clean by the clouds.
The next morning, old peasants worship beside the Pool,
Their drums sound with a *kan, kan*, echoing at the mountain's foot.
Rustic shamans are drunk and satiated; temple doors stay closed,
And desperate bedraggled crows struggle together for leftover offerings.

The dragon leaps into the sky, taking all kinds of sea creatures with it, and lifting the poet's spirits with a demonstration of the immense dynamism of nature.

Pure subjects included smaller bodies of water, such as fresh springs and clear, still pools; also snow, the moon, and any kind of plant or creature that was white, such as cranes, rabbits and plum blossoms, or that had traditional literary associations of purity, such as bamboo, chrysanthemums, tea, and the like. Certain historical figures belonged to this category too because of their fondness for pure subjects, most notably the poet Tao Yuanming (c. 365–427). The following two examples of poems on pure topics give a clear idea of the contrast between this category and the previous one. Pure poems tend to be more subdued in tone and regular in meter and rhythm, while still making use of simple, prosaic diction and gentle humor. Thus, the effect on the reciter is calming rather than exhilirating but still transcendent in terms of creating a serene vision of a dustless, trouble free world:

Yongshu's White Rabbit [Mei Yaochen, 1057][37]

How strange that Chang'e did not carry out her duties carefully,
She let this jade-white rabbit escape and descend to our mortal world![38]
But fate decreed that it would not fall into the jaws of hunting dogs:
An old fellow of Chuzhou managed to catch it and bring it back home.
Its frosty fur was soft and fine; the pupils of its eyes deep black,
He put a silk leash around its neck with red and golden threads.
He galloped off to present it to the Governor as an extraordinary pet,[39]
And now [the Governor] has gone to live in the Mountains of the Immortals![40]

Up in the moon they grow concerned: there's no-one to pound the elixir,
Beside the osmanthus tree, the pestle and mortar are surely lying idle.
But I just want to pluck its fur and make a white-haired writing brush,
I'll grind my ink and write out my poem to bring a smile to your face.

The white rabbit comes from the realm of immortals and inspires its owner to ascend to otherworldly realms himself, even if only in his imagination.

The following poem continues the lunar theme, adding to it a calm and clear stretch of water:

Enjoying the Moon at Flying Canopy Bridge [Ouyang Xiu, 1049][41]

Heaven's form gathers lightness and purity,
Water's power comes from silence and emptiness.
When clouds disperse, wind and ripples grow still,
Then the nature of Heaven and water is revealed:
Their limpid radiance and utmost clarity of feature,
Above and below, contain and reflect each other.
And positioned between the two of them,
Brightly suspended, a chilly mirror.
And what shines radiant in its overflowing glow?
Ten thousand creatures, fresh and luminescent.
Even more so with the souls of human beings:
Can it fail to awaken their senses?
And as for me at this wondrous moment,
Free and easy, I chant my solitary song,
Confusion and darkness are joyfully washed away,
Following the flow, I swim to my heart's content!
My human heart expands and gains release
As the Moon rises higher and moves into the distance.
I only fear the clear night will come to an end:
Time and again, I glance at the handle of the Dipper.[42]

Whether Ouyang is actually swimming in this pure, fresh water or just imagining himself swimming, his poem recreates the mood of a tranquil moonlit night so vividly that the reader can hardly resist being drawn into a similarly relaxed and serene mental state.

Finally, strange subjects included exotic foods, such as clams, olives, and ginkgoes; rare antiques and decorative objects like ancient swords, inkstones, and painted screens; and odd-shaped or strangely coloured rocks. The category also included, paradoxically, subjects that were so unpoetic that they became strange when made the main focus of a poem, especially when treated in a humorous manner, such as snoring, hangovers, insects of various kinds, and sweating through a hot summer's day.[43]

Since I have translated many of these strange poems in other chapters, I will give just one example here by Ouyang Xiu, entitled "Offered in Answer to Shengyu's Poem on a Bulgy-Headed Fish" (written in 1058). This poem illustrates most of the ancient stylistic features mentioned above, and is a particularly arresting example of Northern Song mock argument, or caricatured reasoning:[44]

> I've heard that within the ocean's greatness,
> The species of creatures are truly innumerable.
> Insects and shrimps stay among the shallows,
> Sea-snails and shellfish pile up like mountains;
> "Hairy shrimps" and "antler minnows":[45]
> In one pint are hundreds of thousands.
> As for harvesting, each has its season,
> And people consume them all over the world.
> Tiny creatures may resemble those described above,
> But large ones include the utterly unfathomable:
> Amidst the vastness of breaker and wave,
> An "island" rises for just a moment.
> In an instant it sinks, seen no longer,
> Now, you discover, it was a creature's protruding spine!
> Sometimes one is beached, coming up with the tide,
> Violently it dies, as if suffering exile.
> Coastal dwellers call each other together,
> With knives and saws, they struggle to hack and slice.
> Shockingly, the segments of bones fill a cart,
> The points of its tusks are sharp as swords and halberds.[46]
> The stink is perceptible for several tens of miles,
> Its lingering odour takes ages to disperse.
> Now I know that where hundreds of rivers return,
> There must be a power of latent capacity,
> With sunken rarities and secret treasures:
> Ten thousand forms not readily understood.[47]
> Alas, the minuteness of your bulgy-headed [fish],
> Who transported it to the nation's capital?
> Dry and withered, with hardly any flavour,
> After preparation and washing, it's a waste to fry it up!

From this I know there are exotic creatures,
But is it worthy to be offered to fine guests?
And yet one morning we received your poem:
From that time on its false name was made![48]

Although this poem does not purport to be more than a comic deflation of the undeserved popularity of the bulgy-headed fish, perhaps a more serious point lurks beneath the surface, namely, that like the tiny fish, petty people also too easily exploit their connections to gain a fine reputation in the capital, while those of infinitely greater talent and profundity are left in distant oceans, unknown and unrecognized until they are washed up dead on the beach, "as if suffering exile" (line 16). It is easy to see how this poem works to release the poet's inner tensions and grievances and help balance his emotions.

The content of these poems, whether dynamic, pure, or strange, allows poet and reader to escape from pressing problems of the everyday world and enter an exotic or inspiring imaginative realm. Even if this escape is only temporary, it acts in concert with the rhythm, meter, and other stylistic features of the poem to overcome preoccupation with negative moods and emotions, and restore equanimity—or regular circulation of *qi*—to the poet's mind and body.

THERAPY AND POETIC EXCHANGES

Having established how Northern Song poets view poetic composition and recitation as emotionally balancing, hence therapeutic, and what kinds of poems they considered most beneficial for this function, we should not overlook the social dimension of writing poetry during this period—the fact that virtually all these poems were composed either at social gatherings or as direct responses to poems presented by friends and acquaintances. How does this social context influence our account of Mid-Northern Song use of poetry as a form of therapy or emotional release?

Obviously, it is during times of great personal suffering and crisis that the healing properties of poetry are most necessary. In the Northern Song, a frequent cause of suffering for scholar-officials, who composed most of the poetry surviving from the period, was political disgrace and exile to remote, ill-developed parts of the empire. Such a shattering experience would certainly cause a buildup of resentment, frustration and other negative emotions in the victim's mind and body. Particularly unbearable was the indefinite length of the sentence, which could drag on for a decade or more. In several recorded cases, exiles died before they were pardoned and recalled to the capital. Among poets of the Northern Song, for instance, both Su Shunqin and Su Shi died as a result of their exiles.[49] Even if death did not occur, illness was almost inevitable in such circumstances. Ouyang Xiu, for example, recorded in a letter to Mei Yaochen that his second exile in 1045 led to a prolonged bout of sickness lasting almost two years.[50] Clearly, any relief from the emotional strain of such an experience would be most welcome and might even help to save the exiled person's life.

Unfortunately, two obstacles stood in the way of the exiled person finding emotional solace through poetic composition. First, separation from friends and even family in an unfamiliar, remote place immediately deprives the writer of the normal audience for his poetry. Therefore, much of the impetus for composition disappears. Second, the misery and depression brought on by exile is more likely to impede creative expression than encourage it. Writing poetry, like any other nonessential, or entertaining activity, at first sight is pointlessly inadequate as a way to overcome such deep pain and may have been politically risky too.[51]

Despite these obstacles, the social nature of poetic composition had a more positive aspect; friends of the exiled poet would normally continue to send their compositions to him through trusted emissaries.[52] Besides the immediate consolation such poems provided, as evidence of friendly support in difficult times, they triggered the exile's sense of social responsibility, obliging him to respond in kind. Moreover, the friend's poem supplied a ready-made topic, in most cases a dynamic, pure, or strange topic, so that the exiled poet would focus on a similar mood-altering and transcendent world when writing his response. Finally, it was quite acceptable for the poet to take rhyme words directly from his friend's poem to use in his response. Thus, some of the creative groundwork of composition was already completed.

Relating this process of poetic exchanges to Chinese medical theory, besides the circulation of *qi*, or emotional energy, within peoples' bodies, there is a corresponding circulation of *qi* throughout the universe and between people in society: An exiled person was temporarily cut off from this circulation and deprived of all his normal social relationships, suffering mentally and physically as a result. Yet, aided by poetry exchanged through correspondence, he could again participate in the wider social circulation of emotional energy, releasing his inner mental tension back into the world in a socially acceptable way, and possibly preventing emotional imbalances from developing into physical sickness.

Exile was not the only experience Northern Song scholar-officials faced that caused deep emotional suffering. Working in the central government was doubtless equally stressful and the relief provided by poetic composition with trusted friends was just as necessary. Yet, the consolations provided by poetry are more clear-cut when seen through the concentrated lens of exile. This chapter concludes with a case study of the poems exchanged by Ouyang Xiu, Su Shunqin, and Mei Yaochen after Su's demotion and exile to Suzhou in 1044 and Ouyang's banishment to Chuzhou in 1045, focusing on the therapeutic aspect that Ouyang Xiu, in particular, found so invigorating.

EMOTIONAL RELEASE BY CORRESPONDENCE: EXILE POETRY OF THE MID-1040s

It was probably Mei Yaochen who initiated the numerous exchanges of poems between these three friends following the collapse of the Qingli Reforms and the exile of most of the reformers. Since Mei was only a minor provincial official at the time, he did not suffer exile, and throughout his life he was in the habit of composing poems and sending them to his friends so frequently that most found it impossible to keep up with him.[53] In 1044, Mei sent a number of poems to Su Shunqin, including one entitled "Seeing Off Su Zimei", in which he compared his friend to Qu Yuan, the ancient righteous exiled official—in other words, a suitably dynamic subject. Su responded with a number of his own poems, three of which are extant.[54]

However, it was not until the following year, 1045, when the exiled Ouyang joined the fray, that we begin to see the connection drawn between healing and poetic exchanges. In his poem "While Sick, Sent to Shengyu [i.e., Mei Yaochen] in Place of a Letter," Ouyang starts by describing the gloom of exile, with its deleterious effects on his health, and his subsequent loss of enthusiasm for worldly pleasures:[55]

I remember last year when you visited from Yue,
It happened I was departing on a mission, in a hurry to leave the city.
At that time it was early Fall, and the crabs were just getting plump,
4 I regretted I couldn't drink with you and give you a proper reception.
Earlier this year my sickness flared up when I had too much wine to drink,
For the whole spring I abstained from alcohol; my vital energy sagged.
Sometimes I manage to fill my mouth with sweet and fat [delicacies],
8 But the bugs in my belly aren't used to them and fight back like hostile enemies!
If a single satisfied stomach makes me suffer so much now,
It's no surprise my once-generous salary caused me to endure such punishments! . . .[56]
. . . With our armies at peace and few official duties, normally I would be content,
12 But my heart and mind are in decline even though I'm not too busy.
As days lengthen and the weather warms, all I wish to do is sleep,
Sleeping soundly, I really detest the clamour of spring turtledoves,
Northern Pool is less than a hundred steps from the city wall,
16 The ice has melted in its limpid waters, and fish are leaping and splashing,
But all this time I haven't once managed to take a walk and visit there,
For beautiful scenery, all I can do is listen to travellers' descriptions! . . .

Following this plaintive lament, Ouyang claims that only his friendship with Mei can give him any pleasure in life now, and poetry exchanges are the only activity that he still finds worthwhile, since drinking wine is out of the question:

. . . I don't have many friends now, and you are the only one I miss,
32 How can I get to see you, and forget my worries for a while?
In your kitchen the wine is fine, but it's too far for me to reach,
I think of you, a habitual drinker, loosening your clothes and relaxing.[57]

Master Guo sent me a message, but he hasn't arrived here yet,
36 I long to see your latest poems with a deep hunger and thirst,
Everything I did in my youth I have now put firmly behind me,
Love for poetry is all that remains, and my heart has never tired of it,
You have plenty of leisuretime: you can write me some compositions,
40 Don't refuse to copy them yourself, on a sheet of smooth Teng[zhou] paper,
Lessen the force of your brush for me, so I have some chance to match you,
And don't use inaccessible rhymes to prevent me trying to catch you!

Mei certainly complied with Ouyang's request for a poem very quickly, since Ouyang's collection contains another poem from 1045 entitled "Reading [Mei] Shengyu's *Pan* Peach Poem."[58] The *pan* peach was a magical Heavenly fruit that matured once every three thousand years and could confer immortality when consumed. Therefore Mei's original poem probably belonged to the category of pure and transcendent topics—although we cannot be sure, as it is no longer extant. But in his response, Ouyang virtually ignores the peach, focusing instead on praising the outstanding talents of Mei and Su Shunqin. In the process, he makes some further interesting comments about the healing powers of poetry. In one passage he declares:

. . . Recently your poem on the *pan* peach
Arrived by courier from the north,
It released me from thoughts of sickness and decline,
4 Warm like a ray of springtime sun . . .

These lines bear comparison with Ouyang's comments on how zither playing helped him forget his illness, quoted earlier. His preface on zither playing dates from the following year, during the same period of exile (1047). Feeling better already, Ouyang then describes himself trying to write a responding poem—fulfilling his social obligation to Mei:

. . . Happily I set about trying to match you,
I rinsed my inkstone and sat in the main hall,
But my ink-filled brush seemed to get stuck,

4 I felt distracted, as if something was missing.
I'm an old rooster with tough beak and talons,
It's not easy to advance on my battleground,
I'll retreat first, without doing battle,
8 I may run away, but I will not surrender!
I still want to call for [Su] Zimei,
Zimei, who lives across the pounding river waves,
Although he is certainly worn and haggard,
12 He retains his noble and unbowed will,
With his strong vital energy [*qi*] he is truly fit to oppose you,
You'll compete as equals for victory or defeat . . .
. . . Delightful, that such joys exist in the world:
16 In one draught, we'll drain a hundred winecups!
But it's so hard to meet when we're living apart:
How can our noble plan be fulfilled?

Though Ouyang claims he is unable to put brush to paper, and therefore must rely on Su Shunqin to match Mei's poem, in fact he has co-opted his creative block and made it the main subject of his poem. In other words, instead of bottling up his frustration at having no inspiration, he has released it in a humorous poetic form and thereby overcome it. Notice also the clever way in which he brings Su Shunqin into the poetry exchange, complimenting him and sending him the poem, thereby obliging him to compose a response as well. Doubtless Ouyang's intention is to help release the exiled Su from thoughts of sickness and decline too.

Over the next few years, the three friends exchanged numerous poems expressing their mutual concern and support, encouraging each other to continue writing, and occasionally indulging in lighthearted teasing and poetic banter. Ouyang Xiu especially benefitted from these exchanges, as he makes clear in his poems and letters of the period. In one letter to Mei Yaochen, for instance, he declared:[59]

> I received your six poems [on travelling to Lang Hill]; also the poems on the paulownia blossoms and birdcalls . . . I have been living here [in Chuzhou] for a long time, and every day I am finding it more interesting. My official study is as peaceful as a monk's cloister, and when I tire of reading books, I can drink and play tiddlywinks instead . . . My mother has been sick very often over the last year or two, but since the end of summer she has felt much better. We have plenty of food and drink to satisfy us, and I would say that I have not been as happy as this since our Luoyang days ended. I have written a con-

siderable number of poems, too many to copy down in full here. Until the next time we meet I hope you will look after yourself.

He even laughs at his own situation, portraying himself in a caricatured way as the Drunken Old Man, and describing his comical inebriated exploits in several poems sent to his friends.[60]

We find further evidence of Ouyang's belief that poetry could change mood and overcome harmful emotional imbalances in his constant attempt to persuade Su Shunqin to continue composing poems during his exile. It seems that, having discovered how invigorating poetic composition and exchange could be for himself, he was anxious to see Su reap similar benefits. He was also concerned that Su was cutting himself off completely from social circulation with his friends, due to fear of political recriminations.[61]

Ouyang's attitude is very clear from his poems of the mid-1040s. Besides the *pan* peach poem quoted above, in which Ouyang asked for Su's help to compete with Mei Yaochen's poetic talent, other poems to Su frequently concluded with flattering and consoling remarks like the following:[62]

If a gentleman only possesses life, he won't be long abandoned,
With new poems and fine wine, now you can outlast the year.
And even though you wouldn't permit a vulgar guest to visit,
4 Don't begrudge passing down your excellent lines to the world!

In other words, as the rest of the poem makes clear, Ouyang sees Su as an immortal of the East living in a beautiful paradise that a mere mortal cannot visit. But Su should still send poems down to the world of vulgar folk, so that he does not feel cut off from the world, and so that he has a reason to outlast the year.

One of the most interesting exchanges between Ouyang and Su Shunqin involved their poetic descriptions of a moon-colored inkstone screen.[63] We see here a topic that is at once strange and transcendent. Ouyang first describes how the translucent hue and lunar pattern on the stone draw him into an otherworldly imaginative universe full of "wonders." Using a humorous conceit, he declares that the real moon must have fallen from the sky onto his writing desk! Yet, since he still sees the real moon moving across the Heavens every night, he finds himself at a loss to explain the identity of his strange, unearthly stone. He censures himself for even attempting to describe it, and passes the task on to Su, a man completely at home in the realm of spirits and immortals, and thus perfectly qualified to evoke the cosmic power of the stone in verse:

"*Song on a Moonstone Inkstone Screen, Sent to Su Zimei*" *[1047]*[64]

The moon ascended from the bed of the sea,
And rose up to the South-East of the Heavens;[65]
Then just as it reached the centre of the Heavens,
It sent down a ray to Thousand Zhang Pool.[66]
At the pool's heart the wind was still: the moonlight did not stir,
Its upturned reflection radiated, entering a violet stone cliff.
In moon's glow and water's purity, the stone shimmers cleanly,
How inspiring, this Soul of Yin, descending to seep into its heart!
Ever since the moon penetrated into the heart of this stone,
The Two Fires in the Heavens were divided into three.[67]
Its pure glow lasted for eons, without erosion or destruction,
Yet supreme treasures of Heaven and Earth cannot be hidden or sealed.
Heaven's Lord cried out for the Duke of Thunder:
By night He wielded a huge axe to destroy the towering cliff.
He chopped down this single slab from a height of eighty thousand feet,
Brightly shining, the cold mirror now lies in a jade compact box.[68]
The toad and the white rabbit both managed to escape to the Heavens,
All that's left is an osmanthus shadow extending long and slender.[69]
Jingshan was able to obtain it; he could not bear to part with it,[70]
Giving it to me, he was of a mind to ask for a thousand gold pieces!
He himself claimed that every time it encountered a full moon night,
From a dark room, the stone's glow would radiate beyond the eaves!
How great are Heaven, Earth, and all between:
Their ten thousand wonders cannot be fully expressed.
Alas! I cannot help going too far,
Longing to probe the depths of every matter.
I wish to take all that two eyes and ears can perceive,
And put up a fight with Creative Transformation for every tiniest hairtip!
Dazzling, the Three Heavenly Bodies proceed,[71]
Of them, sun and moon are especially awesome and stern.

If they were made to descend [to Earth] and line up with creatures below,
The multifarious ranks of species would disappear for ever!
But what of this stone: what kind of object can it be in the end?
I have a mouth that wishes to explain, but alas, it seems clamped shut.
I marvel at the heart of Master Su:
Lined up in ranks, the myriad phenomena are all contained within it!
Not only is his heart expansive, his boldness is also great,
He constantly creates compositions to startle the vulgar and ignorant.
Since I was able to obtain this stone,
I haven't seen Master Su at all, and my heart is full of regret:
Without first having to undergo the guidance of a master craftsman,
What apprentice would dare to execute complex carving and chiselling?[72]
I'll call an artisan to make a painting of the stone and take it to you,
I hope you'll give your opinion—and don't be constrained by modesty!

How could Su Shunqin ignore such flattery and refuse to produce a responding poem! While Su doubtless found such poems consoling, it is interesting to see how Ouyang has created and used this idealized image of Su, just as he used other transcendent or strange poetic objects like the stone itself, to evoke an inspiring vision and alter his own mood. We could say such exchanged poems had multiple, if partly delayed, therapeutic functions: first, they allowed Ouyang to focus on transcendent topics (Su the immortal; moon-hued stones) and lift his own mood; next, they would also have lifted Su's spirits with their compliments and encouragement, and obliged him to write a matching poem, distracting him from gloomy sentiments; and finally, they virtually guaranteed that Ouyang would receive a response from Su, and be further inspired to continue these positive exchanges.

Su's responding poem does not add much new material to that of Ouyang, but he continues the transcendent theme with tongue-in-cheek evidence to support Ouyang's hypothesis that the stone has celestial origins.[73] Thus, he claims the reason Chang'e, goddess of the moon, cannot be seen in the moonstone screen is because she must have gone off in a futile search for the escaped toad and rabbit, and never came back. He adds other examples, from Ancient writers, of Heavenly Bodies entering tiny objects—for example, he notes that clams were supposedly able to suck in lunar foam when the moon set in the Western Sea, and form pearls within their wombs (i.e., miniature full moons). Likewise, the curved tusk of the walrus was supposedly formed from a sympathetic reaction to the crescent moon.[74] Su explains these phenomena with the theory that "there are objects which respond to each other despite lacking emotions / No matter whether they are hidden and tiny, or high and far away." He concludes by arguing that this moonstone is actually superior to the real moon because now its transcendent glow will never wane.

Su implies that people, who have emotions, should use their poems to respond to each other at a distance and these poetic exchanges will give them the power to persevere and thrive like the glowing stone filled with the moon's cosmic energy.

WAS POETRY REALLY THERAPEUTIC?

It is interesting that whereas Ouyang Xiu claimed that his health benefited greatly from his various artistic activities during exile, especially from poetry exchanges, Su Shunqin soon succumbed to illness and died in 1048. We cannot immediately conclude that poetry had no positive effect on Su—in fact, Ouyang Xiu wrote, Su often released his resentment about his unjust punishment in songs and poems.[75] Yet, this discrepancy between the two writers reminds us that the powers of poetry were limited. Moreover, some Northern Song literati even considered poetic composition to be more often harmful than beneficial to the practitioner. They felt that it could easily distract scholars from serious tasks like moral self-cultivation and working to improve the society around them. They also worried it might exacerbate any emotional imbalances afflicting poets, tempting them to become self-indulgent, and by extension, even more susceptible to illnesses.[76]

Anti-poetry advocates were very suspicious of scholar-officials like Ouyang and Mei who enjoyed organising banquets at which they would spontaneously compose and exchange poetry. They saw such gatherings as little more than disguised debauchery—not least because female entertainers often frequented such banquets. The famous Southern Song philosopher Zhu Xi (1130–1200) later summed up this view in a harsh criticism of Ouyang Xiu: "He cultivated his literary works but made no effort to cultivate his personality. All day long he sang songs, drank wine, and sought to enjoy himself."[77]

Though such a jaundiced view of poetry was not typical in the Northern Song period, even those who generally appreciated the value of poetic composition and clearly enjoyed writing poems themselves did occasionally express ambivalence about its effects. Ronald Egan cites a number of statements by Ouyang Xiu and contemporary poets warning against the potential dangers of being carried away by writing poetry, especially poems composed in a florid style.[78] Some of these comments are not intended to be taken seriously. For instance, Ouyang's teasing poem to Mei Yaochen entitled "Answering Shengyu's 'Don't Drink Wine'" begins:

> You say don't drink wine;
> I say *don't write poems*:
> Flowers bloom, leaves fall, insects and birds grow forlorn,
> All four seasons the hundred creatures disturb my cogitations,
> Mornings I chant, shaking my head; evenings I knit my brows, . . .
> How can this compare with drinking wine and losing all awareness?[79]

Since Ouyang expresses his argument against poetry within a poem that is particularly lighthearted in tone, we need not assume this is Ouyang's final word on the subject.

Elsewhere, he occasionally makes the point in a serious context, for instance in his comment to a Buddhist monk poet that "poetry is to [official] writing as floating dust is to Mount Tai."[80] But, judging by the fact that Ouyang and most of his scholar-official contemporaries continued to compose poems in great numbers and evaluate poetry very highly for the rest of their lives, we should surely interpret such isolated remarks as a warning against excessive indulgence in poetry, or in any other activity, to the detriment of one's social responsibilities and relationships, rather than as a general attack on the dangers of poetic composition.

Such a conclusion is supported by Mei Yaochen's response to the two poems on the moonstone screen. Though certainly humorous in his intent, Mei spends all his time deflating Ouyang's and Su's extravagant hyperbole regarding this lump of colored rock, and mocking their continuous poetic prattling about it:

Reading the Moonstone Screen Poem [Mei Yaochen, 1047][81]

I observed the two of you composing poems that discussed a moonlike stone:
Yet the moon is up in the Heavens,
And the stone was beneath a mountain,
4 So how could traces of the moon possibly have "entered" into the stone?
Enough! Master Ouyang Xiu:
You know you cannot explain it, but still you don't stop your prattling!
Do you want to silence everyone who follows you, and give them nothing to say?
8 And yes Master Su, it's true that you are extremely wild and expansive,
But what's the point of stretching your analogies to "walrus tusks" and "clams"?
Walruses and clams are vital and active: they do have thoughts and feelings,
But stones lack any emotion or thought—that negates your claim straightaway!
12 I say that though the traces on this stone may indeed resemble the moon,
It cannot move through the Heavens, or mark the months of the year,
Neither has it ever emitted the slightest glimmer of light,
Nor is it anything like a lamp to illumine the night:
16 It is merely a rounded patch in a hard lump of rough jade ore,
And its texture bears no comparison with a precious disc of jade.
Yes, it may contain a lone osmanthus spreading its boughs,
But Chang'e and the jade white rabbit are nowhere to be seen;
20 Without these two creatures, how can it possess any spiritual power?
And simply to use it as an inkstone screen: well why treasure it for that?
Alas, my talent is limited and I cannot describe it any more,
But I've briefly evaluated your two poems: this may be of some benefit!

The extremely critical, vituperative attitude that pervades this poem gives a clear signal that it is not meant to be taken as a serious evaluation of his friends' behavior. Rather, the work is a lighthearted joke, thinly disguised as the ravings of a pedantic logician. Instead of churning out yet another poem idealizing strange objects and talented people, Mei prefers to adopt this curmudgeonly persona and to surprise (or shock) the recipients into laughter. At the same time, he reminds his friends that too much poetry about transcendent objects may be just as harmful as preoccupation with sorrow, if it leads them to lose touch with down-to-earth reality. Implicit in his remarks is a more general principle that imbalances of any kind in life may not be good for one's health.

Nevertheless, we must view these kinds of admonitions in the broader context of Ouyang's and Mei's poetic practice and literary criticism, and against the background of the continuing popularity of poetic composition among the vast majority of Northern Song literati. From this perspective, we can draw the following conclusions about their attitude towards the emotionally releasing powers of poetry—an attitude shared by many other Northern Song literati. First, Ouyang and Mei regularly assert that writing and reciting poetry could help people to release emotional tension in a relatively safe and constructive way. Second, Ouyang in particular draws a direct connection between unbalanced emotions and mental and physical illness. He claims that poetry, like other artistic practices, helps balance one's emotions and prevent or cure such illnesses. Third, through their poetic practice, both Ouyang and Mei emphasize that the benefits of exchanging poetry are greater than simply writing for oneself as a private expression of feeling. Yet, Mei was generally more guarded in his assertions about the therapeutic benefits of poetry, despite being much more prolific and dedicated than Ouyang in his actual poetic productivity. He made it clear that overindulgence in poetry writing, or any other cultural activity, to the detriment of one's social responsibilities, such as family duties and official work, could be harmful. To receive the benefits of poetic composition, one had to maintain a balance between the demands of one's art and those of society.

In other words, although the content of poetry need not focus on serious and moralistic concerns, the aim of writing poetry was to help one become better integrated into society, both by maintaining health through release of emotional tension, and by strengthening bonds with others through poetic exchanges. Hence, poetry should not stop at reviving one's individual mental and physical health—by releasing blocked emotional energy (*qi*)—but it should also extend to improving one's social health as well by reintegrating one into the social environment. This is the process of circulating positive emotional energy within society and this is what poets like Mei Yaochen would have considered the most important therapeutic function of poetry.

CHAPTER FIVE

Poems Promoting Ancient Culture

In chapter 2, we see how Mid-Northern Song poets used games to promote what they saw as ancient poetic style. In this chapter, we examine Northern Song poets' fascination with all things ancient, and their frequent celebration of ancient writers and ancient cultural objects in their poetry. First, I explain why Mid-Northern Song literati considered certain past poets to be more ancient than others, a judgment that often had little to do with chronological sequence and more to do with the style that they adopted. Next, I examine the ways in which Mid-Northern Song poets imitated and addressed the ancients both directly, with works written in the style of past poets, and indirectly, with poems on ancient objects. Finally, I argue that the continuing survival of ancient poetry and other cultural objects gave Northern Song poets hope that their own writings and vital energy (*qi*) would last into future generations. To this end, they expended much effort celebrating their cultural life in poetry and describing their appreciation of the various cultural objects that they collected, so that future readers would view them as worthy inheritors of the ancient tradition and would see fit to preserve the written traces of their lives too. Poetry was thus a vehicle for imbibing vital energy from long deceased writers and cultural figures, then transmitting or recirculating this energy into the future, even beyond the poet's individual death.

LINEAGES OF ANCIENT POETS

Mid-Northern Song literati, like their Mid-Tang predecessors, had a habit of tracing lineages of orthodox past writers and thinkers—those whom they felt had inherited and transmitted the living cultural tradition of the ancient sages. Besides lists of Confucian teachers and prose masters, they also created lineages of poets.[1] Apart from an obvious analogy with Confucian family and ancestral lineages, these lists of past writers give us a clear idea of what stylistic features Northern Song poets considered most vital to the survival of poetry. Ouyang Xiu's version of poetic lineage is representative of Northern Song literati taste and if we simply pay attention to the poets and anthologies listed, it seems to differ little from Mid-Tang lineages except for its inclusion of Mei Yaochen as a worthy Song heir:[2]

> In ancient times, harvest songs and temple purification [songs] were composed by the great music masters, and each of the feudal states also had poems to describe its local customs and situation.[3] Even for [games like] tiddlywinks and ring the bottle, they would still be sure to craft songs to clarify the purpose [of the games] and make their guests happy . . . Su [Wu, d. 60 BC] and Li [Ling, d. 74 BC] in the Han, then Cao [Zhi, 192–232] and Liu [Zhen, d. 217] in the Wei received [the Way of poetry] in its correct and original form. From the Song [420–79] and Qi [480–502] onwards, [poets] only received it superficially or in distorted form, and it was neglected. But during the Tang, among those who followed [Chen] Zi'ang [661–702], Li [Bai, 701–762], Du [Fu, 712–770], Shen [Quanqi, c. 656–c. 714], Song [Zhiwen, c. 656–712] and Wang Wei [c. 699–761], some received its pure, ancient and bland tone, and some received its relaxed, harmonious and noble rhythm. The followers of Meng Jiao [751–814] and Jia Dao [c. 793–c. 865] also received the vital energy of its sadness and hidden sorrows.
>
> Since that time, there have been those who received it, but it was not pure. Now, Shengyu [Mei Yaochen] has also received it. His style is best suited for getting to the roots of human emotions and describing scenes and objects. It is crafted, yet elegant; correct, yet full of variety; chattering, it is like the spring; bleak, it is like the fall. Anyone who reads [his poems] could feel happy yet could also feel sad. Exhilarated and relaxed, unconsciously their hands will tap and their feet will dance. Thus, he has certainly received it in a very profound way.

Two interesting points that emerge from examining this lineage help us understand Northern Song criteria for ancient poetry. First, what distinguishes the lineage from earlier examples is the interesting reason Ouyang gives for the supremacy of truly ancient verse, especially the *Classic of Poetry*, over all later poetry. He claims that the kinds of poems found in the *Classic* celebrate seasonal and ancestral rituals, describe local customs and situations, and are all-inclusive in subject matter and mood. Given the proper social purpose, such as a host making his guests happy, the most mundane activities, including drinking games like tiddlywinks, are suitable poetic topics. Second, despite his obvious admiration for truly ancient verse, the great majority of poets in Ouyang's lineage are not ancient in chronological terms. Most lived less than four hundred years before him, during the Tang dynasty, but they inherited and passed on some kind of living spark that Ouyang considered an essential element of ancientness.

Elsewhere, in various commentaries on the *Classic of Poetry*, Ouyang is one of the first scholars to question whether all the poems in the *Classic* were serious political allegories. Though he agrees that many poems reflect the common peoples' indirect censure or praise of their rulers, he maintains that some were obviously folksongs; simple expressions of the joys and sorrows of ordinary people, without political overtones.[4] One of Ouyang's most original insights lay in using this reinterpretation of the *Classic* to justify the breadth of subject matter and mood of his own poetry and the poetry of his contemporaries, especially its lighthearted, trivial side. Thus, in comparing Mei Yaochen's poetry with those of the ancients listed above, it is the variety of mood as well as Mei's ability to make the reader react with visceral pleasure, that Ouyang considers most praiseworthy.[5]

Of course, Northern Song literati also composed serious poetry on weighty themes. But in their comments on poetic style, they attempt to broaden traditional, moralistic definitions of what constituted ancient—and therefore exemplary—poetry. As long as the act of poetic writing helped bring people together and communicate with each other in a civilized, enjoyable way (as they imagined it had in ancient times), they were unconcerned if the content of their poems promoted a narrow idea of correct moral behavior.

Despite their claims to emulate the ancients, when we turn to specific comparisons between Northern Song poetry and ancient poems, we see very little stylistic common ground. Grammar, diction, meter, and rhymes are generally quite different from the basic four-syllable folk songs in the *Classic of Poetry*, with their repetitive refrains and simple archaic rhythms. Even less ancient poetry, such as the five-syllable verses of the Han and Wei, deals with a narrower range of moods and subject matter than the work of the better-known Northern Song poets, and it is less inclined toward wit and humor. So, beside the rather vague injunctions to include all topics and focus on the social activity of composing poetry together how did Song literati express ancient characteristics in their poetry? They did so in two primary ways: first, stylistically, by imitating comparatively recent poets—especially Mid-Tang poets—whom they considered worthy inheritors of the ancient tradition; and second, in the content of their poems, by describing ancient objects and artifacts, which they felt evoked the heroic and untrammeled values of the past world.

MID-TANG POETS AS ANCIENTS

The most sustained work of literary criticism from the Mid-Northern Song period, Ouyang Xiu's *Remarks on Poetry*, focuses almost exclusively on three groups of poets:

1. his contemporaries, such as Mei Yaochen, Su Shunqin, and Shi Manqing;
2. earlier Song poets, including the so-called Xikun School, which followed the style of the Late-Tang poet Li Shangyin (c. 813–858), and another group that imitated the plain style of Bai Juyi (772–846);
3. Mid- to Late-Tang poets, especially Han Yu, Meng Jiao, and Jia Dao.

Ouyang barely mentions any poets earlier than the Mid-Tang.[6]

In his other comments on poetry, scattered through various collections of anecdotes, notes, and prefaces, earlier poets occasionally make an appearance—for instance, in the poetic lineage quoted above—but Ouyang Xiu makes little attempt to characterize their style with any precision, as he does with the Mid-Tang poets.[7] One of his isolated, rather dismissive, comments on the poetry of Du Fu is typical of the neglect Ouyang and his contemporaries displayed towards most poets before the Mid-Tang period:

"Du Fu's poetry," he claimed, "surpasses that of Li Bai in only a single aspect: his painstaking attention to small details. As for natural talent overflowing spontaneously, [Du] Fu could not even come close [to Li]."[8]

When we look at Ouyang Xiu's and Mei Yaochen's poetry, we notice a similar tendency to focus on more recent poets as stylistic models, especially the Mid-Tang circle of writers around Han Yu. References to Mid-Tang poets occur in both direct and indirect ways. Several of Ouyang's and Mei's poem titles explicitly state they are written "in imitation of" a Mid-Tang poet.[9] Though it is not always obvious they have one particular poem in mind, they often manage to capture the strange hyperbolic diction and sense of cosmic disorder that characterize early ninth-century Yuanhe style. Here is an example by Ouyang Xiu, apparently composed on his journey into exile:[10]

Encountering Wind at Luan City: Imitating the Style of Han [Yu] and Meng [Jiao's] Linked Verses [1045]

At year's end, the clogged atmosphere is foul,
Winter disperses, provoking a seasonal battle.
A light breeze revives the warmer pulse,
Orders are given to spread the New Year.
Distant echoes: its approach seems slow,
Then dashing wildly, its forces spread unchecked.
Toppling city walls, they fight to battle drums,[11]
Charging over the countryside, they overcome troops of Yin;[12]
Swept clean away, no trace of mist remains,
Crushed and destroyed, no stalks can make a stand.
The Five Mountains shake their lofty towers,
The Nine Cauldrons seethe, frying and boiling.[13]
Jade stones split open from burning mountain ridges,
Waves and breakers roll in from the overflowing ocean.
I hear in the distance the markets close at noon,
With struggles and shouts, confusion shakes the night.
The gloom reaches its apogee, clouds are drained of color,
Yin becomes exhausted, and fire is born.
Lightning's whips repeatedly crack and swish,
Thunder's chariot-wheels add their clamorous rumble.
Crevices and caves produce a thousand reverberations,
From darkness and gloom emerge a hundred strange creatures.
Fox spirits hide in the desolate thickets,
Ghostly flames flee, glimmering greenly.[14]

Excited by anger, the gods increase their terror,
But suddenly they cease, giving respite to our ears.
Barbarian troops now possess the moon's corona,
Travelers on the river expect the crocodile's splash.[15]
Floating [like] leaves, a thousand boats are lost,
Flying in the sky, ten thousand tiles are scattered
Brave hunters spur their horses to gallop forth,
As my boat grows stable, I consider the rest of my voyage.
Afraid of being crushed, I repeatedly shift my seat,
Praying in the darkness, I keep adjusting my hat-strings.[16]
The frozen [ice] melts, rousing hibernating creatures,
And withered [plants] revive, about to send out shoots.
With my sick frame, I'm sad at this mountainous journey-stop,
These cold days of Spring I long for the clinking wine-bowl;
A rooster loudly crows as Heaven and Earth grow white,
And climbing to a plateau, I gaze at the brightening sun.

After a violent cosmic battle between the forces of *yin* and *yang*, the latter prevails, allowing spring warmth to revive dormant creatures and plants. The poem bears some resemblance to the battle between fire and water in Han Yu's "Fire in the Luhun Mountains," although Ouyang's imitation is considerably less imaginative and grotesque than Han's work.[17]

Besides such examples of direct stylistic imitation, Mid-Northern Song poets frequently compare themselves to Mid-Tang writers in their poems. This tendency provides a clue to help us understand the link between the Northern Song, the Mid-Tang, and ancient culture. Ouyang Xiu and Mei Yaochen consistently depict Mid-Tang writers as a group of diverse talents bound by a common desire to transmit the essential vitality of ancient culture. For example, Ouyang Xiu compares Mei Yaochen to Meng Jiao—and by extension, himself to Han Yu—in the following poem from 1045:[18]

In their writings Han [Yu] and Meng [Jiao]
Were two heroes matched in strength,
Their poems were punctuated with laughter and wit,
Like thunder and lightning striking in the wilderness.
Among the massed birds, none dared to respond to them,
So like a pair of phoenixes they called to each other.
Meng in his poverty was weighed down by suffering,
Han in his wealth overflowed with abundance,
The poor one pecked at refined seeds,
The rich one dazzled with patterned plumage;

Producing new life, one sounded in the *gong* mode,
Harvesting sorrows, the other sounded in *shang*;
Though their two pitches were not the same,
Their matching tones echoed in perfect harmony.
When Heaven produces rare and unique [sounds],
They occur seldom and do not last long,
They have been silent for two hundred years,
[Like] priceless buried jewels hidden from the light,
When [Meng] Jiao died it was not [Jia] Dao
But [Mei] Shengyu who dug up his treasure;
Suffering in the world, he hides away,
But his lonely chant sounds frostily in the night;
Its freezing cold enters one's flesh and bones,
Its pure echoes sadden the heart and linger long . . .
. . . I stretch my neck and try to match his singing
When my strength gives out, I still force myself on;
I certainly know that I'm not his equal,
I simply want to transmit the flavor of past songs.

In this poem, once again we see that the vitality of past writers must be transmitted in poetry today, though here, Ouyang expresses the point using metaphors of birdsong (lines 5–14, 22–25) and buried treasure (17–20). Yet this vitality is not necessarily restricted to a single poetic style: indeed, Ouyang notes that Meng Jiao's poetry is completely different from Han Yu's, though equally harmonious (lines 7–14). Likewise, their poetry does not limit itself to a single serious mood, but is punctuated with laughter and wit (lines 3–4), something that Ouyang Xiu seems to associate closely with its ancient vitality.

Like Ouyang Xiu, Mei Yaochen frequently speaks highly of Mid-Tang poets, as Jonathan Chaves has shown.[19] Chaves says of Mei that "he considered himself to be participating in a circle of poets comparable to the men of letters who gathered around Han Yu". Chaves also discusses poems in which Mei evaluates Han Yu and his circle:[20]

> "Some of them [i.e., Han Yu's circle] wrote many words of suffering; / Others devoted themselves to an untrammeled manner." Ouyang Xiu, Mei intimates, wishes to emulate Han's catholicity and to preside over a new literary circle. The same names appear in still another poem. Here Han Yu is said to have had universal genius. He swept away opposing views like so much dust. Zhang Ji [c. 765–c. 830] and Lu Tong [d. 835] vied in the "new and strange." Meng

> Jiao was praised most of all for being "outstanding." In modern times, Ouyang Xiu is like Han Yu, a vast ocean or a mighty mountain. Shi Yannian and Su Shunqin are like Lu Tong and Zhang Ji respectively. Mei himself is like Meng Jiao.[21]

Often such casual name dropping was also a sign that a more indirect or disguised imitation was taking place. Mei Yaochen's poem "Ancient Willow Tree," of 1049, contains the couplet: "My friend has evaluated Han [Yu's] poems [saying], / His perilous rhymes are ancient and unparalleled."[22] Coming at the end of a long description of the willow tree, this statement seems out of place until we investigate what Mei's friend, almost certainly Ouyang Xiu, wrote about Han Yu's rhymes. In his *Remarks on Poetry*, Ouyang gives the titles of two poems that exemplify Han's skill at rhyming in easy and difficult rhyme categories. For the latter, Ouyang declared: "When [Han] received a difficult rhyme . . . his true ingenuity was revealed through difficulty, and the more perilous it became, the more wonderful [the result]. An example of this type is 'While Sick, Presented to Eighteenth Zhang.'"[23] Han Yu's poem contains forty-four lines with a rhyme on every other line (i.e., twenty-two rhyme words). Turning to Mei's "Ancient Willow Tree," we find that it contains thirty lines with fifteen rhyme words, fourteen of which are taken from Han Yu's poem. Mei was obviously attempting to reveal his own "ingenuity through difficulty" by setting himself the task of emulating Han Yu's rhyming skill.

Mei does at least signal that some kind of imitation is taking place in this poem. Yet Northern Song poets sometimes adopted rhymes from Mid-Tang poems without hinting that they were doing so. Ouyang Xiu, for instance, uses thirteen of the rhyme words from the same poem by Han Yu in his own poem "Lu Mountain High," written in 1051.[24] Ouyang does not refer to Han explicitly in this poem. We can merely infer from his praise of Han's rhymes in his *Remarks on Poetry* and Mei's earlier example that he was engaging in a clever rhyme-matching game.

Later poets, such as Su Shi and his contemporaries, occasionally used such indirect references to Tang poets, especially unattributed rhyme matching, as a means of adding political bite to poems. Friends who were alerted to the technique would have noticed the unusual rhyme scheme, and would recall its Tang source, a poem that doubtless expressed a quite different message from the poem borrowing its rhymes.[25]

Among the poets of Ouyang Xiu's generation, however, we do not note a clear political motivation for matching the rhymes of Mid-Tang poets. If they were using these poems to criticize their superiors or opponents indirectly, it is so well hidden that any such interpretation is mere speculation. Instead, for poets like Ouyang Xiu and Mei Yaochen, the main reason for imitating Han Yu and his contemporaries is that they admired the ancient vitality of their style. Han Yu's poem "While Sick, Presented to Eighteenth Zhang," is a bravura display of comic and imaginative metaphor and simile. The difficulty of the rhyme scheme forces Han to jump between widely divergent topics in the space of a few lines, giving a sense of surprise and incongruity. It displays many stylistic features Northern Song poets considered ancient and that they wished to promote among fellow literati. In the couplet quoted above, Mei Yaochen declares that even Han Yu's rhymes were ancient, though perhaps he meant the difficult rhyme led to a rough and jumpy poem that gave the flavor of ancient verse. Yet, in other poems, Han Yu consciously uses ancient rhyming words drawn from the *Classic of Poetry*; rhymes already dissonant by the Tang period due to the evolution of Chinese pronunciation, in order to create an archaic and rough effect. Ouyang Xiu praises the untrammeled style of one such poem in his *Remarks on Poetry*:[26]

> When [Han] was given easy rhymes, he would overflow into dissonant rhymes like a mass of waves that cannot be held back, in and out of harmony, impossible to channel into one constant form . . . I once compared him to a skilled carriage driver. When driving along a broad highway, he could let the horses gallop freely where they wanted at top speed; but reaching a winding riverbank or narrow pathway, he could then slow the horses to medium pace without a single stumble. Certainly he was a supreme craftsman in the world!

Clearly, Mid-Northern Song poets felt an affinity to the poets of the Mid-Tang because in their lifestyles and their poetic styles they embody the vitality of the ancients, despite the fact that their poetry was markedly different from truly ancient verse.

There were some exceptions to the Northern Song fixation on poets from the Mid-Tang and afterwards. These were Li Bai (701–762) and certain Wei-Jin period poets, especially Ruan Ji (210–263) and Tao Yuanming (c. 365–427).[27] Li Bai is an obvious choice because of his plain, untrammeled style, frequent use of irregular meters, and constantly stated mission to "revive the ancient" (*fu gu*). As he states in one of his prefaces: "Since the Liang [502–557] and Chen [557–589] periods, the powdery and superficial have reached an extreme. If I do not revive the ancient Way, then who else will care to do so?"[28] And he composed a whole series of poems with the title "Ancient Airs," clearly intended to be Tang dynasty equivalents of the "Airs of the States" from the *Classic of Poetry*.[29]

Ouyang Xiu was particularly fond of Li Bai's poetry. Beside his claim that Li was superior to Du Fu, he composed a poem that directly imitates Li's style, which Ronald Egan has termed "a fantasy on the Tang poet Li Bai . . . filled . . . with allusions to Li Bai's poetry and phrases drawn from it."[30] When particularly satisfied with one of his other poems, Ouyang delightedly declared that he had actually managed to outdo Li.[31] Though he praises Han Yu more frequently than Li Bai, we can see from his poetry that Ouyang generally preferred Li's clarity of diction rather than Han Yu's allusive and difficult obscurity. Ouyang combines this clarity with the wit, humor, ingenuity and strangeness of Mid-Tang poetry to produce his "ancient" Northern Song style.

By contrast, Mei Yaochen's favorite pre-Tang poets were Tao Yuanming, and, to a lesser extent, Ruan Ji. As Chaves demonstrates, Mei especially appreciated what he called the "even and bland" (*pingdan*) tone of these Wei-Jin poets, particularly Tao:[32]

> . . . Poetry is basically stating one's feelings;
> There's no need to shout them out loud!
> When you realize that the poem should be even and bland,
> You'll devote yourself to Yuanming morning and evening.

Chaves also notes that in Northern Song poetics, even and bland was often interchanged with ancient and bland—for instance, Ouyang Xiu used both phrases to characterize the poetry of Mei Yaochen.[33] Hence, Mei's imitation of plain diction, directly expressed emotions, and simple natural descriptions of poets like Tao Yuanming, is his own distinctive attempt to transmit ancient style, a style which he traces back ultimately to the *Classic of Poetry*.[34]

Chaves finds it peculiar that the terms "even and bland" or "ancient and bland" are frequently juxtaposed with phrases like "wild words" or "strange and skilful effects."[35] As a result, he gives an extremely broad definition of "even and bland," which incorporates the unpolished diction and quiet intimate tone of Tao Yuanming and Ruan Ji, and the wild strangeness of Han Yu and Zhang Ji.[36] Rather than attempt to subsume both these distinct styles under the term "even and bland," however, I agree with Ronald Egan that Mid-Northern Song poets considered both the plain "even and bland" style and the strange "untrammeled" style as alternative, but equally effective, ways to emulate the ancients.[37]

It could well be that Mei Yaochen generally preferred to produce "even and bland" poems, whereas Ouyang Xiu preferred writing strange poems replete with hyperbolic diction. But there are plenty of strange and wild compositions in Mei's collection too whereas Ouyang composed countless tranquil and serene poems during his second exile in the 1040s and in his old age. Likewise, in theoretical statements, Mid-Northern Song poets generally avoid reducing ancient style to a single consistent set of characteristics. Instead, they prefer to describe complementary pairs of stylistic features. Ouyang Xiu's *Remarks on Poetry*, for instance, is peppered with praise for both "untrammeled, unrestrained" (*haofang*) poems and "refined, carefully thought out" (*jingsi*) poems.[38] And in his most famous evaluation, Ouyang juxtaposes the work of his two friends, Mei Yaochen and Su Shunqin, claiming their styles are completely different. But he could not decide whose poetry he preferred. Mei, he claims, "concentrates on clarity and concision," and his poetry "resembles a beautiful, elegant lady: / Who, though old, still retains her charm. / His recent poems are especially ancient and tough . . . / Their true flavor only strengthens over time." By contrast, Su Shunqin's poetry is "particularly untrammeled: / Ten thousand caves howling with a single cry! . . . / He is like a thoroughbred racehorse, / Once he starts, he cannot be reined in; / Or like pearls and beads overflowing before one's eyes: / Impossible to follow them all at the same time."[39] Though certainly exaggerated to a comic degree, Ouyang's characterization clearly embraces at least two polarized poetic styles, both of which he considers worthy of comparison with the ancients, yet are seriously under-appreciated by his contemporaries: "Such ancient goods are hard to sell at present," he concludes.[40]

My analysis of Mid-Northern Song references to ancient poetic style demonstrates that, despite their claims to uphold the tradition of the *Classic of Poetry*, in their poetic practice Mid-Northern Song poets normally emulate either the "untrammeled" or "even and bland" styles of more recent writers, especially those of the Mid-Tang. Yet, they also temper Mid-Tang obscurity with the clear diction of Li Bai or the simplicity of Tao Yuanming. They justify their focus on these relatively recent poets by arguing that they had inherited the essential vitality of the ancients—their power, simplicity, strangeness, directness, breadth of interest, and even humor—qualities to which they aspired in their own poetry. They also admired the Mid-Tang poets for developing and sustaining a civilized, urbane group relationship, and for constantly celebrating their friendships in verse. Hence, Mid-Northern Song poets saw no contradiction in claiming that, through imitating these relatively recent poets and establishing a kind of imaginative dialogue with them, they were keeping alive an extended lineage directly linking them to the living vitality of the ancient Confucian poetic tradition and its roots in the *Classic of Poetry*.

CELEBRATING THE ANCIENT THROUGH ARTIFACTS

It is not only through developing stylistic bonds with earlier poets that Mid-Northern Song literati prove their affinity with the ancient sages. Many of them were also avid collectors of ancient objects, ranging from bronze or stone vessels, and antique weapons to paintings, calligraphic scrolls, ancient jades, and excavated household items such as incense burners and screens. Although Tang writers also composed poems about ancient artifacts and collectibles, it was Northern Song poets like Mei Yaochen and Ouyang Xiu who, by the sheer numbers of such works that they produced, transformed the topic into a whole new sub-genre.[41]

It is clear from their poems that Mid-Northern Song literati saw antiques as survivors from heroic, sometimes tragic, ages. Antiques were evocative objects that triggered the kinds of noble, dynamic, and unrestrained moods poets associated with the ancients. Such objects acted on their imaginations in a way similar to the works of past poets and resulted in similar kinds of "ancient" poetic responses. For example, in an early work by Ouyang Xiu on an ancient tile that had been made into an ink-stone, the object triggers an impassioned, lengthy description of the collapse of the Han dynasty and the division of the Empire into separate kingdoms. The main subject of the poem is Cao Cao (155–220), from whose Bronze Sparrow Tower this tile supposedly came. In the notes to my translation, I provide enough background information to make Ouyang's compressed historical allusions comprehensible to modern readers.

Answering Xie Jingshan's Song on the Gift of an Ancient Tile Inkstone [1037][42]

When fire numbered four hundred, the scorching spirit of Han dispersed,[43]
The one who sought to take its place would come from the high roads of Wei.[44]
Extreme treachery and utmost cruelty are not easy to take on,
Only now did [Cao Cao] realize the strong foundation of Wen and Jing.[45]
Just when he brandished a long beak to peck at all under Heaven,
Brave and heroic opponents rose, numerous as spines on a porcupine.
Dong, Lü, Jue and Fan died in quick succession,
Shao, Shu, Quan and Bei engaged in mighty battles.[46]
The weak submitted to defeat, while the strongest emerged victorious,
Countless talented virtuous minions toiled to bring him this reward,
And yet it seemed that, within his grasp, he did not dare to take it,
Instead he allowed those adult locusts to breed their pestilent young.[47]
His son, Pi, right from the start was devoid of all sense of shame,
He dared to claim that like Shun and Yu he received the mandate of Yao.[48]
By his treachery he did receive it, but he lost it just the same way:
Who could have guessed that three horses would eat from his single "trough"?[49]
Cao Cao, in his ascendancy, had struggled with heart and soul,
His curses and shouts were hail and thunder raising a typhoon wind.[50]
When weapons of battle were finally stilled, and countless enemies defeated,
All his trusted ministers were gone, his loyal supporters depleted.[51]
Warriors had offered their toasts of wine, had honored his noble presence,
How lofty he seemed in Bronze Sparrow Tower, soaring giddily on high!
Flowing melodies echoed around, clear wine-goblets circulated,
Wondrous dancers on every side revolved their slender waists.
But one day they looked out and saw only a massive tree guarding his tomb,
How lonely then his tapestries, emptily swinging in the soughing wind.[52]

At that time the bleakness was already deplorable enough,
How much more in later ages do we mourn these former dynasties!
The lofty tower has long since toppled, slowly becoming level ground,
And this tile, as soon as it fell, was buried in choking weeds.
Half obscured beneath patterned moss and sullied by barren earth,
It had to endure the blood of battles, and scorching of rural burning.
But ruined leather and broken nets can still find useful employment,
And someone chiseled and carved [the tile], forming a hollow inkwell.
The powerful strokes of Jingshan's brush are sturdy as a crossbow,
His phrases are lean, their diction hoary: he writes with bold gestures.
But as for me, seizing it by force, how can I use [this precious tile]?
My official papers pile up in mounds, splattered in red and black inks.
Transferred around from north to south, I've never once left it behind,
I wrapped it in several layers of silk, and carefully sealed the package.
There have been times when my inner thoughts were about to fly and scatter,
My moods became completely tangled, hard to separate the strands;
Travelling by boat, I often feared being seized by the Water Deity,
Frequently, in gloomy darkness, I battled through winds and waves;
Stubborn by nature, this object has lasted, bearing an essential strangeness,
I constantly dread its metamorphosis into a spirit or monster!
Back in the capital, wherever I go, I'll hand it around for appreciation,
I love it and wouldn't exchange it even for a jeweled sword of Lu.[53]
The long song that you gave to me is strange yet also powerful,
Though I wish to repay you, I'm ashamed to say I possess no jasper or jade.

Ouyang, inspired by the tile ink-stone, recreates the turbulent years preceding and following the Han collapse: Cao Cao's meteoric rise to power, when the Bronze Sparrow Tower was the scene of elegant parties hosted by beautiful ladies; his failure to unify the Empire; and the subsequent decline of his kingdom of Wei. He concludes the historical summary with a contrast between the glorious days of Cao Cao's prime, and the sad, lonely surroundings of the abandoned Bronze Sparrow Tower after Cao's death, now a monument to the vicissitudes of political struggle (lines 21–26). Finally, in the last eighteen lines, Ouyang returns to the ink-stone itself, which has somehow survived since the days of the Three Kingdoms. He declares that since the ink-stone has come through such a checkered history—(originally part of the Bronze Sparrow Tower roof, then surviving repeated battles over the centuries, sullied and worn down by blood, moss and earth, before being carved out into something useful), it must contain an essential and strange energy. Those who grind their block of ink on this tile will mix some of its mysterious power with that ink and produce writing like his friend Xie's, "sturdy as a crossbow, / . . . phrases lean, . . . diction hoary," full of "bold gestures" (lines 35–36). Though claiming to be devoid of such talent himself, Ouyang still hordes the tile, taking it with him wherever he goes. He knows its vitality and power to survive can protect him against storms and calm his agitated mood—a mood doubtless provoked by his exile at the time of writing (lines 41–45). His only fear is that the tile will transform itself into a spirit and disappear, leaving him bereft of supernatural protection (line 46).

Ouyang's tile ink-stone poem is a representative example of the Mid-Northern Song's untrammeled and unrestrained ancient style, and uses a single object to evoke a massive tableau of violent, larger-than-life imperial history. By contrast, several of Mei Yaochen's poems on ancient artifacts, with their careful observations and minute description, clearly belong at the "even and bland" or "refined thought" edge of the ancient-style spectrum. In some of these poems, Mei focuses exclusively on a precise description of the object in question—for instance in his "Poem on a Crossbow Trigger."[54] However, in most cases, Mei shows just as much interest in the people admiring the object—their conversation, wine drinking, and laughter—as he does in the objects themselves. His purpose is to record such civilized social gatherings of antique collectors in the clearest possible manner, providing documentary evidence of these scholars' affinity with the ancient cultural tradition.

One such poem, whose title immediately supplies the context, is representative of this dual focus on ancient objects and present connoisseurs:

Drinking at Secretary Liu Yuanfu's House with the Scholars Jiang Linji and Chen Heshu, We Viewed a Silver Pheasant, a Peacock, a Tripod with Wild Duck Design and the Seal of Zhou Yafu, an Inlaid Jade Treasure, and a Dragon and Bird Decorated Knife of Helian Bobo [1058][55]

Our host was a scholar at Phoenix Pool,
Two of the guests were from Tianlu Pavilion.[56]
We all congregated at East Terrace to drink,
Our refined discourse was spiced with wit and banter.
In a cage to the south, [our host] kept a silver pheasant,
In a cage to the north, he kept a peacock,
One was plain white, its plumage like rippling water,
One had turquoise feathers, threaded with slender gold.
Loudly we praised a duck-handled tripod,
Far superior to those [fake] dragon-headed spoons;
The jade seal linked it to the Tributary Duke,[57]
We debated whether his style name was Ya or E;
Sword-shaped figures were inlaid on this lucky jade,
Such a precious charm, and crafted with fine distinction;
To conclude the diversions, we examined Helian's knife,
Dragons and magpies were welded onto the scabbard belt.
Whenever he brought out an object to admire,
[Our host] always urged the assembled guests to drink,
He also made three of his cloudy haired [women]
Pass the wine around: so refined and beautiful.
Certainly it would not bring pleasure to the vulgar,
But we attained joy from admiring the ancient . . .[58]

Mei writes only a line or two on each precious object, focusing his attention mainly on the refined behavior of the participants. A particularly interesting feature of this poem is Mei's observation that the antique viewing is really a kind of drinking game—since each new object requires another round of drinks—with beautiful female entertainers passing the wine around. Thus, Mei implies, rather than merely carousing with women and getting drunk in mindless fashion, as the vulgar do, these scholars have added a level of cultivation to their entertainment, raising it from mere sensual pleasure to the status of ancient joy (lines 21–22). As a result, he feels, the occasion deserves recording in verse and preserving for the future.

A similar mix of ancient objects and modern context occurs in another poem by Mei on some scrolls of precious vintage paper from Clear Heart Hall, a gift from Ouyang Xiu.[59] Though the paper is not old in comparison with the ancient objects above, it survived for almost a century in pristine condition through times of political turmoil before the Song. Hence, Mei considered it a valuable antique. In his poem, Mei emphasizes, in comical terms, the difficulties of admiring and preserving ancient objects, and by extension, of adopting a cultured, ancient lifestyle, when one is poor and surrounded by rambunctious children:

Yongshu Sent Me Two Scrolls of Paper from Clear Heart Hall.[60]

Yesterday morning a man arrived; he came from the Eastern Commandery,
I opened the seal on the letter he delivered: two scrolls of ancient paper,
Smooth as ice in spring, and dense textured as a silk cocoon,
Surprised and joyful, I ran my hands over them: my heart began to wander!
Shu notelets are worm-eaten and brittle: they cannot last very long;
Shan paper is thin and unresponsive: really just a pain!
Your letter said you had sent [this gift]; I should treat it like precious treasure:
"Take care not to cut off strips and mindlessly give them away!"
In days when Duke Li of Jiangnan held power over his kingdom,
One hundred cash was not sufficient to buy a single sheet;
Only in Clear Heart Hall could you find an object like this
Spread out for writing on silent desks, without a speck of dust.
But then, when the kingdom was destroyed, was there anything that survived?
In the royal storehouse, empty and bare, only moss and lichen flourished;
All that remained were some library books and this [precious] paper,
They carted it into the capital, without a thought for its worth.
And now, another sixty years have passed since those troubled times:
It lay abandoned within a great hall, stacked and piled in the corner . . .

. . . Now you have passed some sheets to me, I'm embarrassed for two good reasons:
I lack your control of the brush, and I cannot match your brilliance.
Flustered, I gather up [the paper], but I have no trunk or cabinet,
Daily I guard it from my children; I fear they'll rip it to shreds!
Lacking a fine calligraphic hand, I am merely filled with longing:
A lingering sadness, like Zishan's, arises [in my breast].[61]

Mei appreciates the paper especially for its evocative power, its ability to conjure up a world of lost grandeur, and to endure despite the destruction all around it. Yet he also makes sure to portray himself as a bemused and whimsical recipient of this precious gift. Perhaps he hopes to associate himself with the vital power of the paper—one wonders whether the poem itself was written on a sheet of the paper—and in this way both his reputation and poetry might survive into the future. Certainly this theme of literary survival is expressed explicitly in a later poem by Ouyang Xiu on the same topic. If he and his friends copy their poems onto this special paper, he argues, then perhaps their names and achievements will last as long as the paper, protected by its vital strength:[62]

. . . A century of fighting, and shedding of battlefield blood—
A whole kingdom's songs and dances—are now just ruined terraces.
At that time the hundred things were all exquisite and fine,
But most of what survives has been abandoned to rampant weeds.
So where on earth did you manage to obtain paper such as this,
Pure, strong, glossy and smooth: a volume of one hundred leaves?
When work matters and official duties allow us the joy of leisure,
In towers and halls we'll sing and respond, matching each other's heights.
The written word, since ancient times, has always managed to survive,
How do you know that what we produce will not last into the future?

Such poetic records make it clear that Mid-Northern Song poets' fascination with writing about the past and the ancient—whether surviving poetry or excavated objects—is, at least partly, an attempt to leave traces of their vitality for future ages. Ouyang expresses this hope more directly when he thanks his friend Mei

Zhi (995–1059) for carving one of his earlier poems onto stone and setting it up by an ancient pavilion he had renovated:[63]

> . . . You chiseled my heptasyllabic lines on a square slab of stone,
> And in one day, a hundred copies were spread around the capital.
> The ancient people for whom I long all received treatment like this:
> 4 Thus were their inspiring names passed down for hundreds of years!
> After I die, this weighty memorial will record my rise and fall,
> Holding wine cups, people will weep there, mourning the mountains and rivers.
> And though your leaving an appreciation was only an incidental act,
> 8 Future ages will pass it down, and will not let it decay.

POETRY, PROSE, AND POSTERITY

If the main function of compositions about ancient objects is to enable poets to leave traces of themselves for future ages, one would think weighty and formal written genres, such as histories, funeral inscriptions, and government memorials are more likely to survive than lighthearted and informal poems. Certainly the Northern Song witnesses a great flowering of prose writing, especially private historical accounts and classical commentaries, in which most of the well-known poets are enthusiastic participants.[64] Yet, as we saw in our discussion of poems and friendship, poetry held a major advantage over most prose genres in that it was perfectly suited for recording personal feelings, informal relationships, and all manner of unofficial events and activities—the kinds of details histories normally pass over in silence. Ouyang Xiu explains this important function of poetry in a comment on the Tang poet, Wang Jian (c. 767–c. 830):[65]

> The one hundred Palace Lyrics by Wang Jian mostly relate events within the Tang Imperial Palace. All those matters with which the histories, biographies and stories did not deal can usually be found in his poems. An example is: "Within the Palace, for several days there were no shouts or cries, / Then they circulated Prince Teng's butterfly illustrations."[66] Yuan Ying—Prince Teng—was the son of Emperor Gaozu [r. 618–627]. Neither the New nor Old Tang

> Histories described his abilities. Only the "Record of Famous Painters" briefly noted that he was good at painting, and even then did not mention his skill at doing butterflies. And the "Judgments on Painting" merely says: "He was skilled at doing butterflies, as can be seen from [Wang] Jian's poem." . . . All those who excelled at minor arts in Tang times—for instance, "Great Aunt Gongsun dancing with swords"; "Cao Gang playing the *pipa*"; and "Mi Jiarong singing"—are found in the poetic lines of the Tang greats. As a result, they have become famous in later generations.[67]
>
> At that time, there were numerous superior people who hid their virtue, went into reclusion in mountains, forests and rural fields, and were no longer heard about in the world. But [those with] lower skills and peripheral arts found a medium of expression, so [their names] were passed down and never decayed. . . .

With this view of the function of poetry, it is hardly surprising that much of Ouyang Xiu's and Mei Yaochen's poetry—whether on ancient objects and past poets or, for that matter, on current topics—deals with their own everyday concerns, personal tastes, opinions, and social relationships, and includes trivial details more formal genres overlook. They believed poetry concerned itself with these themes in ancient times, and they hoped that by writing such poems, their own words would survive as evidence of their broad humanity and spiritual vitality. In this way, they viewed themselves as part of an orthodox, cultural lineage, inheriting the spirit of the ancients and passing it down to their descendants.

CHAPTER SIX

Poetry as Humanization of Nature

In his seminal study of Song dynasty poetry, Yoshikawa Kojiro gives a rather disappointing evaluation of Song poems on nature:[1]

> Song poetry is deeply interested in human beings, and to that extent its treatment of nature is apathetic and lacking in distinction. In earlier ages there had been poets who had made it their special task to sing of nature, particularly of its more picturesque aspects . . . such as Xie Lingyun [385–433] . . . Wang Wei [701?–761], Meng Haoran [689–740], Wei Yingwu [c. 737–791], and Liu Zongyuan [773–819] . . . But in the Song we no longer find such "landscape poets."

Elsewhere in his study, Yoshikawa praises the merits of Song poetry very highly, comparing Northern Song poets like Su Shi and Ouyang Xiu favorably with some of the greats of the Tang dynasty. He justifies this positive comparison by demonstrating that from the Mid-Northern Song onwards, poets promoted different artistic aims from their Tang predecessors. Their changed social environment and philosophical views led them to produce poetry that was intellectual, discursive, consciously rough in style, inclusive in subject matter, and more optimistic in outlook than most poetry of the Tang.[2] If one adds wit and humor to the equation on the Song side, this characterization retains much validity, especially when limited to the Mid- and Late-Northern Song periods.[3]

However, Yoshikawa drew the line when he came to Song nature poetry. He found himself unable to appreciate the obvious ways in which Song poets humanized the natural world and natural objects. He declared that Song poets' overemphasis on human beings distracted them from the important task of describing the natural world in an unmediated way, and he remained singularly unimpressed by the clever structures and entertaining content of much Song nature poetry.

Against Yoshikawa, one could easily find support for a contrasting view that the "landscape poetry" of Xie Lingyun and Wang Wei is actually more highly stylized and artificial than much Song dynasty nature poetry and reveals obvious human concerns behind its apparently unmediated descriptions of nature.[4] That is beyond the scope of this chapter however. Rather, I will challenge Yoshikawa's negative conclusions by reexamining the functions of Mid-Northern Song poems on natural themes. While poets of this period certainly did humanize the natural world in their poetry, they had perfectly valid aesthetic and social purposes for doing so. Moreover, they produced numerous, vivid descriptions of natural objects and phenomena that poets of earlier ages neglected or treated perfunctorily. In other words, their greater attention to mundane concerns and details of everyday life led them to extend the range and functions of natural topics beyond the stylistic and topical restrictions that bound earlier nature poets.[5]

My argument has two main strands that correspond to the two major ways in which Mid-Northern Song poets treated the natural world. First, I demonstrate that these poets viewed cosmic disorders and aberrations—such as floods, earthquakes, and droughts—as signs that human society was irredeemably corrupt, or that those in charge of government were seriously neglecting their duties. This idea had its roots in ancient Chinese correlational theories systematized by Han dynasty thinkers such as Dong Zhongshu (179–104 BC). Whether or not poets like Ouyang Xiu and Mei Yaochen actually subscribed to these theories, they certainly made effective use of them as poetic devices to release their inner frustrations about the state of contemporary society.

Yet second, Mid-Northern Song poets also celebrated exceptional natural objects—including both unusual creatures or wild plants and processed natural objects such as olives, quality tea, and cultivated flowers. Unlike disorders and aberrations, which were signs of a general human corruption, these exceptional objects stood out against the corruption that surrounded them by their natural purity, vital energy, or transcendent flavor. These qualities reminded the poets of themselves—a group of exceptionally talented and virtuous literati standing out against a corrupt and ignorant society that misunderstood and maligned them. As a result, they composed and exchanged countless poems about such objects in order to revive their spirits and to sustain and celebrate their friendships.

Of course, the distinction between the aberrant and the exceptional is not always clear, and some Northern Song poets displayed a certain ambivalence towards the more unusual objects that they described. We see this most clearly in Ouyang Xiu's poem on pictures of peonies and in Mei Yaochen's playful criticisms of his friends' infatuation with white pets. Still, this occasional ambivalence does not negate the central purpose of Mid-Northern Song nature poetry, which was to allow its writers to release emotional tensions in a socially acceptable way, while simultaneously cementing their human relationships.

The lighthearted mood of many of these nature poems adds further weight to the contention that Mid-Northern Song literati generally saw poetic composition and exchanges as a channel to transform negative emotions and to find consolation from sharing difficult experiences with likeminded friends. Even in the poems of the period on natural disasters, we frequently find caricatures, witty personifications, and ridiculous hyperbole, all of which help to transform what could easily have been tiresome jeremiads into entertaining and incisive works of art. And in poems that they exchanged on exceptional natural objects and creatures, Mid-Northern Song poets incorporated still more humor and clever banter to lighten the tone. To purists, the intrusion of such humanizing features into the natural world may seem awkward and inappropriate. But many readers will find welcome relief in these poems from the earnest sublimity of much earlier Chinese nature verse.

NATURAL ABERRATIONS AND HUMAN CORRUPTION

Since the former Han dynasty, possibly earlier, a systematic if arbitrary scheme of correlations between natural phenomena and human behavior strongly influenced Chinese philosophy and government.[6] Court astrologers studied the skies for evidence of unusual heavenly conjunctions that would presage momentous political upheavals. Government officials engaged in elaborate ceremonies in an attempt to keep the dynasty in harmony with the cosmos and ward off natural disasters. These ceremonies occurred frequently during the Northern Song, as attested by several poems and official writings in the collections of Ouyang Xiu and Mei Yaochen recording prayers for rain, for an end to floods, for favorable winds and the like.[7]

At the same time, both Ouyang and Mei often expressed the view that such ceremonies would have little effect without strenuous effort by government officials to introduce more rational policies to cope with inevitable natural disasters. Ouyang Xiu, for instance, wrote a prose piece in 1040 entitled "The Origins of Abuses," in which he argues that all natural phenomena are cyclical, including floods, earthquakes, and droughts, and even though the timing of these cycles is irregular, disasters would certainly strike in the future. Therefore, instead of waiting for the next flood or drought before taking desperate and inadequate relief measures, the government should store surplus food and supplies whenever there was a good harvest. If Imperial stores could be built up enough over three good years to last the country for one bad year, when disaster did strike, the government would not have to rely so much on prayers to Heaven.[8]

Despite this skepticism towards the more arbitrary aspects of correlation theory, Ouyang Xiu and Mei Yaochen did not hesitate to make use of natural-human correlations as a poetic device. Some of their early works even seemed to accept the idea that the Song emperors—as intermediaries between Heaven, Earth, and human beings—could wield their superhuman virtue to overcome natural disasters. For example, in his impressive and lengthy composition "At Gong County, Watching the Yellow River for the First Time" (completed in 1033), Ouyang recorded a terrible recent flood caused by the Yellow River suddenly changing its course. He vividly personified the River as a God that angrily attacked the common people:[9]

> . . . Just last year, the River turned wild, shocking the people of Hua,
> Soaking and spilling, spreading asunder, its angry flood couldn't be tamed.[10]
> The people of Hua fled in haste, like startled hornets swarming,

4 Seeing them scatter, the River God laughed at the entertaining game!
Seething and gnashing, its fierce mouth gaped open wider than a gate,
Every day it chomped on timber, devouring millions of bundles . . .

Ouyang describes the River's power for another twenty lines, then concludes with a highly flattering portrait of the Song Emperor Renzong (r. 1023–1063), demonstrating his concern for the people by admonishing the River God. The God is suitably chastened, and immediately returns to its correct channel:[11]

. . . In the Bright Palace, the Son of Heaven, sagelike and divine,
Saddened by the River's inhumaneness, sighed and cried "Alas!"
The River God was stubborn by nature, not readily taking commands,
4 But shaken by the ruler's supreme sincerity, it was stunned into awestruck submission:
Channeling the current, it retreated in shock back to its former course,
Shutting its mouth, it no longer dared harass the local officials.
Respecting the boundaries, keeping its course, it descended directly East,
8 Without spilling out of its ordained channel even as much as an inch!
Since that time, the yearly stars have completed a full revolution,
The farmers' cattle feed on straw in abundance; the region produces a surfeit.
The people of Hua live by the River, drinking from the River's flow,
12 They plough by the banks of the River, and irrigate the River's dykes.
I rejoice that the River is transformed from a dangerous threat to a blessing,
Oh, how marvelous the Bright Palace and the Sagely Son of Heaven!

Though certainly written in a caricatured style, this poem clearly subscribes to the idea that Heaven (or Nature) will listen to the sincere requests of the virtuous Emperor—the "Son of Heaven"—to spare his people. At the same time, one wonders whether Ouyang sincerely believed that a simple cry of "Alas," even from the Emperor's lips, could really have returned the Yellow River back to its original course.

A similarly rosy picture of the Emperor's beneficent power and the correlation between human virtue and natural harmony appear in a later poem by Ouyang, dated 1041, celebrating a successful imperial petition to Heaven for a snowfall. Heavy snow was beneficial because it moistened the soil, allowing seeds to germinate, and it also froze the larvae of pests like locusts and malarial flies, preventing them from multiplying and causing diseases and famine later in the year. Near the start of the poem, Ouyang offers the following paean to the Emperor's virtue:[12]

> . . . How divine, His Majesty! Supreme in benevolence and sageliness!
> With deep concern he faithfully prays, radiating utmost sincerity.
> His sage-like person shares a common substance with the Heavens,
> 4 Before he even utters his request, the Heavens already hear him.
> Suddenly pooling their frigid severity, the Watery Ministers return,
> As New Year turns, the withered plants freeze into clear and icy purity.
> The cold wind gathers reinforcements, then charges, gusting and blowing,
> 8 Hailstones accelerate onto dry tiles, a downpour that will not cease . . .

Despite praising the Emperor in this fulsome fashion, elsewhere in the poem Ouyang makes it very clear that the root cause of the unseasonal warmth still had to be addressed. He declares that only major reforms to Song military policies—such as removing "treacherous generals"—and a concerted effort to stamp out the invading Xixia in the West would permanently free ordinary Chinese people from the burden of supporting the war effort. This, in turn, should lessen Heaven's displeasure and put an end to such inauspicious and abnormal climatic phenomena:[13]

> *Yin* and *yang* are out of joint, disrupting the Five Phases,
> In mid-winter mountain valleys grow warm and their ice melts away.[14]
> When *yang* energy disperses above the surface of the ground,

4 How will the ten thousand plants send up their shoots from beneath the earth?
Supreme *yin* ought to be deployed now, but finds itself under-employed:
Isn't this because our treacherous generals have escaped execution and demeaned the Imperial law!
This caused a pestilent wind to arise and sneak through every chink and crack,
8 Silently striking exhausted commoners with deadly contagious diseases . . .
. . . for now our host and the nation may forget their worries and agitation,[15]
But ought we simply to rejoice that we'll receive a bumper harvest?
We still should remember the cold armor penetrating into the bones
12 Of over a hundred thousand soldiers camped beyond the border regions!

Few Mid-Northern Song poems on natural objects and phenomena are as overtly political as these. Because writing poetry was often a means for Song scholar officials to indulge in imaginative escape from the burdens of their offices, one commonly finds them using correlational ideas in support of their fantasies of retiring and living in reclusion. The general assumption behind such poems is that when natural aberrations occurr frequently, it is a sign that the times are utterly corrupt. Hence serving in the government could be both dangerous and futile. Far better to simply retreat into private self-cultivation and await a more auspicious era.

Mei Yaochen gave a subtle and gently humorous example of this point of view in his poem "Floods on the Thirteenth of the Fifth Month":[16]

Who could have known that the mountain waters
Would suddenly come flowing outside my house?
And who could have known that the road before my gate
4 Would allow ready access to boats from the creek?
Desperate snakes climb up bamboo stems,
Crowds of worms wriggle to the edge of my terrace,
Though my home is built on higher ground,
8 It's surrounded by a sea of flowing waters.
Floating duckweed comes through holes in the fence,

Severed roots glide past the roofs of houses,
The local officials try to save the city bridge,
12 And halt their carriages before the city hall,
They should show concern for us living out here,
But the waters are so wide, they can't even see us.[17]
A dangerous current overflows the main river,
16 Spreading endlessly, it leaves no dry land,
The masses of frogs are truly in their element,
All night and day they croak on without end.
Shoals of fish escape our pond at the back
20 Following the waves away: no-one can block them,
Although they flap their tails, pleased at their freedom,
Down by the river plenty of nets and hooks await them!
The local urchins roam about in their packs,
24 Leaping and splashing: all learning how to swim,
But I only envy Master Kong Xuanfu,
Who had the sense to board his raft and simply float away.[18]

Faced with such serious floods, a clear Heavenly warning that the Way is not being followed, Mei feels it would be sensible to follow the example of Confucius, and just float away into retirement. Ouyang Xiu expresses similar sentiments at the conclusion of one of his poems on floods, entitled: "Heavy Rain, Sent to Mei Shengyu", dated 1057: "My official duties are few, and my abilities are meager, / I'm ashamed I've done little to pay back the State. / My life will soon reach its final conclusion, / So why do I not retire to rivers and lakes?"[19]

In some poems from the 1040s and early 1050s, Ouyang Xiu even floated the idea that nature, or Heaven, was itself corrupt and cunning, aiming to destroy human beings while protecting and nourishing other creatures and plants. Observe, for example, the complaints of Ouyang's cantankerous narrator in his "Moved by the Spring: An Irregular Meter Verse," from 1050.[20]

The turtledove calls—on the rooftop,
The sparrows twitter noisily—in among the eaves.
A hundred birds are moved by the warmth of Spring,
4 As if something stirs in their internal mechanism.
Males and females echo in harmony,
All day their cacophony keeps me from my rest!
As for the two trees beneath my terrace,
8 Who would pluck anything from their withered branches?
But the Spring breeze arrives in the course of one night,

And their blossoms and leaves become oh so dappled.
Thus do I know that Heaven's cunning steals our human strength,
12 Steals it to help withered trees grow young rosy faces!
Why is it that human beings, the most vital of ten thousand creatures,
Cannot compare with plants and trees, or birds that soar on the wing?
Ever since Spring came upon us, what thoughts have crossed my mind?
16 Only surprise that, sleeping late, I'm unaware of the dazzling sun rising high over Southern Mountains,
And meeting the hundred flowers as I walk, my eyes feel no attraction! . . .

Such sentiments were doubtless provoked by Ouyang's continuing exile in the provinces even after five long years away from the central government. He released his resentment by lashing out at the natural order itself, which seemed so oblivious to his emotional turmoil.

However, it was more common for Ouyang and his contemporaries to declare that the greed and vulgarity of human beings somehow caused disorder and instability in the natural world, and this is reflected both in natural disasters and in the abnormally rapid mutation of individual species. Ouyang's poem "Drawings of Luoyang Peonies," dated to 1042, makes this argument very clearly through another grumpy narrator:[21]

The soil and terrain of Luoyang are perfectly suited for flowers,
And everywhere its peonies are considered especially rare.
As for the several dozen kinds I once noted down,
4 It is ten years since then, and they are dim memories now.[22]
Opening the drawings is just like seeing familiar faces of friends,
And among them are several kinds that I have never encountered before.
My guest tells me in recent years the blossoms are really exceptional:
8 And frequently they are intermixed to produce novel strains.
People of Luoyang boast in amazement, trying to think up new names,
Buying the seeds, they take no heed of their family's resources.
Weighing and comparing new with old, it's hard to give them ranks,
12 Each has its moment coming to the fore and selling for the highest price.
At that time, among the strains of most outstanding quality,

Were the charm of Wei's Red, and the beauty of Yao's Yellow.
The slender petals of Peace and Longevity rarely bloomed back then,
And Crimson Dots or Jade Banners: well nobody knew about them!
But it's said that even the Thousand Petals once did not exist,
Only when Zuo created his Violet, its fame first spread abroad.
In forty years, these flowers underwent a hundred transformations,
The latest and the finest was the Qianxi [Temple] Crimson.[23]
Though today's blooms are certainly novel, I don't recognize them at all,
I can't believe anyone compares their beauty with the old.
In those days, the flowers that I saw were said to be unparalleled,
Can there be even better ones now? That is surely debatable.
The ancients claimed that nowhere was there any perfect form,[24]
But my fear is that society's tastes are changing faster than the seasons.
The Red Girdle and Crane's Feathers: are they not pretty enough?
But their smiles fade as they're cut dead by the late-arriving beauties!
It's worse for the blooms of Su and He, recorded in the distant past:
They are left behind in an archaic world that admired Ladies Qiang and Shi.[25]
"Creative Transformation is ruthless": that about sums it up,
Or else it is blatantly biased, working so hard in this one place.[26]
I suspect that peoples' hearts have also grown more cunning and false,
And Nature wished to combat their guile with endlessly varying subtlety,
Otherwise why would primal transformations, dispersing over the ages,
Suddenly concentrate all their powers in the space of a few short years?
Struggling for freshness, fighting for beauty: if it isn't brought to a halt,
A hundred years from now, I wonder, how is it all going to end?
No doubt only fresh new flowers will grow finer every day,
But old fogies like us will become more decrepit in every way!

The poem begins in a lighthearted vein as Ouyang, a well known peony connoisseur, looks at the pictures of his favorite flowers, "like seeing familiar faces of friends" (line 5), but his mood soon deteriorates when he comes across several varieties he has never previously encountered (line 6). His guest explains that these are "novel strains" produced in the last few years, which are now extremely popular among the people of Luoyang (lines 7–10). At first, Ouyang admits the various blooms he catalogued back in the 1030s, in his "Record of Luoyang Peonies," were also the result of interbreeding, culminating in the strain he most admires, the Qianxi Temple Crimson (lines 19–20). Yet, he is certainly disgruntled that, having taken such pains to list and describe over twenty of the best peonies, now, only eight years later, his account is obsolete. He vents his frustration in lines 21–22: "Though today's blooms are certainly novel, I don't recognize them at all, / I can't believe anyone compares their beauty with the old!"

Ouyang's mood of skeptical grumpiness remains for the rest of the poem. In lines 27–28, he gives a sardonic illustration of the rapidity with which peoples' tastes change by personifying two older, though still beautiful, varieties, now ashamed to show their faces. Next, he begins to suspect that only an aberration in the natural rhythms of creation would concentrate such extreme beauty in one place. Either "Creative Transformation is ruthless" (line 31), randomly displaying partiality towards certain regions, or, perhaps more convincing in Ouyang's present mood, peoples' hearts have become more "cunning and false" (line 33). As a result, they have attempted to improve upon nature and Heaven has counter-attacked with still more exquisite peonies, forcing people to recognize their limitations (line 34). Unfortunately, the battle is not easily won, and Ouyang predicts disastrous consequences for the future (lines 37–38).

In one sense, this poem reflects the correlational idea that imbalances and extremes of any kind—including extreme beauty—are a sign of cosmic irregularity. Ouyang has already made this point, as early as 1034, in his "Catalogue of Luoyang Peonies," where he argues that extreme beauty, as much as extreme ugliness, is a kind of monstrosity.[27] This cosmic irregularity is in turn the result of human cunning and deceit, and of peoples' insatiable desire to be superior to their fellow human beings, which leads them to manipulate natural processes in order to produce more and more beautiful objects. Ouyang wonders why people of today cannot simply enjoy what they already have, instead of constantly striving for the newest and latest thing. He is also resigned to the fact that the general human tendency towards greed and corruption, and its degenerative effect on natural cycles, cannot be overcome by the virtue of a few good people, especially old fogies like himself.

In their poems of the late 1040s and 1050s, Ouyang Xiu and Mei Yaochen increasingly adopt this negative view of the connection between the natural world and human morality. The underlying assumption is that the present age is seriously imperfect and corrupt—unlike the golden age of the Ancients—and this corruption has infected both human society and the natural world. Yet, rather than causing them to despair, this pessimistic view motivated these poets to search for exceptions to the rule, both in nature, with objects that remained pure and vital in the face of nature's destructive forces, and in society, with outstanding people who resist the corrupt and blindly self-seeking forces that drive the mass of humanity. Not surprisingly, they viewed themselves and their friends as prime examples of such outstanding human beings. Clearly, in seeking out and celebrating a variety of unusual and exceptional natural objects in their poetry, they also celebrate, or at least console, themselves.

POEMS ON EXCEPTIONAL NATURAL OBJECTS AND PEOPLE

A fine example of this search for the exceptional is the following poem by Ouyang Xiu. The old narrator seems to be in a better mood than the characters who narrated the preceding two poems, doubtless because he has found a natural object that can act as a foil for himself:

The Chrysanthemums East of Aspiring for Truth Hall, Planted With My Own Hands, Have Just Started to Bloom in the Tenth Month [1047][28]

Planting flowers for springtime, I always feared being late,
Now that I only plant chrysanthemums, please do not call me foolish:
Spring branches fill the gardens with gorgeous spreads of brocade,
4 But wind and rain in no time will cause them to tumble and fall;
Seeing so many, I soon grow tired, unable to focus my feelings:
Those struggling violets and boasting reds delight only vulgar tastes.
How clear is the high autumn season, when Heaven and Earth grow stern!

8 Hundreds of plants decay and fall; who has time to mourn them all?
Yet look at these golden sepals, just opening out so fragrantly,
In morning sunlight they float over frost, dazzled by their own reflections.
Shining, shining, their clear color, so exquisite you could eat them!
12 Dense, dense, their pure scent, lingering longer in the cold:
Like high-minded men avoiding the clamor, living in secluded solitude,
Or noble ladies, serene in appearance, cultivating elegant refinement.
When they're about to sway and fall, they appear still more exquisite,
16 In return for consoling my loneliness, what reward can I offer them?
I'll bring my wine-cup every day, and come to drink by their side,
Just like finding a friend in need and discussing our plans to retire.
In recent years I've faced many troubles; my strong mind is in decline,
20 My habits differ from people of the world as stillness differs from noise,
So, planting flowers, I do not plant the blossoms of young boys and girls:
Now that I'm old, why should I still run after the youths in their prime?

Blooming in the fall, when most other plants wither, the chrysanthemum is a friend in need, consoling Ouyang's loneliness and inspiring him to poetic creativity despite his troubles and old age. He implies that exceptional objects, and by extension, exceptional people like himself, may survive and even flourish in hard times as compared to the mass of ordinary objects in the world.

This identification with exceptional or neglected objects is a constantly recurring theme in northern Song poetry of the 1050s. It continued even after Ouyang, Mei, and most of their friends returned from exile or provincial postings to serve in the central government during the mid-1050s. In fact, they extended their range of subjects to include not just natural objects like plants and animals, but man-made objects—writing tools, ornaments, domestic utensils, and antiques—along with various kinds of foods and drinks. Unlike some of their earlier works, such as Ouyang's peony poem, there is rarely a hint that any of these exotic or unusual objects are inauspicious symbols of a degenerate world. This is because the whole aim of these poets was now to express their own sense of being different from the common run of corrupt and greedy people. By loudly appreciating unusual objects, they were actually trying to prove their own uniqueness and outstanding talent. They even created eccentric personae—caricatures of themselves—to people their poetry. Ouyang became the Drunken Old Man from 1045, and Mei turned into the Poet Elder (*shi lao*) around the same time. In other words, they portrayed themselves as strange, exceptional objects too: fitting companions for the unusual plants, animals, and artifacts in their poems.

The entertaining conjunction of exceptional natural objects and their eccentric owners appears in numerous poems by Mei, Ouyang, and their literati friends during the 1050s. The most interesting examples come in a series of poetic exchanges celebrating white pets. The series began in 1055, with several descriptions of Ouyang's first pet, a white rabbit, and culminated four years later with a number of lengthy caricatured eulogies to a pair of white cranes and a pair of silver pheasants belonging to a friend, Mei Zhi (995–1059). In most of the extant poems, which take the form of mock debates, Ouyang and Mei Zhi play the role of devoted, if slightly addled, animal and bird fanciers, completely uninterested in the striving ambitions of young people of today. Mei Yaochen, by contrast, pretends to be a decrepit old playboy, arguing against the toil and responsibility of keeping such exotic creatures alive and instead preferring to head into town to watch dancing girls.

Despite their differing personae, all these poets claim to be equally unconcerned with politics and worldly cares. Yet, since they were by this stage all holding central government posts, their unworldly pose was more likely a temporary escapist fantasy than a sincere description of their everyday lives. Writing such poems allowed them to create and share an ideal imaginative world of freedom from strictures, refined pursuit of cultural pleasures, and eccentricity. In this way, they could release some of the inevitable tensions of their political careers without actually having to take leave of mundane human society and become recluses.

To give one example of these mock debates, Mei Yaochen responds to Ouyang and Mei Zhi's pet eulogies by ridiculing their attachment to creatures that would only escape (given half a chance), and cause them sorrow. At the same time, Mei pretends not to notice his own attachment to equally unattainable pleasures—for a wobbly old man like himself—such as carousing with dancing girls. He concludes one poem with the following blunt declaration:[29]

I've heard that these two Masters have quite different inclinations:
One raises a creature of the Moon,
The other raises fledglings of Huating.[30]
4 One fears [his rabbit] will flee to an ocean cave,
The other fears [his crane] will nest on pine boughs.[31]
Though I may be getting old, I have no creatures to burden me,
So I plan to visit the Eastern Quarter and watch the dancing entertainers!

Ouyang counters this challenge by doubting whether Mei, the "Poet Elder," still has enough vigor to consort with dancing girls:[32]

The Drunken Old Man tells the Poet Elder:
"Do not censure us for our stupidity.
Growing old we play with bunnies and care for crane fledglings,
4 But surely you are just as old and decrepit as ourselves!
So why then do you cast us aside,
And head for the Eastern Quarter to watch the dancing girls?
Better watch that the dancing girls don't burst out laughing when they see you:
8 Just take a look at your white-haired, sallow-faced reflection in the mirror!"

Not willing to concede defeat, Mei justifies his weakness for young female entertainers with yet another poetic response, which Ouyang is doubtless too exhausted or overcome by laughter to answer:

Matching Hanlin Scholar Ouyang's Poem 'Answering in Jest' [1057][33]

I don't care if those dancing girls laugh at me for being old:
At least laughter is a sign of pleasure—much better than disgust!
It certainly makes more sense than [keeping] rabbits and [raising] cranes
4 With their feet pounding and scratching, and their beaks constantly pecking,

I doubt they'll allow you to admire their sheen, as "moist as limpid moonlight":
All they desire is to run and fly away; their feelings are so superficial.
That's why you have to close one in a cage and tie the other with a rope:
They simply cannot compare with the slender waist of a beautiful girl!
Now since, my host, I know that you're a generous and worthy fellow,
You're well aware that your first duty is making your visitors happy,
I'm going home to powder my face and dye my whiskers black,[34]
I want you to organize many more banquets and keep on inviting me back!

Part of the humor of these poems lies in the fact that Mei was considerably older than Ouyang, yet he was the one adopting the role of an unreformed playboy and urging Ouyang not to lose his youthful vitality. At the same time, he must have realized that dancing girls were as likely to run from a decrepit old fellow like himself as cranes and rabbits would flee from Ouyang and Mei Zhi, and dyeing his whiskers black would merely make him look ridiculous. Clearly these poets were using poetic exchanges on natural objects to laugh at their own aging and to demonstrate that their sense of humor and inner vitality was intact despite the destructive forces working on their bodies and the corruption of human society disturbing their minds.

EXCEPTIONAL VERBAL FORMS: EMBODYING NATURAL OBJECTS

Not satisfied with simply describing natural objects in verse, Ouyang and Mei also frequently tailored the form and style of their poems to fit the unique features of the objects that they portrayed. See, for instance, the vivid way in which Ouyang uses an irregular meter to give a lopsided impression when comparing his odd-looking, squat rabbit with Mei Zhi's gangly cranes:[35]

The cranes strut and peck,
With green jade beaks and withered pine legs.

The rabbit crouches and hunches up,
With two pointed ears and paws drawn together.

Likewise, the extended line lengths at the close of another poem on the same topic evoke the distance these creatures would travel if they managed to escape from their owners; especially the cranes: "The rabbit will flee to the wide ocean and hide in the bright moon's grotto; The crane will fly to the jade mountains that rise up sheer for three thousand feet and will nest in the green pines."[36]

Indeed, one could argue that these Mid-Northern Song poets were consciously aiming to make their poems as exceptional and unique in style as the natural objects and creatures they chose to describe. Their purpose was to ensure that when their pets escaped or died, or when their favored plants finally faded, they would still possess evocative embodiments of those objects in the form of poems. Their poetry could revive the pleasure of sharing these objects with their friends—even when the object or the friends were present no longer.

This use of unusual poetic style to embody exceptional natural objects is particularly noticeable where the object in question is ugly or unappealing on the surface, yet has certain admirable inner qualities. The ugliness of poems by Ouyang and Mei on such topics is striking. For example, in his poem entitled "Olives," Ouyang begins by giving a theoretical explanation for the strange flavor of these plain-looking fruits: a mixture of sourness and bitterness that finally resolves into a satisfying aftertaste. He then spends the rest of the poem introducing several other common life situations where initial distaste is followed by unexpected benefits. He underscores his point by choosing particularly unpoetic rhyme words, including several exclamations, which readers of the time would certainly have found jarring. The ugliness of the rhymes perfectly accords with the sour / bitter content of the poem, and the reader is left chuckling at Ouyang's ingenuity in producing his own "literary olive." To give some idea of the effect of the rhymes, I have used an equally ugly English rhyme for as much of my translation as I could:

Olives [1050][37]

Five elements correlate with the seasons and directions,
And fire predominates towards the South.
Its scorching heat touches wood's vitality,

And olive groves receive its concentrated stuff.[38]
The sour and the bitter do not readily mix,
But after inner conflict they harmonize well enough.
The frosted olives enter the Capital region,
Coming thousands of miles over river waves rough.
With luck they'll be chosen for a gentleman's banquet,
Placed with the assembled fruits, carefully lined up;
In the Capital region, the fruits are so refined,
Like rounded pearls and shining white jades;
What a shame that this slight and ugly olive,
Having come so far, is dismissed with a "huff"![39]
True, syrup is sweet for boys and girls,
But the aftertaste it leaves: well that's really rough!
Good medicine may be more bitter on the tongue,
Yet it definitely soothes a serious cough,
And likewise, though everyone detests sincere advice,
If it wards off disaster, it's helpful enough.
Since Poetry Collectors no longer do their rounds,
My verse complete, I'll recite it off the cuff!

A younger Ouyang Xiu might have sided with the suspicious diners, who took one look at the unprepossessing olives and dismissed them, preferring to eat sweeter and better-looking fruits. But by this stage of his career Ouyang, exiled to the Southern provinces and himself a Southerner born and bred, identifies strongly with such displaced outsiders. He concludes the poem not by declaring olives to be inauspicious objects revealing the corruption of society, but by trying to persuade his audience to eat them, to realize that what initially seems bitter, sour, and strange, can in time prove itself to be even tastier than what is sweet. The poem is not merely a quirky invitation to try some olives. Obviously, it has an allegorical function as well. The most obvious interpretation is a political one: Ouyang wishes to be recalled from his southern exile to the capital (like the olive), where he can advise the Emperor (the gentleman) on how best to run the government. This reading fits with the compressed allusions to *Han Feizi* in lines seventeen and nineteen which, fully stated, read: "Sincere advice goes against one's ears, but the enlightened ruler, hearing it, knows that it can be used to extend his achievements . . . Good medicine is bitter in the mouth, but the wise person can be persuaded to drink it, knowing that once ingested, it will bring an end to his illness."[40] The reference to "Poetry Collectors" in line twenty-one underscores the political overtones of the poem: just as officials collected ancient folksongs reflecting the needs and desires of the common people and communicated them to rulers of the past, Ouyang wishes his words to reach the ears of the Emperor.[41]

On the other hand, the style of the poem and Ouyang's comments about olives in other contexts suggest a broader, more nuanced interpretation. In an earlier poem, Ouyang famously compared reading Mei Yaochen's poetry with eating olives: "His recent poems are especially ancient and tough, / I chew but they're extremely hard to swallow, / At first it's like when I'm eating olives: / Their true flavor only strengthens over time."[42] As I suggested above, it seems that Ouyang has created his own literary olive here. Though the "olive-poem," with its rough rhymes, seems ugly and strange when compared with the conventional beauty and sweet diction of earlier Song poetry (the other fruits), it actually contains important insights into society and human happiness. Rather than leaving an unpleasant emotional aftertaste—as the sad and empty verbiage of much earlier poetry does—Ouyang's poetry is like good medicine, bitter at first, but effective at curing emotional malaises within individuals and fostering social harmony through its pungent wit.

POETRY PRESERVING OBJECTS, MOMENTS, PEOPLE

Unlike Ouyang Xiu, who ultimately reached the top of the official hierarchy after returning from his second exile, Mei Yaochen spent his whole career in relatively low-ranking official positions. We do not see such an obvious turning point in the subject matter and mood of his poetry during the 1040s, since right from his youth he was able to identify with neglected outsiders and exceptional objects. Indeed, according to Ouyang's several descriptions of Mei, he was something of an archetypal outsider, like buried jade treasure, whom the shallow people of today's world generally fail to notice, but whom later generations will rediscover and properly value.[43]

At the same time, Mei was less effusive than Ouyang Xiu about the consoling powers of the exotic and unusual objects he encountered. Though he composed poems on a huge variety of such objects—even more than Ouyang Xiu—he tended to describe them in a relatively unemotional way. Instead, his main focus and interest is the human context in which the objects were displayed, exchanged, or admired. His poetry provides a humorous and revealing portrait of the humanity, and occasionally the ridiculous weaknesses, of himself and his friends, showing how dependent they were upon their favorite possessions, yet, at the same time celebrating the moments they spent sharing natural and cultural pleasures.

This is not to say Mei was less concerned than Ouyang about the problem of survival. It was simply that he saw a greater need to preserve in his poetry the humanity that gave life and meaning to these exceptional objects. Indeed, he saw poetry as the most exceptional and valuable object because it gave permanence to fragile things, short-lived social occasions, and the people with whom he shared them. Ouyang Xiu would doubtless have agreed that preserving a record of his friendships was more important than celebrating his favorite plant or pet, and he creates some memorable poetic portraits of his friends. But often he was carried away by his enthusiasm for the latest exceptional thing—a translucent stone or a silver plumed pheasant—and Mei had to act as the voice of reason, reminding him that no objects should come in the way of human relationships, and preserving those relationships in verse.

To demonstrate this subtle contrast between Ouyang's and Mei's attitudes towards objects in their poetry, we conclude by comparing their reactions to an exceptionally refined tea—a processed natural object—that Cai Xiang, then Governor of Jian'an, had sent to Ouyang. Both Ouyang and Mei wrote pairs of long poems on tasting this tea, and all four of their works share the same rhyme words. Despite the identical rhymes, however, they still managed to engage in a convincing, if caffeine-fuelled, mock debate over the merits and drawbacks of tea drinking.

In his first poem, Ouyang focuses on the uniqueness and spiritual power of the tea, noting that it came from the earliest crop of young tender tealeaves plucked on distant mountainsides and rushed to the capital. Therefore, only the most refined people could appreciate its true quality and its proper method of preparation; and only exceptional people like Mei Yaochen and himself were worthy enough to drink it:[44]

Ten thousand trees are cold and dull, unable to rouse from sleep,
The tea bush is the only one that has already sent out shoots,
Thus do I know it is an object of supreme spiritual power,
4 Truly fitting that it alone should receive the full bounty of
Heaven and Earth!

. . . Its fresh fragrance and tender hue seem to be newly created,
I cannot believe it has come so far, from the distant borders of the Empire.
. . . It's always been true that pure objects require sincere appreciation,
8 And when I share it with the Poet Elder we endlessly sigh and exclaim.
Contrast the others who soon go off in search of wine to gulp down:
That's like performing the Elegant Odes, but ending with a shrill "Yeehaa!"

Once again, we see Ouyang's preoccupation and identification with an exceptional object from far away, and his exaggeration of both the unique spiritual qualities of the tea and of the refinement of his friend Mei Yaochen, the only person qualified to share his own appreciation for such a pure object.

Mei's answering poem, by contrast, though still politely enthusiastic about the tea, shows less concern with praising the uniqueness or spiritual qualities of the object. Instead he focuses on describing the tea-party that Ouyang organized, taking care to record the event for posterity and to link this exceptional group of literati with refined tea masters of past ages such as Lu Yu (733–c. 804):

Matching the Rhymes of Yongshu's Irregular Metre Poem on Tasting New Tea [1058][45]

Ever since Lu Yu was born into the world of mortal men,
Mortals have learned from his instruction the method for brewing spring tea,[46]
In those days, the plucking of [tealeaves] was still not especially widespread,
4 But some refined ascetics would burn bamboo and boil spring water, promoting [the drink] to the world,
Entering the mountains at dewdrop time, they plucked the tender shoots,
They showed no fear of tigers and snakes that lurked beneath the bushes.
. . . Master Ouyang, Hanlin scholar, displays the same discriminating taste,
He identifies all the grades of tea without a single mistake,
One sunny day, he opened his terrace and ground some leaves to snowy powder,[47]

The assembled guests enjoyed them together: we all praised the outstanding taste.
The Governor of Jian'an enclosed the leaves along with his [latest] letter,
He wrapped and sealed them in green paper, and sent them from the distant coast,
. . . White tealeaves and violet porcelain complemented one another,
To find pure water, we did not have to search for the Magic Toad [Spring].[48]
In a stone jar we heated the liquid, and beat it with a silver whisk,
Fine grains spread over the surface; everyone watched in amazement.
My poet's stomach had long been starved; now nothing could oppose its force:
One sip [of tea] entered my belly and the echoes resounded: "Eeewah!"

In his final couplet, Mei claims this tea and its accompanying refined tea party inspired him to produce a spontaneous poem. At the same time, he hints his poem is actually not very different from the chemical reaction of an empty stomach rumbling when confronted with a potent brew of tea leaves. He also gives a much clearer description than Ouyang of the whole group of friends enjoying the tea together, implying that the social gathering is at least as important as the tea itself for inspiring poetry.

The contrast between the two poets' reactions comes out even more clearly in their second pair of matching compositions. Ouyang, the enthusiast, has by this stage drunk far too much of the tea, and discovered that its effects on his body and mind are much less benign and spiritual than he had anticipated. He and his less abstemious guests find themselves constantly running to relieve themselves and with their caffeine-stoked minds racing, they compose strange, shocking poems that leave their servants laughing behind their backs and send Ouyang's children into fits of terrified wailing:[49]

. . . I boiled it myself and repeatedly poured: I just couldn't get enough,
As I said to myself, "Such joy is truly beyond all bounds!"
No-one mentioned that drinking too long would make my hands tremble,

4 Already I feel sick with hunger; my eyes are starting to blur.
My guests suffer "water problems" and weary of lifting their bowls,
Our mouths become no different from the mouth of the moon-eating toad![50]
My servants and maids watch from the side, puzzled yet also amused,
8 This hobby is strange and eccentric; it's really something to moan about.
And hearing our poem exchanges, so strange as to be quite shocking,
All my children add to the din with their wailing: "Wah, wah, wah!"

Having built up this object into something transcendent and exquisitely refined, Ouyang is now forced to admit that it is more likely to bring him crashing down into the real world of digestive problems and trembling hands than help him transcend his mortal frame. Still, he is at least willing to recognize his error and set the record straight in his poetry.

Mei Yaochen, already a little skeptical of Ouyang's previous claims about the tea, declares in his second poem that he can happily live without the feeling of transcendence that drinking tea provides, especially if it has such unbecoming side effects. Why not simply stick to the familiar relaxing effects of wine, he asks? More so, because this particular brand of tea is so rare and expensive that becoming addicted to it would cause him financial ruin. Rather than sending him such exotic presents, Mei tells Ouyang, he should simply allow him to visit more often as, he implies, friendship is far more valuable than any material object:[51]

Yesterday [Ouyang] gave me some [tea] that he had freshly ground into powder,
He wrapped it in leaves of cattail, and tied them with hempen string;
I could only sip a small amount since it brought a chill to my belly,
4 I managed to avoid becoming so "tipsy" that my hat went all askew:[52]
People say, "Drinking much [tea] may cause your head to tremble and spin,
"But your thoughts remain clear and sober, and the flavor still tastes fine,
"And even though you are in this condition, it beats getting drunk on wine,

"Since when you get drunk you stumble and fall with truly disastrous consequences!"
But I don't want a "pure breeze to rise up beneath my armpits,"[53]
All I want is to look at bamboo then go to admire some blossoms,
. . . As long as you remember our friendship, and let me visit you frequently,
Why do we need these "bells and whistles" to make such a raucous fanfare?

Mei claims to be happy with the simple pleasures of friendship and ordinary literati pursuits like viewing plants and flowers, drinking wine, and exchanging poems. He does not need the richer Ouyang to present him with all kinds of expensive gifts, as if he is on a tribute mission preceded by loud fanfares of ceremonial music. At the same time, Mei is happy to record the whole tea drinking spectacle in verse, since it gives a vivid sense of how he and his refined scholar friends spent their leisure time together.

NATURE AND HUMAN BEINGS

In this chapter we focus on two contrasting ways in which Mid-Northern Song poets dealt with the natural world and natural objects. These poets, in common with the prevailing correlational worldview, frequently viewed major natural aberrations—floods, unseasonal weather, and droughts—as indications the government and human society were corrupt and needed reform. Whether or not these educated scholar-officials actually believed in such a simple and direct correlation between human behavior and cosmic response, they were content to make use of cosmic evidence to add weight to their calls for political reform.

As they grew older, however, they increasingly began to express the idea that the natural world, as a whole, was not necessarily on the side of good government or human virtue; that nature could in fact be ruthless, killing off innocent people and allowing the corrupt to survive and prosper. If they themselves wished to survive, they had to find a way to compete with the creative transformations of nature, to avoid the destructive aspects of natural forces while benefiting from their creative and vital side.[54] Thus, they sought out exceptional objects within the natural world: plants that flourished when everything else decayed; exotic creatures or fruits that stood out in an unfamiliar environment; or refined objects like tea that flourished ahead of other spring plants and imbued the drinker with creative, if sometimes over powerful, energy.

Poetry was the vehicle that allowed them to celebrate these unusual, even trivial, natural objects, and to draw parallels with their own exceptional talents and personalities. With its various linguistic, aural, and formal effects, poetry embodied some of the vitality of natural objects, and long after the objects disappear, poems continue to evoke the positive feelings the poets associated with them. Even more crucial, poetry preserves a vital record of the poets themselves, enjoying these objects with their like-minded literati friends and sharing their witty and entertaining impressions of them.

Ultimately, these Mid-Northern Song poets realized that after the flowers had faded, the creatures had passed away, and the food and drink had been consumed; even after they themselves cease to exist, their exceptional poem-objects might survive into the future. As a result, they continued to challenge the destructive forces of natural and human corruption through the poetic records of their vibrant humanity—a humanity that could be reinvigorated and experienced by any appreciative readers who encountered their poetry in future generations.

Conclusion

In his *Remarks on Poetry*, Ouyang Xiu attributed to Mei Yaochen a characterization of well-written poetry that later became famous. Mei declared that poems should "contain boundless meaning revealed beyond their words."[1] The examples with which Mei illustrates this precept are typically evocative Mid- and Late-Tang couplets that manage to create a lingering mood in the reader's mind—a "meaning"—without actually using words of feeling or emotion. Their skillful description of a scene triggers a mood much deeper than the poem's relatively simple verbal structure and content leads one to expect.

In their own works, however, Mid-Northern Song poets generally preferred the freer and plainer ancient-style genres in which they could express emotions openly and directly, rather than the painstakingly crafted, evocative, regulated verse forms. Nonetheless, Northern Song poems also embody a "meaning beyond their words," not so much by the intangible moods they evoke, but by the various social functions they served. Thus, some of Ouyang and Mei's most trivial and lighthearted verses, full of jokes, caricatures, and mutual mockery, suddenly gain deeper significance when we note that they were sent to an exiled and miserable friend (Su Shunqin), in an attempt to lift his spirits and distract him from thoughts of sickness.

Not everyone agrees with Ouyang's contention that in producing such compositions he and his colleagues were upholding the Confucian poetic tradition, which originated with the *Classic of Poetry*, or, that as long as their poetry helped promote social cohesion, it was perfectly acceptable for them to include base, crude, and comical subject matter. In particular, members of the *Daoxue* school—and especially Zhu Xi in the Southern Song—attacked Ouyang's circle for claiming to follow the ancient moral Way while actually continuing to enjoy a hedonistic and "immoral" lifestyle. Doubtless, the *Daoxue* followers would have preferred these poets to produce only serious works of sociopolitical criticism, or even better, to avoid poetry altogether until they had raised their level of moral self-cultivation.[2]

Yet, whether or not one agrees with Zhu Xi's attacks on the moral fiber of Northern Song literati, it is undeniable that poetry writing became increasingly popular in the Song period and over the next several centuries. As literacy spread to the lower classes, and publication of books became more economical and widespread, numerous poetry-writing manuals appeared and legions of poetry societies—including, by the time of the Ming dynasty, societies of women poets—sprouted up throughout the Empire.[3] This development occurred even as Zhu Xi's ideas gained prominence at Court and his commentaries on the Confucian Classics were adopted as required texts for civil service examinations.[4]

Undoubtedly, the main reason for the continued and increasing popularity of poetry in late imperial China—especially among the newly literate and upwardly mobile classes—was its usefulness in smoothing the development of social relations. There were occasional political crises when important poet-officials suffered persecution for allegedly criticizing the Emperor in their writings, but the vast majority of literate people—including the scholar-officials—composed poetry not for political purposes but because poetry helped them get along with other people, and possibly improve their social standing. This is not to say people wrote poetry purely for materialistic reasons. As demonstrated in chapters 3 and 4, poetry was indispensable as a socially acceptable vehicle for expressing pent-up feelings and overcoming emotional imbalances. In a society like traditional China, strictly regulated by rules of propriety and polite behavior, poetry provided a controlled outlet for powerful emotions that might otherwise have been suppressed, leading to psychosomatic illnesses or erupting in violence.

With their broad-minded approach to poetic content and functions, Ouyang Xiu, Mei Yaochen, and subsequent cultural leaders of the Northern Song such as Su Shi and Huang Tingjian, strongly encouraged the continued development and flourishing of poetry as a genre separate from prose, with its own distinct and equally valuable social purposes. Unlike the *Daoxue* thinkers, they realized poetry allowed people to tread a middle path between the need for private expression or emotional release, and the demands of living as responsible citizens in the wider society. In other words, poetry helped rebalance the circulation of vital energy (*qi*) both within their own bodies and, via their interactions with other people, throughout the world outside. As a result, these poets asserted that poetry fostered the healthy development of individuals and led to a healthier society.

Notes

INTRODUCTION—POETRY AND ENERGY CIRCULATION

1. The calculations are my own, as accurate as a nonmathematician could manage. See *Ouyang Xiu quanji* (Taipei: Shijie shuju, 1991), 2 vols. [hereafter, *Ouyang ji*], contents pages. This is the edition of Ouyang Xiu's works to which I refer throughout this study. For alternative editions, see the Bibliography.

2. See Zhu Dongrun, ed., *Mei Yaochen ji biannian jiaozhu* (Shanghai: Guji chubanshe, 1980), [hereafter, Zhu, *Mei*], contents pages.

3. I discuss such studies below, especially in chapters 1 and 2.

4. "Dry and hard" is a phrase that Burton Watson uses in his translation of the chapter on Huang Tingjian in Yoshikawa Kojiro, trans., Burton Watson, *An Introduction to Sung Poetry* (Cambridge, MA: Harvard University Press, 1967) [hereafter, Yoshikawa], 37. The phrase is from a poem by Ouyang Xiu praising Mei Yaochen and Su Shunqin: see *Ouyang ji*, 11–12. Though Watson actually mistranslates the Japanese here, which should read "*ancient* and hard / tough," and Yoshikawa himself generally praises Song poetry highly, the phrase does accurately reflect the negative view of many scholars towards Northern Song poetic style. See chapter 2 for further discussion of this point, and chapter 5, for discussion of ancient qualities in Northern Song poetry.

5. There were also Song poets who favored dense and obscure poetry in the style of Li Shangyin, notably the Xikun school of the early eleventh century, for which see Yoshikawa, 49–52. Yet these were in the minority.

6. The famous philosopher Zhu Xi (1130–1200), for example, attacked Northern Song poets like Ouyang Xiu and Su Shi for their

supposed hypocrisy. See James T. C. Liu, *Ou-yang Hsiu: An Eleventh Century Neo-Confucianist* (Stanford, CA: Stanford University Press, 1967), 98.

7. This seems to be the view of Ronald Egan, in *The Literary Works of Ou-yang Hsiu* (Cambridge: Cambridge University Press, 1984) [hereafter, Egan, *The Literary Works*]. I partially agree with this view, though with reservations that I discuss in chapter 1.

8. *Ouyang ji*, 299. I quote the relevant passage at length in the conclusion to chapter 2 below. I realize that the term Confucianism has recently become controversial. I use it in the conventional way, as a convenient shorthand to refer to values such as humaneness, righteousness, propriety, wisdom, and sincerity, and the strict social hierarchy of the Five Relationships system. For a good historical introduction to the topic, see John Berthrong, *Transformations of the Confucian Way* (Boulder, CO: Westview Press, 1998).

9. See Yoshikawa, 60, 72.

10. See Jonathan Chaves, *Mei Yao-ch'en and the Development of Early Sung Poetry* (New York: Columbia University Press, 1976) [hereafter, Chaves, *Mei Yao-ch'en*]; and Egan, *The Literary Works*.

11. Egan has demonstrated that Ouyang Xiu's prose style was noticeably more informal and personal in tone than that of his Mid-Tang predecessors. See Egan, *The Literary Works*, 12–78, especially 31–32, 35–36. Nevertheless, in his prose Ouyang rarely engaged in the witty banter and wordplay that was so prevalent in his poetry.

12. For complete information on these studies, see the Bibliography.

CHAPTER ONE. POETRY AS POLITICAL AND SOCIAL CRITICISM

1. For general studies of Song literary theory, including numerous quotations from Song literati, see Guo Shaoyu, *Zhongguo wenxue piping shi* (Shanghai: Xinwenyi chubanshe, 1957) [hereafter, Guo Shaoyu], especially 138–212; and more recently Zhou Yukai, *Songdai shixue tonglun* (Chengdu: Ba-Shu shushe, 1997); and Zhang Hongsheng, *Song shi: rongtong yu kaituo* (Shanghai: Guji chubanshe, 2001). For an insightful survey of the various literati groupings in the Northern Song and their differing interpretations of the Way, see also Peter Bol, *"This Culture of Ours": Intellectual Transitions in T'ang and Sung China* (Stanford, CA: Stanford University Press, 1992), especially chapters 5–6.

2. For writing as a "vehicle for the Way" (Zhou Dunyi's [1017–1073] phrase), see Guo Shaoyu, 156. For Confucianism, see John Berthrong, *Transformations of the Confucian Way*. For a broader approach that encompasses the cosmology of Confucianism including Confucian attitudes towards nature, which complements my own interpretation of Mid-Northern Song poetry, see Xinzhong Yao, *An Introduction to Confucianism* (Cambridge: Cambridge University Press, 2000), especially chapter 3, "The way of harmony."

3. Zhu, *Mei*, introduction, 16. The two poems mentioned are in Zhu, *Mei*, at 164–5, and are translated in Chaves, *Mei Yao-ch'en*, 164–67.

4. Zhu, *Mei*, 16.

5. Ronald Egan notes the lack of overtly didactic poems in Ouyang's collection. Egan implies that there is a contradiction between the lighthearted content and style of much of Ouyang's poetry and his moralistic statements about the functions of writing, a view I question below. See *The Literary Works of Ou-yang Hsiu* (Cambridge: Cambridge University Press, 1984) [hereafter, Egan, *The Literary Works*], 81–84.

6. Zhu, *Mei*, 16–17.

7. *Ouyang ji*, 235, "Grave Inscription for Mei Shengyu." Shengyu was Mei Yaochen's style name.

8. *Ouyang ji*, 235.

9. Ouyang's *Shihua* can be found in *Ouyang ji*, 1035–41.

10. *Ouyang ji*, 299, from a prose piece entitled "Preface to Poems Composed and Exchanged in the Ministry of Rites," dated 1057.

11. Ronald Egan expresses this view in *The Literary Works*, 78–122.

12. Zhu, *Mei*, 117. Zhu dates the poem to 1038. Fan Raozhou refers to the illustrious statesman and reformer Fan Zhongyan (989–1052), then governor of Raozhou. For this poem I have relied to a certain extent on Chaves' translation and analysis in *Mei Yao-ch'en*, 14–15, 179–85.

13. When he attacked Wu, the ancient king, Goujian of Yue, was so impressed with the fierce glare of a bloated frog that he ordered his troops to imitate the frog's aggressive pose.

14. Moye was the wife of a legendary swordsmith, Ganjiang, who on his death, left her a sharp sword telling her to bring up their baby and get him to use the sword to seek revenge on a wicked king. See Gan Bao, *Sou shen ji* ("Record of Searching for the Supernatural") and Karl S. Y. Kao, *Classical Chinese Tales of the Supernatural and the Fantastic* (Bloomington: Indiana University Press, 1985), 73–75.

15. Tuizhi was Han Yu's (768–824) style name. Han composed a poem about strange southern foods in which he claimed to have released a snake because its fierce expression scared him. The poem indirectly expresses Han's discomfort at being exiled to an unfamiliar southern environment. Han also exchanged a poem with Liu Zongyuan (style name Zihou), in which he noted that Liu, also exiled to the provinces, had eaten a dish made from toad meat. For these two poems, see Qian Zhonglian, *Han Changli shi xinian jishi* (Shanghai: Guji chubanshe, 1984) [hereafter Qian Zhonglian], 1132, 1138.

16. As Chaves (181) notes, this saying originated in the *Zuozhuan*. There, of course, it related to physical beauty (*mei*), an attribute that the river-pig fish obviously lacks. Mei plays wittily on the other meaning of *mei*, meaning tasty, reinterpreting the saying to mean that eating great tasting food will lead to disastrous consequences. It is impossible to give both senses of *mei* in the English translation.

17. Chaves, 178–99. His conclusion is that the poem may have political implications, but that without further extrinsic evidence it is impossible to draw any firm conclusions as to whom Mei might be criticizing. Hence it is better to treat the poem simply as a piece of moralistic verse (Chaves 184–85). Though more balanced than most commentators, Chaves seems to neglect the humorous tone of the poem.

18. See James T. C. Liu, "Mei Yaochen 'Biyunxia' yu Qingli zhengzheng zhong de shifeng," in *Dalu zazhi* 17.11 (1958): 341–46. Cf. Chaves 183–84.

19. For the events of this period, see Liu, *Ou-yang Hsiu: An Eleventh Century Neo-Confucianist* (Stanford, CA: Stanford University Press, 1967), 24–51.

20. From *Zhuzi yulei* (Hong Kong: Zhengzhong shuju, 1962) *juan* 140:5413. Quoted in Chaves, 183. For another comment by Zhu Xi on the loose morals of Ouyang Xiu and his circle, see Liu, *Ou-yang Hsiu*, 98.

21. First paragraph from *Ouyang ji*, 1035, an excerpt from Ouyang's *Shihua*. Second paragraph from *Ouyang ji*, 535, a colophon entitled "Written at the End of Mei Shengyu's Poem on the River-Pig Fish." Cf. Chaves, 179.

22. For samples of these comments, see Chaves, 181–83.

23. Chaves, 2–3.

24. For an extended discussion of Northern Song caricatured reasoning, see my "Fowl and Bestial? A Defense of Ouyang Xiu's Poems on White Creatures," *Journal of Sung-Yuan Studies* 28 (1998): 123–53.

25. *Ouyang ji*, 19.

26. Zhu, *Mei*, 61–62. Translated in Chaves, 188.

27. See Chaves' discussion of Mei's poem and some other pre-Song mosquito poems, Chaves, 188–91. Cf. Ouyang Xiu's 1034 poem, entitled "Matching Shengyu's Swarming Mosquitoes," which expresses similar sentiments: *Ouyang ji*, 354–55.

28. *Ouyang ji*, 19.

29. Ouyang considers writing about mosquitoes to be a waste of paper. The phrase translated "leaving its traces," literally "dirtying," could also refer to squashing a mosquito and leaving a stain on one's paper.

30. Yu: a mythical ancient ruler responsible for overcoming various legendary beasts and disastrous floods that plagued the Empire. By depicting the forms of the evil beasts on a tripod, Yu demonstrated his power over them. The Duke of Zhou: another semi-mythical Confucian hero who helped found the Zhou dynasty.

31. The mosquitoes, though tiny, still count as "evil beasts," hence they wish to avenge their mythical ancestors' defeat at the hands of the ancient sage rulers.

32. Or "back and belly."

33. The phrase "closes his eyes" normally refers to someone dying; here the servant is just going back to sleep, but Ouyang's mock heroic scenario imagines him defeated and dying after a brave battle.

34. Mythical auspicious creatures that only appeared when the world was at peace.

35. For a description of this kind of poetry, see James J. Y. Liu, *Chinese Theories of Literature* (Chicago: University of Chicago Press, 1975), 106–16; cf. Zhou Yukai, *Songdai shixue*, 31–41.

36. Zhu, *Mei*, 164–65. Chaves, 166–67.

37. I explore this aspect further in chapter 6 below.

38. See a letter from Ouyang to Mei Yaochen dated 1046, in which he speaks of several poems he has written recently—one of which may have been "Hateful Mosquitoes," and thanks Mei for sending him several compositions matching his own previous poems: *Ouyang ji*, 1284.

39. See also Chaves, *Mei Yao-ch'en*, especiallyly 178–99, for more examples of poems by Mei Yaochen that commentators have attempted to interpret allegorically.

40. Poem in *Ouyang ji*, 53–4. The poem by Mei that Ouyang mentions in his title may be the similarly long composition entitled "Heavy Rain: Ninth Day, Seventh Month, Second Year of the Jiayou Period (i.e., 1057), Sent to Scholar Yongshu [Ouyang Xiu]," in Zhu, *Mei*, 965. Cf. two earlier poems on floods from 1040 by Mei Yaochen, in which Mei regrets his inability to prevent peoples' distress. Zhu, *Mei*, 159; Chaves, 18–19.

41. Fierce monsters: literally *kuixu*, mentioned in Zhang Heng's (AD 78–139) "Prose-poem on the Eastern Capital," and glossed there as "a kind of dragon with scales glowing like the sun and moon." Here, Ouyang uses the *kuixu* to personify the storm. See Li Shan, ed., *Zhaoming wenxuan* (Taipei: Wenhua tushu gongsi, 1995), 3.44.

42. There were supposedly nine years of floods during the reign of the mythical sage emperor Yao.

43. *Ouyang ji*, *nianpu*, 12–13.

44. See Liu, *Ou-yang Hsiu* and Liu, *Reform in Sung China: Wang An-shih and his New Policies* (Cambridge, MA: Harvard University Press, 1959). For a more detailed study of the topic in Chinese, see Shen Songqin, *Bei-Song wenren yu dangzheng* (Beijing: Renmin chubanshe, 1998). Ronald Egan also provides much detail on factionalism among the generation after Ouyang Xiu's: see *Word, Image, and Deed in the Life of Su Shi* (Cambridge, MA: Harvard University Press, 1994) [hereafter, Egan, *Su Shi*].

45. *Ouyang ji*, 363, from poem entitled "Song Rejoicing at Snow in Commissioner Yan's Western Garden," discussed further in chapter 6.

46. Liu, *Ou-yang Hsiu*, 43–46. Named after the Qingli reign period (1041–1048), though the reforms lasted for only about a year after 1043.

47. Cai's poem series, which includes one poem for each person involved, is in Fu Xuanzong et al., eds., *Quan Songshi* (Beijing: Beijing daxue chubanshe, 1992), 7.4748–50. Cf. Liu, *Ou-yang Hsiu*, 34, 49.

48. Liu, *Ou-yang Hsiu*, 49. Liu notes that one forged letter was supposedly from Shi Jie to Fu Bi, and talked of a conspiracy to depose the Emperor.

49. From Pan's *Categorized Selections of Song Gossip (Songbai leichao)*, quoted in Fu Pingxiang and Hu Wentao, eds., *Su Shunqin ji biannian jiaozhu* (Chengdu: Ba-Shu shushe, 1990) [hereafter, *Su Shunqin ji*], 795–6. For more on the whole episode involving Su, cf. Liu, *Ou-yang Hsiu*, 49–50; Shen, *Bei-Song wenren*, 117–25.

50. See *Su Shunqin ji*, 609, for Su's letter to Ouyang Xiu justifying his actions as customary practices.

51. Liu, *Ou-yang Hsiu*, 50–51.

52. See Ronald Egan's discussion of the authenticity of Ouyang's song lyrics, including those used to attack him at various stages of his career, in *The Literary Works*, 161–95.

53. See the Song Code offence under "domestic disorder" (*neiluan*) in Xue Meiqing, ed., *Song xingtong* (Beijing: Falü chubanshe, 1999), 1.14. For more on the trumped up nature of these charges, see Hawes, "Competing with Creative Transformation: The Poetry of Ouyang Xiu (1007–1072)" (PhD. diss., University of British Columbia, 1996), 28–31.

54. The reference to "Master Liu" is a euphemism for a man looking for love. This lyric does not appear in *Ouyang ji*, but is collected in Tang Guizhang, ed., *Quan Songci* (Beijing: Zhonghua shuju, 1965), 156. Translation in Egan, *The Literary Works*, 171. Egan (170–72) doubts the authenticity of this lyric and two others in similar vein.

55. Egan gives some similar examples of erotic lyrics by other well-known Northern Song scholar officials, including Huang Tingjian (1045–1105) and Qin Guan (1049–1100). See *The Literary Works*, 175–76.

56. Liu, *Ou-yang Hsiu*, 65–67.

57. For details of these later accusations, see Liu, *Ou-yang Hsiu*, 79–82.

58. For further discussion of the traditional Chinese idea that poetry expresses one's intent, originating in the Han dynasty "Great Preface" to the *Classic of Poetry*, see Stephen Owen, *Readings in Chinese Literary Thought* (Cambridge, MA: Harvard University Press, 1992), chapter 1.

59. Though detailed discussion is beyond the scope of this study, we should mention here the contrasting case of Su Shi (1037–1101) in the following generation, who was accused of slandering the Court and of lése-majestè in the late-1070s, due to his attacks on the New Policies implemented by Wang Anshi (1021–1086) and his disciples. Most of the incriminating evidence for Su's political attitude was drawn from his poetry and, unlike the Qingli conservatives, Su's accusers found numerous poems that referred directly or obliquely to the New Policies. They then forced Su to explain how each of these poems criticized the government. The record of Su's confession gives us plenty of interesting examples of poetry being interpreted as indirect political and social criticism. There is no doubt that Su intended some of his poems to give a negative view of the New Policies and the suffering they caused the common people. However, three points make us wary of extending this interpretive strategy to other Northern Song poetry. First, a forced confession, probably obtained after prolonged torture, is unreliable evidence for the meaning of poems.

Instead we should stick to comments on the functions of poetry made by Northern Song poets who were not in gaol accused of heinous crimes. Second, Su Shi had already made his opposition to the New Policies abundantly clear in his prose writings, including several government memorials. It is hardly surprising he occasionally refers to the problems caused by these Policies in his poetry. But this does not mean that the poetry he composed at other times in his life also had a political function. Again, we must look to his other comments on the purposes of poetry, and those of his poet contemporaries, for a more balanced view. Third, as Egan notes, Su's occasional use of poetry for indirect political criticism in the 1070s was exceptional in the Northern Song, and several of his friends warned him not to continue writing in this way. By implication, therefore, Su's contemporaries generally did not consider poetic writing as an appropriate vehicle for political dissent. Cf. balanced discussion of the issues in Ronald Egan, *Word, Image, and Deed in the Life of Su Shi*, chapter 2, especially 46–47. For an excellent analysis of Su's trial and the surviving texts, see Charles Hartman, "Poetry and Politics in 1079: The Crow Terrace Poetry Case of Su Shih," in *Chinese Literature: Essays, Articles, Reviews* 12 (1990): 15–44. For a contrasting view that interprets many of Su Shi's poems as veiled political critique, see Alfreda Murck, *Poetry and Painting in Song China: The Subtle Art of Dissent* (Cambridge, MA: Harvard University Press, 2000).

CHAPTER TWO. POETRY AS A GAME

1. For a detailed analysis of the Qing enthusiasm for Song poetry, see J. D. Schmidt, *Within the Human Realm: The Poetry of Huang Zunxian, 1848–1905* (Cambridge: Cambridge University Press, 1994), 79–92. More modern Chinese critics, including even the contemporary wit and scholar Qian Zhongshu, in his *Song shi xuan zhu* (1958; repr., Beijing: Renmin wenxue, 1989), have generally neglected or derided the less serious works of Northern Song poets, focusing instead on their works of social criticism. See also the negative evaluation by Wang Shuizhao in one of his earlier discussions of Northern Song poetry from 1979 entitled "*Songdai shige de yishu tedian he jiaoxun*," in *Wang Shuizhao zixuan ji* (Shanghai: Jiaoyu chubanshe, 2000) [hereafter Wang, *Selected Works*], 81–104. Since the 1990s, Wang's view of Northern Song poetic games has become much more positive, as I show below. In a later note added to the above paper (Wang, *Selected Works*, 104), he blames his earlier erroneous and narrow attitude on political pressure to conform to the Maoist line in literary criticism.

2. "Caricatured reasoning" means using the rhetorical structures and forms of serious intellectual debate to discuss trivial subjects in an

exaggerated way for humorous ends. See my papers entitled "Fowl and Bestial?" and "Mundane Transcendence: Dealing with the Everyday in the Poetry of Ouyang Xiu (1007–1072)," *Chinese Literature: Essays, Articles, Reviews* 21 (1999): 99–129. For Yan Yu's remarks on Song poetry, which were pejorative in tone, see *Canglang shihua*, in *Yushutang shihua ji qita san zhong*, Congshu jicheng edition, 1st. ser. (Beijing: Zhonghua shuju, 1985), 4.7. In particular, Yan accuses Northern Song poets of incorporating prose, arguments, and even cursing into their poetry.

3. See Zhu, *Mei*, introduction, 16. Jonathan Chaves's excellent evaluation of Mei's poetry (*Mei Yao-ch'en*) is much more balanced than Zhu Dongrun's critique; but, perhaps influenced by previous Chinese studies of Mei, Chaves still underplays the wit, humor, and ingenious craftsmanship of many of Mei's poems. More recent Western studies of other Northern Song poets, especially those of the Su Shi generation and later, have paid greater attention to the wit and ingenuity of their compositions. See, for instance, Michael Fuller, *The Road to East Slope: The Development of Su Shi's Poetic Voice* (Stanford, CA: Stanford University Press, 1990), 164–67, 180, 256–60; and Ronald Egan, *Word, Image, and Deed in the Life of Su Shi*, 169–79.

4. Zhu, *Mei*, 16.

5. Wang, *Selected Works*, 96–9.

6. Wang, *Selected Works*, 233. From a paper entitled "*Jiayou ernian gongju shijian de wenxueshi yiyi*" (198–243). See also Wang, *Selected Works*, 52–80 and 174–97, for further papers by Wang giving positive evaluations of Northern Song poetry dating from the 1990s. For another excellent discussion of Northern Song wit and poetic wordplay, see Han Jingtai, "*Lun Songshi xiequ*," in *Zhongguo shehui kexue* 1993.5: 133–147.

7. For brief discussions of earlier poets' literary games, see Han Jingtai, *Lun Songshi*, 134–5; Wang, *Selected Works*, 232–4.

8. *Ouyang ji*, 29. Ouyang composed this poem in 1050. *Ren* (literally, people's) festival was on the seventh day of the first month, according to the traditional Chinese calendar. I have located eight such rhyme-category games in Ouyang Xiu's collected poems, and nine in Mei Yaochen's collection (*Ouyang ji*, 21, 29, 42, 59, 348, 356, 369, 386; Zhu, *Mei*, 32–33, 47, 267, 331, 502–3, 714, 896).

9. The *Guangyun* was first published in 1008. See *Chongjiao Songben Guangyun* (Taipei: Guangwen shuju, 1961).

10. *Ouyang ji*, 29, lines 5–8 of poem.

11. See examples of Mei and Ouyang borrowing Han Yu's rhyme categories in chapter 5 below, section entitled "Mid-Tang Poets as Ancients."

12. *Ouyang ji*, 43. Shengyu was Mei Yaochen's style name. Mei's poem "Don't Drink Wine" is in Zhu, *Mei*, 925.

13. Tuizhi was Han Yu's style name. The phrase "carving liver and sculpting kidneys" refers to painstaking literary composition. In his poem "Presented to Case Reviewer Cui Lizhi," Han Yu included the lines, "I urge you to cultivate yourself in private, and wait for the campaign summons, / There's no need to carve and sculpt, depressing your liver and kidneys" (Qian Zhonglian, *Han Changli shi*, 569). Han is politely telling Cui to stop wasting his energy sending poems importuning Han to recommend him for a high position. But Ouyang Xiu purposely takes Han's words out of context, as a claim that poetic composition inevitably harms one's equilibrium. In the following line (line 7) he then declares that Han Yu ("that old man") contradicted himself by composing a carefully crafted poem to criticize Cui for writing poems. It would be far better, Ouyang argues (in his own poem), simply to get drunk on wine and forget about poetry altogether.

14. Literally "the jagged peaks of ten thousand affairs can all be leveled [or made equal]," probably a tongue-in-cheek reference to the second chapter in the *Zhuangzi* entitled "Discussion on Making All Things Equal," See Wang Xianqian, ed., *Zhuangzi jijie* (1974; repr., Taipei: Sanmin shuju, 1985), 6; Burton Watson, trans., *The Complete Works of Chuang-Tzu* (New York: Columbia University Press, 1968), 36.

15. "Rotting innards" actually refers indirectly to fine wine and good food, which act like medicine to cure one's stomach, as in Bai Juyi's poem, "Sent to Lu Shaoqing": "Excellent dishes and vintage wine / Are truly balm for rotting innards!" *Quan Tangshi* (Beijing: Zhonghua shuju, 1960), 14: 452.5114. "Pickled meat" is a reference to the *Jinshu* biography of Kong Qun, a wine lover. When a friend warned him of the harmful effects of drinking, Kong retorted: "Do you not see that when meat is pickled [in wine lees], it is able to last much longer?" See Fang Xuanling, *Jinshu* (Beijing: Zhonghua shuju, 1962), 46:78.2061. These seem to be two theories claiming that wine drinking will bring good health and long life. Ouyang dismisses both, declaring that, since everyone will die sooner or later, it is better not to waste time on justifications, but just to drink (lines 16–19).

16. Zhu, *Mei*, 926. Yongshu was Ouyang Xiu's style name.

17. I assume this ending refers to Ouyang's foolish attempt to attack poetry while still clearly being attached to poetic composition. Mei, by contrast, sees no contradiction in loving both wine and poetry, since both help him deal with life's troubles.

18. The *Boliangti* was a poetic form that supposedly originated during the reign of the Han Emperor Wu (r.140–80 BC) at a place called Boliang Terrace. The distinctive feature of this form was that every line

bore an end rhyme, in contrast to the alternate-line rhyming of most Chinese poetry. The partial *Boliangti* varied sections where every line rhymed with sections of alternate-line rhyming. There were no fixed rules about how many lines should rhyme in a partial *Boliangti*: this depended on the skill of the poet. For discussion of the origins of the form, and further examples, see Wang Li 王力, *Hanyu shilu xue* (1958; repr., Shanghai: Jiaoyu chubanshe, 1979), 14–15, 366–79.

19. A typical series begins with Mei Yaochen's poem of 1059, "On New Year's Eve I Went with My Host to Climb the Eastern Tower of the Secretariat," which Mei then matched twice himself. See Zhu, *Mei*, 922–23. Ouyang Xiu then composed three poems to match Mei's: *Ouyang ji*, 88. Another series begins with Ouyang Xiu composing a long poem on Fujian tea in 1058, "Tasting New Tea, Presented to Shengyu" and matching it himself (*Ouyang ji*, 49–50); Mei Yaochen then chips in with two matching poems (Zhu, *Mei*, 1008–10). For further discussion of these poems on tea, see chapter 6.

20. For further discussion of Su Shi's expressive use of rhyme-matching, see Alice W. Cheang, "Poetry and Transformation: Su Shih's Mirage," *HJAS* 58: no. 1 (June 1998): 147–82, 169–72, and Alfreda Murck, "Misty River, Layered Peaks: Decoding Landscape Imagery," *The East Asian Library Journal*, 8.2 (Autumn 1998): 17–68. Cheang's article also notes the strong influence of Han Yu on Su Shi, a feature that is evident in my own discussion of the Ouyang Xiu circle. Murck shows Su Shi borrowing rhymes from Du Fu, a poet in whom Ouyang Xiu and Mei Yaochen seem to have shown less interest. I am indebted to both these scholars for their insightful comments on an earlier draft of this chapter. See also Yoshikawa, 39–41, 116–17.

21. See Fu and Hu, *Su Shunqin ji biannian jiaozhu*, 2, 23, 30, 45, 74, 77, 99, 120. Examples of linked verses involving Ouyang Xiu and various colleagues are in *Ouyang ji*, 375–76. Mei Yaochen's collection also contains a number of early linked verses written with various acquaintances: Zhu, *Mei*, 47–49.

22. See, for example, Bai Juyi's series "Matching Twenty Three Poems by Weizhi [i.e. Yuan Zhen]," in *Quan Tangshi*, 13: 445.4982–90. As for Han and Meng's linked verses, see the excellent discussion of these in Stephen Owen, *The Poetry of Meng Chiao and Han Yu* (New Haven, CT: Yale University Press, 1975), 116–36.

23. See Richard Mather, trans., *Shih-shuo hsin-yu: A New Account of Tales of the World* (Minneapolis: University of Minnesota Press, 1976), 34, 321–22. For references to rhyme matching in the later Six Dynasties, see Stephen Owen, *An Anthology of Chinese Literature: Beginnings to 1911* (New York: W. W. Norton, 1996), 325–29.

24. One example of a rather incongruous transition is the sudden appearance of a horse with drooping ears in line 12 of Mei Yaochen's poem on wine quoted above. The rhyme-word *chui* (droop) triggers his imagination and, since it is only a game, he can introduce an unexpected and slightly out of place self-caricature knowing that it will at least give his friends a laugh.

25. I discuss this point further in chapter five below. See a more sustained characterization of Northern Song poetics and aesthetic ideals, based on the literary criticism of Ouyang Xiu, in my "Competing with Creative Transformation," 321–91.

26. See "Colophon on the Chant of the Drunken Old Man," in *Ouyang ji*, 540.

27. Text of poem in Zhu, *Mei*, 882. Ouyang's collection has two other poems with the same title, which Ouyang composed by himself during the same period (the years 1056–1057). However their meters are quite different from the example translated here. See *Ouyang ji*, 45, 113.

28. I use the word "oh" as a rough equivalent for the Chinese syllable *xi* 兮. The poem concludes by declaring that the Drunken Old Man does not bother anybody, and when he leaves at night, the poet somehow misses him.

29. Zhu, *Mei*, 882.

30. There is, for instance, a work by Bai Juyi entitled "Poem [with Lines Increasing] from One Syllable to Seven," which, according to the title note, resulted from a drinking game. See *Quan Tangshi*, 14: 462.5262.

31. In connection with this point, see Ronald Egan, *The Literary Works*, and *Word, Image and Deed in the Life of Su Shi*, 332–36.

32. *Moji ji qita wu zhong*, Congshu jicheng edition, 1st. ser. (Beijing: Zhonghua shuju, 1991), 3.2–3; see also Chu Djang and Jane C. Djang, trans., *A Compilation of Anecdotes of Sung Personalities* (Taipei: St. John's University Press, 1989), 345–47. Cf. Text of lyric in *Ouyang ji*, 1076.

33. Egan, *The Literary Works*, 154–56, notes that Ouyang Xiu enjoyed inserting poem lines from famous past writers into his lyrics, thereby giving them a new context, apparently with the aim of entertaining his fellow literati.

34. *Ouyang ji*, 42–43. Poem dates to 1056.

35. *Ouyang ji*, 36. I translate the whole poem in chapter 4.

36. *Ouyang ji*, 42.

37. Lines 20–22 of poem, in *Ouyang ji*, 42. The second sentence is arguably a single line of 24 syllables, since the rhyme comes on "mist"

(*yan* 煙), and this section of the poem has a rhyme on every line. At the very least, it is a single syntactic unit divided into two long lines, 15 and 9 syllables respectively, with the line break coming on attain (*dao* 到).

38. For Su's poem see Feng Yingliu and Wang Wengao, eds., *Su Shi shi ji* (Taipei: Xuehai chubanshe, 1982), 277–78. Fuller has translated Su's poem and part of Ouyang's in *The Road to East Slope*, 129–31. He notes that irregular meters are uncommon in Su's poetry. Stephen Owen also translates both these poems in *An Anthology of Chinese Literature*, 679–80.

39. For an excellent discussion of Ouyang Xiu's influence and that of other early Song literati on the transformation of Northern Song writing style, especially in the area of ancient style prose, see Egan, *The Literary Works*, 12–78. For more on the "untrammeled" poetic style, see chapter 5.

40. In *Ouyang ji*, 370–71.

41. *Ouyang ji*, 370.

42. *Ouyang ji*, 1036–37.

43. This poem, entitled "Bai tu," is in *Ouyang ji*, 371. For translations of this and Ouyang's subsequent poems on white pets, see my "Fowl and Bestial," 126–47.

44. Preface to Mei's poem "Once Again Describing the White Rabbit," in Zhu, *Mei*, 900.

45. See Ouyang's "Irregular Meter Poem Answering Shengyu's 'White Parrot,'" in *Ouyang ji*, 54.

46. My emphasis. From the poem "Traveling at Night in Shuigu, Sent to Zimei and Shengyu" (dated 1044), in *Ouyang ji*, 11–12. Ouyang later quoted his own lines as a fair representation of Mei's poetry in his *Remarks on Poetry*, compiled in 1071. See *Ouyang ji*, 1037–38.

47. Chaves, *Mei Yao-ch'en*, 178–99, gives many examples of Mei's works on unusual topics, some doubtless resulting from poetry games. See, for instance, the poem entitled "[Xie] Shihou Said that from Ancient Times, No-one Had Ever Done a Poem about Lice, and Invited Me to Write One on the Subject" (Chaves, 191; Chinese text in Zhu, *Mei*, 283). I have translated numerous poems by Ouyang Xiu on similarly odd topics in my "Competing with Creative Transformation": see especially 150 (clams), and 316 (parrot-shaped wine cup). These works resemble the game-poems described above in that they appear to have been composed at banquets or social gatherings and are lighthearted in tone. See also Wang, *Selected Works*, 55, for a list of the incredible variety of foods and drinks about which Su Shi composed poems.

48. Compilers of literary anecdotes enjoyed spotting such games in the collections of their famous predecessors. For example, besides describing some of those I have mentioned here, Wei Qingzhi in his *Shiren yuxie* lists: a poem by Mei Yaochen in which every character is pronounced with an oblique tone (unlike the traditional balancing of level and oblique tones); a poem by Huang Tingjian where the rhyme changes every three lines (normally it would be at most every four lines); and a palindromic composition by Su Shi that can be read in either direction as a respectable poem. See *Shiren yuxie* (1959; repr., Shanghai: Guji chubanshe, 1978), 34–36.

49. See Ouyang Xiu's five quatrains in *Ouyang ji*, 348, and Mei's five quatrains with preface in Zhu, *Mei*, 32–33. The poems of the other participants are no longer extant.

50. *Ouyang ji*, 348.

51. "Preface to Poems Composed at a Small Drinking Party Held Early Fall in the Bamboo Grove of Puming Temple," in Zhu, *Mei*, 32.

52. Following the modern scholar Xia Jingguan's emendation of Pu worthies (*pu xian*) to "past worthies" (*xi xian*): cited in Zhu, *Mei*, 33.

53. In *Han-Wei Liuchao baisan mingjia ji* (Taipei: Wenjin chubanshe, 1979), 3:2376. For an English translation by Richard Strassberg, see Victor Mair, ed., *The Columbia Anthology of Traditional Chinese Literature* (New York: Columbia University Press, 1994), 565–66. The Orchid Pavilion gathering also included a poetry composition game with wine forfeits, and the poems in the Orchid Pavilion Collection were apparently produced during this game. However, in Wang's preface the initial happy mood soon turned to melancholy, as Wang recollected the transitory nature of existence. This contrasts with Mei Yaochen's sustained optimism.

54. See "Preface to Poems Composed and Answered in the Ministry of Rites," in *Ouyang ji*, 299.

55. *Ouyang ji*, 299.

56. From Ouyang's collection of anecdotes entitled *Guitian lu* ("Notes on Returning to the Fields"), in *Ouyang ji*, 1030–31.

57. *Xikun chouchang ji* (Xikun Collection of Responding Poems) (Shanghai: Shangwu, 1935). For a summary of this view, see Egan, *The Literary Works*, 78–84.

58. See my "Competing with Creative Transformation," 370–73.

59. For one example, see the song lyric in my section on games with meter above.

60. *Ouyang ji*, 124.

61. Two of the four surviving linked verses in Ouyang's collection were composed with Fan. See *Ouyang ji*, 375–76.

62. That poetic games could have unintentional political overtones is further suggested by an event following the 1057 examinations: a disgruntled group of unsuccessful candidates tried to mob Ouyang Xiu, the chief examiner, in the streets of Kaifeng, claiming that he had not announced his stylistic criteria for grading, and hence had unfairly failed the students of his conservative opponents. When Ouyang published his anthology of lighthearted poems by the examiners, many candidates complained that the examiners had spent all their time having fun and neglected their job of properly grading the examinations. They were particularly incensed by two poems that compared the busily writing candidates with ants and silkworms. Their demands for a re-mark were ignored, however. See *Shiren yuxie*, 29: 204–5. Translation in Chaves, *Mei Yao-ch'en*, 37.

63. "Ba Zuiweng yin," in *Ouyang ji*, 540. Composed in 1070, two years before Ouyang's death. See also his inscription "Written at the End of Three Quatrains," which states: "In the first poem, Mei Shengyu describes the bamboo partridge; in the next poem, Su Zimei [i.e., Shunqin] describes the oriole; and in the final poem, I describe the song thrush. Our three compositions were produced by coincidence, and at first none of us knew of the other [two]. But when we brought them together, [we found that] their ideas were completely alike. How can one deny that this fortuitous harmony was due to our shared spiritual empathy? Since these two masters have died, from now on I'm afraid I too will have to lay down my brush" (*Ouyang ji*, 535).

CHAPTER THREE. POETRY AND RELATIONSHIP BUILDING

1. Qian Zhongshu, *Song shi xuan zhu*, Introduction, 9–10.

2. Qian, 9–10, does also note the importance of love in *ci*, but does not make it clear that often the same poets would compose both *shi* and *ci*. For more information on Northern Song *ci*, see James J. Y. Liu, *Major Lyricists of the Northern Sung: AD 960–1126* (Princeton, NJ: Princeton University Press, 1974), and Pauline Yu, ed., *Voices of the Song Lyric in China* (Berkeley: University of California Press, 1994). Ronald Egan's chapter on Ouyang Xiu's *ci* also gives a clear discussion of Northern Song *ci* style, with numerous examples by Ouyang and other poets. See *The Literary Works*, 133–95.

3. For one example, see the traditional Chinese commentators cited by Hightower in his study "The Songs of Chou Pang-yen," in James

R. Hightower and Florence Chia-ying Yeh, *Studies in Chinese Poetry* (Cambridge, MA: Harvard University Press, 1998), 292–322, 300–306.

4. Besides the evidence from their *shi* poems, cited below, see also James T. C. Liu, *Ou-yang Hsiu*, 29, 98, and several of the historical anecdotes about Yan Shu, Fan Zhongyan and Ouyang Xiu in Ding Chuanjing's *Songren yishi huibian* (Taiwan: Shangwu, 1935, repr. 1966), 266–7, 309, 344–45, 347. Translated in Chu and Jane C. Djang, *A Compilation of Anecdotes of Sung Personalities*, 277, 279–81, 313–14, 345–47, 352–53.

5. *Ouyang ji*, 353. From poem entitled "Moved by Events, I Write My Feelings, Sent to Mei Shengyu."

6. The final line refers to Ouyang Xiu's move away from Luoyang in 1034, and the subsequent separation from his various friends there, who moved to various positions around the country. Ouyang looks back fondly on their life of pleasure in Luoyang.

7. Zhu, *Mei*, 1076. See also a poem by Mei defending his enjoyment of dancing girls, translated in chapter 6.

8. According to Xia Jingguan, this phrase means the entertainers are sixteen years old, since when the character for melon (*gua* 瓜)is split into its two constituent parts, the inner part looks like "two" (*er* 二) and the outer part looks like "eight" (*ba* 八), and two multiplied by eight makes sixteen. See Xia Jingguan, *Mei Yaochen shi* (Shangwu, 1940), 46. However, the image also surely has erotic implications.

9. In *Ouyang ji*, 47–48. Poem entitled "At Administrator Liu's House I Saw Assistant Professor Yang [Bao's] Maid Play the Pipa. Written in Jest, Presented to Shengyu." The *pipa* is a kind of long-necked lute.

10. In his matching poem, Mei Yaochen is equally clear in condemning Yang's lack of compassion:

> The servant girl is still young and stands out from the vulgar run,
> But in the tenth month she wears a thin robe and only gets millet to eat.
> She says that she waits on Broadly Cultured Yang, of Guanxi:
> Yet "Broadly Cultured" just empties her belly, greedy to teach her tunes.
> . . . She also laughs that collected drawings and paintings fill the house,
> But he's not willing to spend the money to buy her a pearl tiara,
> Instead she's stuck with clumps of chrysanthemums picked from the front terrace!

See "Matching the Rhymes of Yongshu's 'Written in Jest,'" lines 19–22, 26–28, in Zhu, *Mei*, 981.

11. *Ouyang ji*, 13. From poem entitled "Dappled, Dappled, the Turtledoves in the Grove: Sent to My Wife" [1045].

12. Jing refers to Jingzhou, the general area surrounding the county of Yiling (present Hubei province), inhabited by indigenous people referred to as the Man. Ouyang was exiled to Jingzhou in 1036, hence his talk about being forced to flee.

13. For translations of several of Mei's poems of bereavement, and detailed discussion of their style and precedents, see Chaves, *Mei Yao-ch'en*, 19–22, 146–63. Mei also affectionately praised his second wife in verse: see Chaves, 158, 162. Unfortunately, very few women's poems from the Northern Song survive to give a clear indication of the kinds of poetic exchanges that occurred between women and other women or men. Li Qingzhao (1084–c. 1151), China's most famous woman poet, who lived at the end of the Northern Song, wrote in one of her lyrics about being so sad that she "refused invitations from my poetic partners (*shi you*)." See Li's lyric entitled *Yong yu le*, in Hou Jian and Lu Zhimin, eds., *Li Qingzhao shici pingzhu* (Taiyuan: Shanxi jiaoyu chubanshe, 1985, repr. 1991), 168. Li's collection also contains three poems (*shi*) exchanged with named people, both men (207, 220, 230). It is also possible, though doubtful, that Zhu Shuzhen (traditional dates c. 1063–c. 1106), another female poet, lived during the Northern Song, and her surviving collection contains a number of poems exchanged with friends, some matching the rhymes of friends' poems. For some translated poems by Zhu, including exchanged poems, and discussion of her dates, which are very uncertain, see Kang-i Sun Chang and Haun Saussy, eds., *Women Writers of Traditional China: An Anthology of Poetry and Criticism* (Stanford, CA: Stanford University Press, 1999), 100–6, 103, 105. Many Northern Song literati in their biographical sketches of wives and mothers frequently state that along with their stock female virtues, such women could also turn out excellent poetry. See, for example, Su Zhe's grave inscription for Ouyang Xiu's third wife, in Gao Xiufang and Chen Hongtian, eds., *Su Zhe ji* (Beijing: Zhonghua shuju, 1990), 418–20. Ouyang Xiu even helped a friend to publish his sister, Xie Ximeng's, collected poems, and wrote a preface to promote the collection. Ironically, however, only this "Preface to Ms. Xie [Ximeng's] Poetry" has survived—doubtless since it was from the hand of a famous male writer—and we have little idea what Xie's poetry was actually like. Ouyang's preface is in *Ouyang ji*, 292; translated by Ronald Egan in Chang and Saussy, 725–7. Perhaps more detailed study of Song dynasty anecdote and short story collections would reveal further evidence of women using poetry to build and sustain relationships. Besides the educated wives and daughters of literati, there were also, of course, the female entertainers, many of whom were literate and almost certainly exchanged song lyrics, if not *shi*, with their male admirers. See examples by one Lady Wei (fl.1050) in Chang and Saussy, 86–89. Much more evidence of women's poetry

exchanges survives from the Ming and Qing dynasties. Besides the generous selection of examples in Chang and Saussy's anthology, there is also the sustained description of a poetry club established by the female characters in Cao Xueqin's *Dream of the Red Chamber* which, though fictional, probably records similar events in the author's life and the lives of his female relatives.

14. In *Ouyang ji*, 1370. "Three years old" in the first sentence is equivalent to the traditional Chinese "four *sui*."

15. For a general study of Song and post-Song educational methods, see William Theodore de Bary and John W. Chaffee, eds., *Neo-Confucian Education: The Formative Stage* (Berkeley: University of California Press, 1989).

16. *Ouyang ji*, 61. "Book-reading."

17. The two marked phrases in this couplet both refer to assiduous study. See Chen Xin and Du Weimo, *Ouyang Xiu xuanji* (Shanghai: Guji chubanshe, 1986; repr. 1999), 198–99, n. 4.

18. For more details on the development of the examination system during the Song, including a discussion of the importance of poetry in the exams, see John W. Chaffee, *The Thorny Gates of Learning in Sung China: A Social History of Examinations* (Cambridge: Cambridge University Press, 1985, repr. 1996), 4 and 71–73.

19. Su's poem is in *Su Shi shiji*, 20–21. For Ouyang's poem, see the preceding chapter.

20. *Su Shi shiji*, 50–51, poem entitled, "Ouyang Yongshu's Supreme Joy Pavilion in Yiling County." Cf. Further exchanges between Ouyang and Su in the 1070s, in *Su Shi shiji*, 275–77, 364–65. See also three admiring poems by Su Zhe to Ouyang, in Chen and Gao, *Su Zhe ji*, 57, 68–69.

21. For Su's dazzling early career, including examples of Ouyang Xiu's enthusiastic praise of his talents, see Egan, *Word, Image, and Deed*, 3–53. Su Xun, the father of Su Shi and Su Zhe (1039–1110), had already paved the way for his sons by developing social relations with Ouyang Xiu and his colleagues in the mid 1050s, including poem exchanges. See Wang, *Selected Works*, 214–15, and for poems exchanged with Ouyang and Mei, see *Quan Songshi*, 7.4360, poem by Su Xun entitled "Ouyang Yongshu's White Rabbit," and Zhu, *Mei*, 950–51, poem by Mei entitled "Su Mingyun [Xun's] Wooden Mountain." As for another great statesman of the Northern Song, Wang Anshi, although he did not take the examinations under Ouyang's administration, Ouyang and Mei also exchanged poems with him in the 1040s and 1050s, and both gave glowing assessments of his talents, with Ouyang recommending Wang for a government post. See *Ouyang ji*,

57; Egan, *The Literary Works*, 20–21, 115–16; Liu, *Ou-yang Hsiu*, 153–54, and Chaves, *Mei Yao-ch'en*, 40–42.

22. See chapter 1, note 59. Cf. Egan, *Su Shi*, 2, esp. 46–47. Hartman, "Poetry and Politics in 1079," 15ff.

23. First couplet from "Seeing Off Scholar Jiao Qianzhi," *Ouyang ji*, 30; remaining lines from "Hot Summer Days: Presented to Masters Jiao and Xu," *Ouyang ji*, 30–31.

24. *Ouyang ji*, 36. "Seeing Off Master Xu to Mianchi."

25. Lit. "If there were a dragon gate in the world, you could visit it too." Dragon gate traditionally referred to the home of a famous scholar, to which disciples would flock.

26. An allusion to the first chapter of *Zhuangzi*, usually interpreted as a person of small attainments looking up to one of vast wisdom. See Wang Xianqian, *Zhuangzi jijie*, 2.

27. *Ouyang ji*, 235. "Grave Inscription for Mei Shengyu."

28. For examples of such evaluations, see Chaves, *Mei Yao-ch'en*, 128–30.

29. See Liu, *Ou-yang Hsiu*, 49–51, and Chaves, *Mei Yao-ch'en*, 27–28. Chaves points out that Mei was very quick to dissociate himself from Li Ding, composing a poem in which he effectively compared Li with a spoilt child, who could not enjoy a banquet himself, so he overturned the cauldron of food. Thus, as Mei demonstrated, poetry could also be used to publicize breaking off relations with others.

30. For Ouyang's attitude to religion and poetic relationships with Buddhist monks, see Liu, *Ou-yang Hsiu*, 155–72, and Egan, *The Literary Works*, 32–33, 39–40, 70, 95. Cf. several admiring poems addressed to Taoist and Buddhist recluses late in Ouyang's life, *Ouyang ji*, 62, 64–65. For Mei's views, see Chaves, *Mei Yao-ch'en*, 176–78. Mei's poems to monks and other "followers of the Dao" are too numerous to list individually: see some examples in Zhu, *Mei*, 17, 86, 150, 192, 226, 408–9, 521, 763, 949, and 990.

31. *Ouyang ji*, 25.

32. For Su Shi's attitude to Buddhism, see Beata Grant, *Mount Lu Revisited: Buddhism in the Life and Poetry of Su Shi* (Honolulu: University of Hawaii Press, 1995); for his Daoist practices, see Zhong Laiyin, *Su Shi yu daojia daojiao* (Taipei: Xuesheng shuju, 1990). For an interesting discussion of poems by Huang Tingjian influenced by Buddhist ideas, see Stuart H. Sargent, "Huang Tingjian's 'Incense of Awareness': Poems of Exchange, Poems of Enlightenment," *Journal of the American Oriental Society* 121.1 (January–March 2001): 60–71.

33. An interesting discussion of mutual influences between Late Northern Song literati interested in Buddhism and monks interested in literature is in Zhang Hongsheng, *Song shi: rongtong yu kaituo*, chapter 6. For support given by local literati-officials to Buddhism during the Song period, see also Huang Chi-chiang, "Elite and Clergy in Northern Sung Hang-chou: A Convergence of Interest," in Peter N. Gregory and Daniel A. Getz, eds. *Buddhism in the Sung* (Honolulu: University of Hawaii Press, 1999), 295–339. For religious synthesis, see Kenneth Ch'en, *Buddhism in China: A Historical Survey* (Princeton, NJ: Princeton University Press, 1964), and Gregory's introductory chapter in Gregory and Getz, 1–20.

34. See comments to this effect by Ouyang's son in *Ouyang ji*, 1369.

35. *Ouyang ji*, 800–1. "Memorial Discussing Lü Yijian."

36. *Ouyang ji*, 28. A variant title reads "In Answer to Lü Gongzhu's Poem." The West Lake mentioned in this poem was in Yingzhou. In several of the poems he composed in Yingzhou, Ouyang favorably compared the beauty of this West Lake with its more famous namesake in Hangzhou.

37. Orchid and angelica, both sweet-smelling plants, had ancient associations with worthy and talented people.

38. For more examples of poems exchanged between Ouyang and Lü Gongzhu, see *Ouyang ji*, 34, 35, 81, 393. Cf. the evidence that Ouyang's son provides of his father's magnanimity towards former enemies and his attempts to avoid continuing personal grudges: *Ouyang ji*, 1371–72.

39. For Ouyang's letters to Mei, see *Ouyang ji*, 1278–91. Mei's letters are no longer extant.

40. *Ouyang ji*, 346. "Seven Poems on Seven Friends."

41. *Ouyang ji*, 347. "Self-Portrait."

42. The two phrases in this couplet refer indirectly to receiving blessings by associating with people of great moral worth. See Chen and Du, *Ouyang Xiu xuanji*, 3–4, n. 3.

43. See *Ouyang ji*, 1279, where Ouyang, known by the group as Precocious Elder, writes to Mei Yaochen, the Poet Elder, questioning whether he should be counted as a member of the Eight Elder group, since he is still so young.

44. *Ouyang ji*, 353. For other examples of poems from the Luoyang period, see *Ouyang ji*, 1–3, 347–49; and *Mei Yaochen ji*, 27–45.

45. Ouyang refers to all his friends by their style names: Xishen was Xie Jiang (995–1039); Shilu was Yin Shu (1001–1047); Zijian was Yin Yuan

(996–1045); Yanguo was Fu Bi (1004–1083); Jidao was Wang Fu (n.d.); Zicong was Yang Yu (n.d.); Ziye was Zhang Xian (992–1039); Cigong was Sun Yanzhong (n.d.); and of course, Shengyu was Mei Yaochen.

46. Two mythical ancient sages associated with the early development of Chinese culture.

47. Xie An (320–385): a famous Jin dynasty aristocrat, known for his unbridled character.

48. The Immortal of Lang was the nickname of the mid-Tang poet Jia Dao (c. 793–865), known for his painstaking craftsmanship.

49. Zhang Xu (c. 658–748): renowned Tang calligrapher, best known for his "wild cursive" script, supposedly written when he was drunk.

50. For twelve poems on Mount Song by Ouyang, see *Ouyang ji*, 347–48; for Mei's echoing poems, see Zhu, *Mei*, 42–45.

51. *Ouyang ji*, 353.

52. For a letter by Xie Jiang describing a further trip to Mount Song, and Mei Yaochen's answering poem, see the appendix to *Ouyang ji*, 1381–83. Cf. other poems and recollections of Luoyang by Mei translated in Chaves, 5–9.

53. *Ouyang ji*, 299–300. "Preface to Poems Composed and Answered in the Ministry of Rites."

54. See, for example, the selection of parting poems in Stephen Owen, *An Anthology of Chinese Literature*, 374–88. See also Yoshikawa, 28–35, for the contrast in mood between Tang and Song poetry.

55. Yoshikawa, 5–6, 24–28.

56. For evidence supporting this view, see chapter 4, Poetry as Therapy.

57. *Ouyang ji*, 93.

58. Zhu, *Mei*, 939, poem entitled "Seeing Off Scholar Fang Yun After He Failed the Examination," dated by Zhu to 1057. Another such poem is found on the same page, addressed to one of Mei's nephews.

59. The word that I translate "selected" (*deng*) was also used to refer to candidates who passed the examination.

60. Mengzhu: name of an ancient marshy lake, near present Shangqiu, Henan Province.

61. *Ouyang ji*, 35. This poem is translated in chapter 4.

62. Zhu, *Mei*, 257.

63. I assume Mei is referring to rank sea mists that obscure the sun and moon, causing people to catch chills.

64. For a reconstruction of the Middle Chinese pronunciation of this rhyme category, based on the *Guangyun*, see Hugh Stimson, *The Jongyuan In Yunn: A Guide to Old Mandarin Pronunciation* (New Haven, CT: Yale University Press, 1966), 205–24, under column headed MC.

65. *Ouyang ji*, 58.

66. Mei Sheng (d. 145 BC): well-known Han prose-poem writer and statesman. Zou Yang (fl.195–168): another famous Han dynasty literary figure. Ouyang here praises Qian Weiyan, Governor of Henan, for gathering so many talented young scholars in Luoyang, just as the Han Prince of Wu (r. 195–154) invited literary talents to make his court cultured and to give political advice. See Michael Loewe, *A Biographical Dictionary of the Qin, Former Han and Xin Periods (221 BC–AD 24)* (Leiden: Brill, 2000), 435–56, 753–54.

67. Holding the nose while chanting gave a sonorous tone to the poem.

68. That is, Mei was still poor, and low in status.

69. Ouyang claims that Mei was too poor to afford a full day's rice, despite his outstanding writing talent. Obviously, this is an exaggeration, since Mei became a middle-ranking central government official by the mid-1050s, hardly a subsistence position.

70. *Ouyang ji*, 60–1. Poem entitled "Moved by the Two Masters," written some time between 1060 and 1063.

71. *Ouyang ji*, 7. "Weeping for Manqing." Manqing was Shi Yannian's style name.

72. Literally "dragons and fish," but most fish don't coil.

73. Literally "Yan and Yu": Yan Zhenqing (709–785) and Yu Shinan (558–638), two outstanding calligraphers of the Tang period.

CHAPTER FOUR. POETRY AS THERAPY

1. For two interesting collections of essays on therapeutic uses of poetry in the West, see J. J. Leedy, ed., *Poetry Therapy* (Philadelphia & Toronto: J. B. Lippincott, 1969), and Morris R. Morrison, ed., *Poetry as Therapy* (New York: Human Sciences Press, 1987).

2. For a more extended definition of *qi*, including many compound words in which it appears, see Manfred Porkert, *The Theoretical Foundations of Chinese Medicine* (Cambridge, MA and London: Massachusetts

Institute of Technology Press, 1974, repr. 1980), 167–176, especially 173ff. A less rigorous, but more accessible, summary of Chinese medical theory, including an account of its historical development, is Manfred Porkert and Christian Ullmann *Chinese Medicine*, trans. Mark Howson (New York: William Morrow, 1982).

3. As yet, I have not come across any Chinese secondary sources directly relating poetry to healing, though there have been articles on the therapeutic effects of practicing calligraphy, and many Chinese studies, noted later, discuss the benefits of poetry for releasing emotional tension. For calligraphy, see the discussion and references in Jean Francois Billeter, *The Chinese Art of Writing* (Geneva: Editions d'Art Albert Skira, 1990), 168–73, 198. A fascinating study by John Hay has also shown how collecting and painting rocks, another favourite hobby of Northern Song literati, related to the circulation of vital energy (*qi*) that rocks were thought to contain. Therapeutic effects could be felt by those who contemplated and handled the rocks. See Hay, *Kernels of Enery, Bones of Earth: The Rock in Chinese Art* (New York: China Institute in America, 1985). For a broader discussion of East Asian cultural practices and their relation to the body-mind, see also Yuasa Yasuo, trans., Shigenori Nagatomo and Monte S. Hull, *The Body, Self-Cultivation and* Ki-*Energy* (Albany: State University of New York Press, 1993).

4. Porkert, *The Theoretical Foundations*, 167–76, especially 173ff.

5. Porkert, *The Theoretical Foundations*, 173–74; *Chinese Medicine*, 84.

6. Porkert, *Chinese Medicine*, 173–77.

7. Ibid.

8. See the fascinating paper entitled "Emotional Countertherapy" in Nathan Sivin, *Medicine, Philosophy and Religion in Ancient China: Researches and Reflections* (Brookfield, VT: Variorum, 1995).

9. *Ouyang ji*, 290–91. The *gong* mode referred to in the text was the first of five musical modes based on the pentatonic Chinese scale.

10. I discuss these events in more detail in chapter 1, and in the final section of the present chapter.

11. *Ouyang ji*, 531, 532. From colophon entitled "Written at the End of a Manuscript by Mei Shengyu."

12. "Shoot" could also be understood in a figurative way as "descendant."

13. For further examples of the supposed healing and life-prolonging effects of Chinese calligraphy, see Billeter, *The Chinese Art of Writing*, 168–73, 198.

14. *Ouyang ji*, 1044.

15. For the full text of this poem, see Zhu, *Mei*, 1071. Zhu dates the poem to 1059. For Ouyang Xiu's calligraphy comments and exercises, see *Ouyang ji*, 1043–52.

16. As the modern scholar Wang Shuizhao notes, Mei Yaochen had a habit of rewriting his friends' prose pieces, and even their letters, in the form of poems. See this poem and other examples partially quoted in Wang Shuizhao, "Bei-Song Luoyang wenren jituan yu Song shi xinmao de yunyu," in Wang, *Selected Works*, 174–97, especially 180.

17. For Ouyang and Mei's views on calligraphy, and several examples of their poems about calligraphic tools, with an emphasis on the therapeutic effects of such poems, see my "Plucking Hairs to Save the World? Northern Song Poets on Their Writing Tools," unpublished paper presented at Association for Asian Studies Annual Meeting, San Diego, 2000. Cf. Ronald Egan, "Ou-yang Hsiu and Su Shih on Calligraphy," *Harvard Journal of Asiatic Studies* 49.2 (1989): 365–419.

18. From Hu Zi, *Tiaoxi yuyin conghua* (Beijing: Renmin wenxue, 1981), 29: 201–2. Ouyang's poem on Mount Lu is in *Ouyang ji*, 35–36. I translate it later in this chapter.

19. See *Ouyang ji*, 535, from a colophon entitled "Written at the End of Mei Shengyu's Poem on the River-Pig Fish."

20. For a comprehensive study of the different meanings of the concept of *qi* as it appears in Chinese literary criticism, see Di Huanning, *Qishi lun* (Beijing: Minzu chubanshe, 2002).

21. From Han Yu's "Letter Responding to Li Ao," quoted in Guo Shaoyu, "Zhongguo wenxue piping shang zhi 'shen' 'qi' shuo," *Xiaoshuo yuebao* 19 (1929): 129. For an English discussion of the relation between *qi* and literature in traditional China, which includes a slightly different translation of this passage, see David Pollard, "*Ch'i* in Chinese Literary Theory," in Adele Rickett, ed., *Chinese Approaches to Literature from Confucius to Liang Ch'i-ch'ao* (Princeton, NJ: Princeton University Press, 1978), 43–66, especially 45–50. For Han Yu's influence on Ouyang Xiu and contemporaries, see chapter 5, and Egan, *The Literary Works*, 14–17, 20, 104–5.

22. From Ouyang's "Grave Inscription for Mei Shengyu," in *Ouyang ji*, 235.

23. See "Shi Manqing shiji xu," in *Su Shunqin ji*, 708–9.

24. See Huang Tingjian's "Shu Wang Zhizai Jushan zayong hou" (Written After Wang Zhizai's Miscellaneous Verses on Mount Ju), quoted in Han Jingtai, "*Lun Song shi xiequ*," 141.

25. From Mou Xian's "Yu Haowen shigao xu," (Preface to Yu Haowen's Poetry Manuscript), quoted in Zhou Yukai, *Songdai shixue tonglun*, 64–65.

26. Zhou Yukai, *Songdai shixue*, 62–73.

27. Zhou Yukai, *Songdai shixue*, 67.

28. *Ouyang ji*, 35–6. Compare the similar ancient and rough style of the poem mentioned by Ouyang Xiu in connection with healing: Mei's "Hearing A Guest at Fan Raozhou's Party Talk of Eating the River-Pig Fish," translated in chapter 1.

29. That is, Daoist recluses and Buddhist monks.

30. "Many-faceted," or "with many joints," literally means a tree having many knots in the trunk, but was later extended to refer to a person whose character has numerous talents.

31. "Dark robes" were worn by low-ranking officials.

32. This poem shares the same rhyme category as a poem by Han Yu that Ouyang once cited to illustrate Han's skill at using difficult or narrow rhymes. See *Ouyang ji*, 1040–41.

33. See Porkert, *Chinese Medicine*, 240, for the tendency of traditional Chinese medical treatise writers to attribute their techniques and theories to semi-mythical, ancient doctors or rulers like the Yellow Emperor, in order to give them more authority. This tendency may seem highly illogical to us today, but was accepted by Song scholars in all areas of rational inquiry. For example, in his preface to the Daoist text entitled *Huangting jing*, Ouyang argued that the views of the Wei-Jin Period writers on prolonging life, though acceptable in places, could not compare to the wisdom of Confucius' disciple Yan Hui and the mythical Great Emperor Yu: see *Ouyang ji*, 471. Partial translation and discussion in my "Competing with Creative Transformation," 333–34.

34. Yoshikawa, 24–28.

35. For a fuller discussion of this point, see my "Mundane Transcendence: Dealing with the Everyday in the Poetry of Ouyang Xiu," 99–129.

36. *Ouyang ji*, 18–19. I use the variant title given for the poem: the original character was *bai* 百 ("one hundred") rather than *bai* 柏 ("cypress").

37. Zhu, *Mei*, 896.

38. Traditionally a white rabbit was supposed to live on the moon, next to an osmanthus tree, grinding an elixir of immortality for the moon-

goddess Chang'e and other immortals who lived there. Mei refers to this legend again in lines 9–10.

39. Ouyang Xiu was governor of Chuzhou from 1045 to 1048, during his second exile.

40. Literally "Mount Penglai," a mythical island in the Eastern Ocean where immortals supposedly dwelt. Here Mei uses it as a tongue-in-cheek way of referring to the Hanlin Academy in the Northern Song capital, to which Ouyang was promoted in the mid-1050s. Compared with his previous provincial postings, this position seems Heavenly.

41. *Ouyang ji*, 28.

42. When the Big Dipper constellation slants down in the sky, it is a sign that morning is coming.

43. For further translations of many strange poems by Ouyang Xiu, see my "Mundane Transcendence," *passim*. For Mei Yaochen, see Chaves, *Mei Yao-ch'en*, 178–218. Cf. Egan's slightly different categorization along with examples in *The Literary Works*, 85–89 (pure works), and 99–112 (dynamic and strange works).

44. *Ouyang ji*, 56. Shengyu was Mei Yaochen's style name. The poem by Mei that Ouyang is responding to is no longer extant.

45. I cannot find Ouyang's term "hairy fish" (*maoyu*) in any reference work, though several mention "hairy shrimp" (*maoxia*), hence my translation. As for "antler minnows," Ouyang's original term is "deers' antlers" (*lujiao*), which is defined merely as "a small variety of fish" in most reference works. The name suggests that the fish has protruding tentacles of some sort.

46. The reference to sharp whiskers, or tusks, seems to indicate a walrus rather than a whale, though the rest of the description is much more whale-like.

47. Or "not understandable in only one way."

48. An original note explains that people in the capital didn't know of this fish until a provincial official sent some up from the coast, and Mei Yaochen managed to obtain a portion. See also Ouyang's letter to Mei, dated 1057, in which it is clear that it was Ouyang who gave Mei the fish (*Ouyang ji*, 56, 1288).

49. Though both were pardoned just before they died, neither made it back to the capital. This high mortality rate is less surprising when we consider the relatively unhygienic living conditions of the time, especially in remote regions.

50. See *Ouyang ji*, 1284, letter dated 1046.

51. See Ouyang Xiu's comment about Su Shunqin, who in the immediate aftermath of his exile "hid himself and did not want to meet anyone, afraid of possible slanderous attacks." *Ouyang ji*, 1283, letter to Mei Yaochen dated 1044.

52. Again see numerous references in Ouyang's letters to poems that he received from Mei and other friends in the first three years of his second exile: *Ouyang ji*, 1283–84.

53. For Mei's prolific output, see Chaves, *Mei Yao-ch'en*, 48–49.

54. See Zhu, *Mei*, 251, 257, 260. "Seeing Off Su Zimei" is translated in the preceding chapter. For Su's responses, see *Su Shunqin ji*, 150–52, 160.

55. *Ouyang ji*, 12.

56. A reference to Ouyang's exile which, he claims sardonically, resulted from too much good fortune in his previous official career.

57. Literally, "frequently removing your clothes," a figure of speech implying relaxation.

58. *Ouyang ji*, 15. The subtitle of this poem is "Sent to Zimei [i.e. Su Shunqin]". Mei's original poem on the *pan* peach is not extant.

59. *Ouyang ji*, 1284. The poems by Mei that Ouyang mentions are all responses to Ouyang's own previous poems. Several of the letters on this and the preceding page of *Ouyang ji* include similar upbeat comments and references to the joys and consolations of exchanging poems. See also a letter dating from Ouyang's previous exile in 1038, in which he talks of Mei's poetry as able to "clear away my gloom and soothe my longing to meet up with you. Among the gifts of an old friend, none can surpass [poems]." *Ouyang ji*, 1281.

60. For some translations of Ouyang's Drunken Old Man poems and his famous prose record describing the Pavilion of the Drunken Old Man that he had built in Chuzhou, see Egan, *The Literary Works*, 85, 88–89, 215–17.

61. See *Ouyang ji*, 1283, letter to Mei Yaochen dated 1044.

62. *Ouyang ji*, 20. From Ouyang's poem entitled "Green Waves Pavilion," written to commemorate Su's newly built residence in Suzhou in 1047. For a detailed analysis of this poem, and Su's prose record and poetry about the Pavilion, see my "Competing with Creative Transformation," 186–95.

63. *Ouyang ji*, 27. Decorative inkstone screens, often made from strange-colored or odd-shaped rocks, were used by literati to prevent ink splashing onto their writing paper from the inkstone (or inkwell). Ouyang describes this particular stone further in a brief preface to the poem: see *Ouyang ji*, 474.

64. Ibid.

65. Traditionally the moon was believed to reside in a cave beneath the Eastern Sea during the day, only emerging from there at night.

66. One *zhang* being equivalent to about 3 metres.

67. "Two Fires" refers to the sun and moon.

68. The mirror is the round, white moon form in the stone, surrounded by the violet (jade) stone, like a "compact box." See prose description at *Ouyang ji*, 474.

69. Toad, osmanthus, and rabbit were supposedly all found on the moon.

70. Zhang Jingshan (n.d.), Ouyang's friend and fellow collector.

71. Three Heavenly Bodies refers to the sun, moon and stars.

72. In other words, Su is like a master craftsman; Ouyang is his apprentice. He hopes that Su will guide him by writing a suitable poem for the screen.

73. See poem in *Su Shunqin ji*, 276–77.

74. *Su Shunqin ji*, 276.

75. See Ouyang's grave inscription for Su in *Ouyang ji*, 221, final column.

76. Egan notes this anti-poetry view among early Song practitioners of ancient-style prose, such as Mu Xiu (979–1032), Shi Jie (1005–45), Liu Kai (c. 968–?) and Yin Shu (1001–1047): *The Literary Works*, 81. Egan also shows that some later thinkers, such as Cheng Yi, considered even prose composition to be potentially harmful when the writer focused too much on perfecting literary style rather than on practicing and promulgating moral self-cultivation (ibid. 22–23).

77. Quoted in Liu, *Ou-yang Hsiu*, 98. Liu notes that actually Ouyang's behaviour was quite normal among Northern Song statesmen and officials.

78. Egan, *The Literary Works*, 80–1.

79. *Ouyang ji*, 43. I translate this poem in full, along with a matching work by Mei, in chapter 2.

80. *Ouyang ji*, 26. Translated in a slightly different way by Egan, *The Literary Works*, 81. We should read Ouyang's statement here in the context of the rest of the poem: he argued that without becoming a scholar-official, it was pointless for the monk to study poetry (especially the *Classic of Poetry*), since poetry should help people fulfill their social functions better, but to remain as a Buddhist monk was to follow an inherently anti-social path. He ended the poem with a reference to Han Yu, who once persuaded a monk to return to society and become an official. Hence the poem was first of all a criticism of Buddhism rather than of poetry, and second, an affirmation of the *social function* of poetry, as opposed to versifying merely for private enjoyment, a point which I expand upon below.

81. *Mei Yaochen ji*, 562.

CHAPTER FIVE. POEMS PROMOTING ANCIENT CULTURE

1. For examples of such lineages from the Tang and Northern Song periods, see Guo Shaoyu, *Zhongguo wenxue piping shi*, 138–42, 146–49.

2. *Ouyang ji*, 532. From prose piece "Written at the End of a Manuscript by Mei Shengyu."

3. "Harvest songs" were songs composed by music masters at ancient imperial sacrifices or great audiences; "Purifying the [Ancestral] Temple" is the title of the first of the "Lauds of Zhou" in the *Classic of Poetry*. I assume that here Ouyang is referring to the whole section of "Lauds" in the *Classic*. The reference to poems of the feudal states presumably refers to the "Airs of the States" section of the *Classic of Poetry*.

4. For more on Ouyang's attitude to the *Classic of Poetry*, as revealed in his commentary on the text, see Steven van Zoeren, *Poetry and Personality: Reading, Exegesis, and Hermeneutics in Traditional China* (Stanford, CA: Stanford University Press, 1991), 159–89. For a punctuated edition of Ouyang's commentary on the *Classic* with useful introductory materials and comparisons with Zhu Xi's commentary, see Pei Puxian, *Ouyang Xiu 'Shi benyi' yanjiu* (Taipei: Dongda tushu youxian gongsi, 1981).

5. See also Ouyang's comparison of the lighthearted poems composed by himself and his colleagues during the 1057 civil service exams with the *Classic of Poetry*, quoted in chapter 2.

6. Ouyang's *Remarks on Poetry* are in *Ouyang ji*, 1035–41. There is one entry on Du Fu, but it emphasises the neglect of Du's poetry. Another two entries name Li Bai and Du Fu in passing, yet without quoting their poems. See *Ouyang ji*, 1036, 1037–38. For an excellent detailed survey of Mid-Tang and early Song influences on Mei and Ouyang, see Chaves, *Mei Yao-ch'en*, chapter 3.

7. See my extended discussion of Ouyang's various comments on poetry in "Competing with Creative Transformation," 321–91, especially 332ff. Cf. Owen, *Readings in Chinese Literary Thought*, 359–91, which translates many passages from Ouyang's *Remarks on Poetry*.

8. *Ouyang ji*, 1044, from his *Calligraphic Jottings*. Zhang Jian tries to argue that in fact Ouyang thought no less of Du Fu's poetry than of Li Bai's, but he provides little concrete evidence for his assertions. See Zhang Jian, *Ouyang Xiu zhi shiwen ji wenxue pinglun* (Taiwan: Shangwu, 1973), 51; Hawes, "Competing with Creative Transformation," 343 n. 66.

9. For flagged imitations of Mid-Tang poets by Ouyang and Mei, see *Ouyang ji*, 23, 26, 37, 45, 77; *Mei Yaochen ji*, 65, 410, 497–500, 930.

10. *Ouyang ji*, 77. For excellent analysis of the Yuanhe period style, including discussion of Han Yu and Meng Jiao's linked verses, see Owen, *The Poetry of Meng Chiao and Han Yu*, 116–36.

11. Ouyang adopts the metaphor of attacking forces to refer to the spring storm, hence my use of the third-person plural "they."

12. *Yin*: the polar cosmic force associated with cold, winter, water and the night.

13. "Five Mountains" probably indicates Mounts Tai, Hua, two Mount Hengs, and Song, peaks representing east, west, north, south and central China respectively. The Nine Cauldrons were bronze vessels supposedly forged by the mythical Emperor Yu (founder of the first Chinese dynasty, the Xia) to represent each of the Nine Regions of the Empire.

14. Ghostly flames: the phosphorescent lights emitted by decomposing corpses left above ground. Usually in poetry these flames indicated the aftermath of a real battle, but here Ouyang imagines them in his figurative description of the "battle" between *yin* and *yang*.

15. Perhaps the "barbarian troops" line refers to an eclipse of the moon, or simply clouds partially obscuring it. As for "crocodile's splash," literally "crocodile's cry," the traditional belief was that crocodiles would make noise before heavy rain.

16. Ouyang is afraid that due to his slovenly official dress, Heaven will punish him in the storm, hence he must "adjust his hatstrings" (i.e., tidy himself up).

17. For a translation of "Fire in the Luhun Mountains," see Owen, *The Poetry of Meng Chiao and Han Yu*.

18. *Ouyang ji*, 15. Excerpt from "On Reading the *Pan* Peach Poem."

19. Chaves, *The Literary Works*, 81–86.

20. Chaves, *The Literary Works*, 82. In the quotation I have altered names in Wade-Giles to *pinyin*.

21. The first poem that Chaves cites is Mei Yaochen's "Sent to Yongshu after We Parted," full text in Zhu, *Mei*, 468, dated by Zhu to 1048; the second poem is "Matching the Rhymes of Yongshu's 'Clear-Heart Hall Paper, Answering Liu Yuanfu,'" in Zhu, *Mei*, 800, dated 1055.

22. Full text in Zhu, *Mei*, 524–5.

23. *Ouyang ji*, 1040–1. Han Yu's poem is in Qian Zhonglian, *Han Changli shi*, 63–71. Eighteenth Zhang was the poet Zhang Ji. Cf. English translation in Owen, *The Poetry of Meng Chiao and Han Yu*, 52–53.

24. *Ouyang ji*, 35–6. Translated in chapter 4.

25. For an interesting discussion of this technique as used by Su Shi, see Alfreda Murck's "Misty River, Layered Peaks."

26. *Ouyang ji*, 1040–1. For Han Yu's use of archaic rhymes, see Qian Zhonglian, 89–90 nn. 23 and 25; 93 n. 62; and 96–8.

27. Obviously there are brief references to numerous other poets scattered through Ouyang's and Mei's writings. For further examples, see Chaves, *Mei Yao-ch'en*, 69–107, and Zhang Jian, 49–54. Yet Li Bai, Tao Yuanming and, to a lesser extent, Ruan Ji were the poets whom Northern Song literati in Ouyang Xiu's circle most frequently emulated and praised in their writings besides Han Yu's contemporaries.

28. Quoted in Guo Shaoyu, "*Zhongguo wenxue pipingshi shang zhi 'shen' 'qi' shuo*," 127.

29. See Zhu Jincheng and Qu Tuiyuan, eds., *Li Bai shi ji jiaozhu* (Shanghai: Guji chubanshe, 1980), 91–187.

30. Egan, *The Literary Works*, 99–100. Egan translates the poem. In quoting Egan, I have altered Li's name to *pinyin*. I use the modern mainland Chinese pronunciation of Li Bai, rather than Western sinologists' hybrid version, Li Bo (or Li Po in Wade-Giles).

31. Quoted in Hu Zi, *Tiaoxi yuyin conghua*, 200. Egan (*The Literary Works*, 115–6) translates this poem, entitled "Song of Mingfei, Answering a Poem by Wang Jiefu [i.e., Wang Anshi]." In the same passage, Ouyang also compared his poem "Lu Mountain High!" to Li Bai's poetry, claiming that Li was the only poet who could have matched it. As the anecdote states, normally Ouyang did not boast of his writing talent, but on this occasion he was rather drunk.

32. Chaves, *Mei Yao-ch'en*, 116. Quoting from Mei's poem "Answering [Song] Zhongdao's Poem Sent while He Was Feeling a Little Sick," full text in Zhu, *Mei*, 293. Cf. Chaves, 101–7.

33. Chaves, *Mei Yao-ch'en*, 116, 120.

34. Chaves, *Mei Yao-ch'en*, 80, 114.

35. Chaves, *Mei Yao-ch'en*, 115, 120.

36. Chaves, *Mei Yao-ch'en*, 124, 133.

37. Egan, *The Literary Works*, 106.

38. *Ouyang ji*, 1035–41. Cf. my discussion of this use of complementary pairs, with several translated examples from Ouyang's *Remarks*, in "Competing with Creative Transformation," 370–72.

39. *Ouyang ji*, 1037–78.

40. *Ouyang ji*, 1038.

41. For some statistics comparing the numbers of Tang and Song poems on such objects, see Stuart Sargent, "Poetry of Awareness, Poetry of Exchange," 1–2.

42. In *Ouyang ji*, 358. See also a shorter work on the same object entitled "Ancient Tile Inkstone" (*Ouyang ji*, 359). Jingshan was the style name of Xie Bochu, a young scholar whom Ouyang befriended during his first exile in Yiling in the mid-1030s.

43. According to the commentator in Gao Buying, ed., *Tang Song shi juyao* (Beijing: Zhonghua shuju, 1959), 323, there are various references in the official histories to the Han (206 BC–AD 220) as a dynasty of fire, and to the "scorching heat" of this fire dispersing after four hundred years. In the first two lines of this poem, I have added Han and Wei for the sake of clarity.

44. "Come from the high road" is a paraphrase of *dang tu gao*, literally "higher on the road," or alternatively, "blocking the road with its height." According to Gao, *Tang Song shi juyao*, 323, this phrase is part of an obscure riddle prophecy recorded in the *Chronicle of Wei Kingdom*, predicting that Wei would overthrow the Han dynasty.

45. Based on the rest of the poem, I interpret the subject here to be Cao Cao. Wen and Jing were two early Han emperors whose virtue supposedly placed the Han dynasty on a strong footing, allowing it to last for several centuries.

46. Dong Zhuo (d. AD 192) overthrew Emperor Shao in AD 189 and placed a puppet ruler, Emperor Xian (r. 190–220) on the throne. Lü Bu (d. 198), after working with Dong Zhuo, betrayed and murdered him in 192. The other two men mentioned in line 7, Li Jue and Guo Fan, formed a loose coalition and seized power in the new capital, Chang'an, after Dong Zhuo's death. Through political misjudgment, Li and Guo

allowed the Emperor to return east to Luoyang, the former capital, in 195, where Cao Cao captured him the following year. In line 8, Yuan Shao (d. 202) was a strong regional leader defeated by Cao Cao at Guandu in 200. Shao's cousin, Yuan Shu (d. 200), was actually a long-term enemy: the two cousins had struggled for supremacy on the eastern side of the Empire until Cao Cao decisively defeated Shu in 197. Later, Liu Bei (161–223) and Sun Quan (182–252) allied to defeat Cao Cao at Chibi ("Red Cliff") in 208, destroying Cao's hope of unifying the Empire under his control.

47. Locusts are clearly pests: it is possible that Ouyang is referring to Cao Cao's enemies in the other two of the Three Kingdoms, Wu and Shu-Han, whose successors continued to plague Wei with raids and campaigns. Wei never managed to unify the empire. Cao Cao himself died in 220 and was succeeded by his son Cao Pi.

48. According to the *Chronicle of Wei Kingdom*, Cao Pi forced the last emperor of the Han to abdicate in favor of himself. In the edict recording the event, the Han emperor declared that they were emulating the abdication of the mythical sage Emperor Yao in favor of the equally sage-like rulers Shun and Yu. For a translation of this episode from a slightly different source, see Achilles Fang, *The Chronicle of the Three Kingdoms (220–265): Chapters 69–78 from the Tzu Chih T'ung Chien of Ssu-ma Kuang* (Cambridge, MA: Harvard University Press, 1952), 37 n. 35.1. Fang notes that the Han Emperor also gave his two daughters to be Cao Pi's wives, emulating Yao's presentation of his two daughters to Shun. However, Cao was already married, unlike Shun, and had a notoriously large harem. See Fang, 37, 40 n. 38.

49. "Trough" (*cao* 槽) is pronounced identically to the Cao family surname (曹). The "three horses" (*san ma* 三馬) possibly refer to the Si*ma* 司馬 family, who usurped the Wei Kingdom and set up the Jin Dynasty in AD 265. Support for this interpretation comes from the passage in the *Jinshu*—"three horses eat together from one trough"—which Ouyang quotes almost verbatim in this line, and which was supposed to have been a dream vision about Sima Yi, posthumously known as Emperor Xuan of Jin, that Cao Cao had before his death. See Fang, *Jinshu*, Xuandi ji ("Annals of Emperor Xuan"), 1.20. Another possibility is that the single "trough" refers to the Empire, and "three horses" are the Three Kingdoms who continued to struggle for it in the face of Cao Cao and Cao Pi's efforts at unification.

50. Lines 13–16 referred to Cao Pi; here, the subject is once more Cao Cao in the days of his prime.

51. This line literally reads: "Zhou had destroyed Fang and Shao; Yao had lost Gao." Since this is virtually impenetrable, I have chosen to

paraphrase. The allusions in the first clause are apparently to Fang Shu and Shao Bohu (also known as Duke Mu of Shao), semi-mythical ministers who loyally served King Xuan (c. 827–782 BC) at the beginning of the Zhou dynasty, and are mentioned briefly in the *Classic of Poetry*. The final three words refer to Emperor Yao and his trusted minister Gao [Yao], supposedly the creator of laws and punishments. See *Tang Song shi juyao*, 324. I take the line to mean that after all his battles and political maneuvers, Cao Cao no longer had any trustworthy advisors and ministers left to guide his rule, hence Wei Kingdom could not last very long.

52. "Tomb" in the preceding line is actually "Western tomb," the place where Cao Cao was buried. Cao Cao apparently told his former concubines (the dancers in line 24) to stay in Bronze Sparrow Tower and continue dancing for him after his death, and on certain days to look towards his grave. The Tower was decorated with ornate tapestries. See *Tang Song shi juyao*, 324–5.

53. I haven't found a specific reference to swords made in Lu (around present Shandong Province), but Ouyang was a collector of antique weapons, and composed a poem on an ancient Japanese sword. See *Ouyang ji*, 372; and full translation by Burton Watson in Yoshikawa, 10–12.

54. Chaves translates and discusses the "Poem on a Crossbow Trigger" in *Mei Yao-ch'en*, 213–15. Chaves' whole section on "Antiquities and Works of Art" (199–218) provides much interesting information on the kinds of objects that Northern Song literati collected, with several translations of poems by Mei and others.

55. Zhu, *Mei*, 1057–58. Zhou Yafu (d. 143 BC), a famous Han general, helped to pacify both internal rebellions and external incursions by Xiongnu invaders. Helian Bobo (r. AD 407–425), descended from Xiongnu peoples, ruled Xia Kingdom, one of sixteen northern states established during the Six Dynasties period. Cf. a similar dual focus on objects and their collectors in another poem by Mei describing two ancient knife-coins, in Zhu, *Mei*, 635; translated in Chaves, *Mei Yao-ch'en*, 210–11.

56. Phoenix Pool refers to the Secretariat, where Liu Chang worked; Tianlu Pavilion was the name of the Imperial Library in the Han, here indicating that Jiang and Chen were eminent scholars.

57. This was the official title of Zhou Yafu, whom Mei notes in the following line was referred to in some texts as Zhou Efu. See Xia Jingguan, *Mei Yaochen shi*, 43.

58. The poem ends with Mei's rather conventional reflections on how quickly time passes and how the events of today soon become yesterday's memories.

59. This hall was part of the royal palace of Li Yu, last ruler of the Southern Tang kingdom (937–975), defeated during the Song reunification.

60. Zhu, *Mei*, 156. Zhu Dongrun dates the poem to 1040 based on internal evidence. Yongshu was Ouyang Xiu's style name.

61. Zishan was the style name of Yu Xin (513–581), who composed a famous "Rhapsody Mourning for Jiangnan" (*Ai Jiangnan fu*). The gift of Clear Heart paper reminds Mei first of the sadness of Li Yu, who briefly ruled the area of Jiangnan before losing his kingdom to the Song dynasty (see line 9 of Mei's poem), and who spent the rest of his life composing melancholy songs remembering the past. But the paper then brings to mind Yu Xin's earlier lament on the destruction of Jiangnan, implying that the cycles of growth and decay repeat themselves endlessly. Of course, Mei's noble sadness seems somewhat incongruous when placed within the domestic setting of the penultimate couplet!

62. *Ouyang ji*, 38. Poem entitled "Matching Liu Yuanfu's 'Clear Heart Paper,'" dated 1055. Cf. alternative translation of complete poem by Stephen Owen, *An Anthology of Chinese Literature*, 686.

63. *Ouyang ji*, 59–60. Poem title: "Fifteen Years after I Rebuilt the Returning Geese Pavilion at Huazhou, Mei Gongyi [i.e., Mei Zhi] Went to Be Governor of this Region; He Obtained My Poem and Carved It on Stone, Also Sending Me a Seven-Syllable Poem, Which I Now Answer" (dated 1056).

64. For some of these prose-writing activities, see Yoshikawa, 11, 22; and for detailed descriptions of important works of scholarship by Song writers, see Yves Hervouet, ed., *A Sung Bibliography (Bibliographie des Sung)* (Hong Kong: Chinese University Press, 1978).

65. From Ouyang's *Remarks on Poetry*, in *Ouyang ji*, 1038. Wang Jian, a Mid-Tang poet and friend of Zhang Ji, was known for poetry of social criticism. Ouyang does not mention this aspect here, concentrating instead on his "Palace Lyrics." Chinese texts of these works are found in *Wang Jian shi ji* (Shanghai: Zhonghua shuju, 1959), 88–96.

66. From no. 60 of Wang's "Palace Lyrics," in *Wang Jian shi ji*, 92.

67. References, respectively, are to Du Fu, "Ballad on Watching Great Aunt Gongsun's Singing Girl Dancing with Swords," in William Hong, ed., *Du shi yinde* (Taipei repr. of Harvard-Yenching Institute Sinological Index Series: Supplement 14, 1966), vol. 2, 192; Bai Juyi, "Listening to Cao Gang's *Pipa*, Also Shown to Zhonglian," in *Bai Xiangshan ji*, vol. 4, *juan* 56, 97–98; and Liu Yuxi (772–842), "Given to the Singer Mi Jiarong," in *Quan Tang shi* 11.4116–4117 (*juan* 365).

CHAPTER SIX. POETRY AS HUMANIZATION OF NATURE

1. Yoshikawa, 45.

2. Yoshikawa, 6–8, 28–34.

3. For wit and humor in Northern Song poetry, see chapter 2 and my "Mundane Transcendence."

4. See, for example, Kang I-Sun Chang's study of Xie Lingyun's craft in *Six Dynasties Poetry* (Princeton, NJ: Princeton University Press, 1986); see also Stephen Owen's discussion of Wang Wei entitled "The Artifice of Simplicity," in *The Great Age of Chinese Poetry* (New Haven, CT: Yale University Press, 1981).

5. Of course, as Yoshikawa himself notes, some earlier poets had already paved the way for this expansion of subject matter, most notably Du Fu and the circle of poets around Han Yu in the Mid-Tang. Yoshikawa, 12, 29, 64–65.

6. For a summary of Han cosmology, especially Dong Zhongshu's correlation theory, see Fung Yu-lan, *A History of Chinese Philosophy*, vol. 2, trans. Derk Bodde [hereafter Fung Yu-lan] (Princeton, NJ: Princeton University Press, 1953), 7–87. Joseph Needham also deals with Han correlational theory in some detail, in *Science and Civilisation in China*, vol. 2, History of Scientific Thought (Cambridge: Cambridge University Press, 1956), 216–345.

7. *Ouyang ji*, 68, 81, 105, 386; Zhu, *Mei*, 139, 554, 709. See also Liu, *Ou-yang Hsiu*, 155ff., for further discussion of these practices.

8. *Ouyang ji*, 420–3. In various other writings, Ouyang expressed even more clearly his skepticism about any human ability to influence Heaven and the natural order through words alone. See examples cited in Liu, *Ou-yang Hsiu*, 155–6.

9. In *Ouyang ji*, 351. Gong County was in the region of present Central Henan Province, on the south bank of the Yellow River. I translate the full poem in my "Competing with Creative Transformation," 303–6.

10. Hua refers to the region of Huazhou and its environs, in present Hua County, Henan Province, facing the former course of the Yellow River to the north.

11. *Ouyang ji*, 351.

12. *Ouyang ji*, 363, lines 9–16 of poem entitled "Song Rejoicing at Snow in Military Commissioner Yan's Western Garden," dated 1041.

13. *Ouyang ji*, 363 lines 1–8, 29–32 of the same poem.

14. The Five Phases, or Elements (*wu xing*) were water, earth, metal, fire and wood. According to Han correlation theory, every object in the world was supposedly formed from a particular combination or interaction of the five. If the normal balance of the Five Phases was disrupted, unusual climatic phenomena and other inauspicious signs would result.

15. The "host" was Yan Shu, the Military Commissioner Yan of the title, whose garden Ouyang was visiting. "For now" means now that the Emperor had successfully prayed for snow. Ouyang argues that even though the climate has returned to normal, the border campaign must still be concluded swiftly to prevent the common soldiers from suffering further. Reportedly, Yan Shu was very offended by Ouyang's poem, seeing it as a slight on his own military command. See Ding Chuanjing, *Songren yishi huibian*, 266.

16. Zhu, *Mei*, 792–93. Zhu dates the poem to 1055. See also two other poems by Mei Yaochen from 1040 in which he blames his own incompetence as a provincial official for "causing" floods in the region: Zhu, *Mei*, 159; Chaves, *Mei Yao-ch'en*, 18–19.

17. Literally, "cannot distinguish an ox from a horse," a phrase used by *Zhuangzi* (Chapter 17, Autumn Floods) to describe the huge breadth of the Yangtze River after autumn floods, so wide that one could not distinguish these two kinds of animals on the other bank. See Wang, *Zhuangzi jijie*, 90.

18. Kong Xuanfu was a respectful way to address Confucius originating during the Tang dynasty. The final couplet alludes to the *Analects* 5.7: "The Master said: 'The Way does not prevail. I shall take a raft and float out to sea.'" See Simon Leys, trans., *The Analects of Confucius* (New York: W. W. Norton, 1997), 20.

19. *Ouyang ji*, 53. I translate the full poem in chapter 1.

20. *Ouyang ji*, 35. My emphasis.

21. *Ouyang ji*, 13–14.

22. Ouyang composed a "Record of Luoyang Peonies" in 1034, in which he listed the varieties of peony and their cultivation methods, and discussed why Luoyang was such a suitable environment for these flowers. See *Ouyang ji*, 526–31. Needham translates and discusses substantial portions of the "Record" in *Science and Civilisation in China*, vol. 6, part 1, 394–408, 402–5.

23. All of the names capitalized here, and those that follow in the poem, were varieties of peony mentioned by Ouyang in his prose account. See his list of twenty-four varieties in *Ouyang ji*, 527.

24. "Perfect form" is an allusion to the chapter entitled "Making All Things Equal" in *Zhuangzi*, in which the author describes how famous beauties like Lady Li and Mao Qiang, so admired by human beings, would cause birds and fish to flee in fear at the sight of them. *Zhuangzi* used this observation to prove that our likes and dislikes are totally subjective, and that all values, whether aesthetic or moral, are relative. See Wang, *Zhuangzi jijie*, 1.25.

25. Su and He were the family names of two peony cultivators of the Tang Dynasty, hence their strains were considered old-fashioned by the Song. Qiang and Shi refer to Wang Qiang (better known as Wang Zhuojun) and Xi Shi, two legendary beauties of ancient China who were long since deceased and forgotten, like these out-of-date peonies.

26. In Luoyang.

27. See *Ouyang ji*, 526.

28. In *Ouyang ji*, 23.

29. Zhu, *Mei*, 927. From "Matching Hanlin Academician Yongshu's 'Rhapsody on Longing for a White Rabbit,' and Answering His 'Recalling Cranes,'" 1057.

30. The rabbit came from the Moon; and the region of Huating had been famous for its cranes ever since the poet Lu Ji (261–303) wrote about raising them at his home there.

31. Traditionally the Moon was believed to reside in a cave under the ocean during the daytime, only rising into the sky at night. A mythical rabbit supposedly lived on the Moon.

32. *Ouyang ji*, 44. "Playfully Answering Shengyu."

33. Zhu, *Mei*, 928.

34. Mei responds here to Ouyang's taunt that his hair was white and his complexion sallow.

35. *Ouyang ji*, 44. "Playfully Answering Shengyu."

36. *Ouyang ji*, 43–44. "Irregular Meter Poem on Longing for My White Rabbit, in Playful Response to Mei Gongyi's Composition 'Recalling My Crane.'"

37. *Ouyang ji*, 29–30. Interestingly, Mei Yaochen used several of these same rhyme words, along with some others, in a poem describing a bad hangover: an even more "ugly" topic! See Zhu, *Mei*, 333; Chaves, 139–40.

38. For a summary of the theory that certain directions, and the flora and fauna living there, are influenced by the dominant "element" in

that region, see Needham, *Science and Civilisation in China*, vol. 2, 261–62. Needham's Table 12 on these pages gives the following combinations: fire goes with summer, the south, and bitterness; wood goes with spring, the east, and sourness. Hence, the olive combines the sourness of wood (since it is a tree) and the bitterness of the southern region in which it grows to produce its unique flavor.

39. *He* 訶, an exclamation expressing censure: one of Ouyang's harsh rhymes. In other words, the olive is completely ignored, since people do not dare to taste a strange-looking object from so far away.

40. From the chapter "*Waichu shuozuo shang*." See Tang Jingzhao and Li Shi'an, eds., *Han Feizi jiaozhu* (Jiangsu renmin chubanshe, 1982), 370.

41. Cf. the clear parallels between olives, poetry collectors, and politics in an earlier poem on the same topic by Wang Yucheng (954–1001), in *Xiaoxu ji* (Taiwan: Shangwu, Guoxue jiben congshu ed., 1968), 62; partially translated in Chaves, *Mei Yao-ch'en*, 126.

42. *Ouyang ji*, 11–12, from poem "Travelling at Night in Shuigu, Sent to Zimei and Shengyu," dated 1044. There are some minor textual variants to this poem in the version quoted by Ouyang in his *Remarks on Poetry*. One has "bitter and tough" in the first line, which may fit better with the olive analogy. See *Ouyang ji*, 1037–38.

43. *Ouyang ji*, 235, 295, 531, 1037–38.

44. *Ouyang ji*, 49–50, poem dated 1058. I translate and discuss Ouyang's two poems on Jian'an tea in my "Mundane Transcendence," 112–16.

45. Zhu, *Mei*, 1008. Jian'an was in South East China, by the sea (around present Fujian province).

46. Lu Yu (733–c. 804), a famous Tang dynasty tea master, and author of the *Tea Classic* (*Chajing*), which contains detailed instructions on how to brew the drink. See a readable, but slightly unreliable, translation by Francis Ross Carpenter, *The Classic of Tea* (Boston and Toronto: Little, Brown, 1974).

47. The best Jian'an tea leaves, ground into powder, were whitish in color, hence were often compared to snow.

48. Toad Spring, in Xiazhou (present Henan Province), was a place where magical spring water emerged from a rock face. Within this water were tadpoles, which presumably grew into toads, hence the name. If one used the water in offering ceremonies, it would guarantee rain. Han Yu composed a poem about this place: see Qian Zhonglian, 807, especially

n. 1. It seems that Mei had trouble using Ouyang's rhyme word "toad" here, thus he had to resort to a rather far-fetched image.

49. *Ouyang ji*, 50. "Once Again Matching the Rhymes."

50. According to Chinese myth, a three-legged toad supposedly ate up the Moon during eclipses. Ouyang seems to be using the image to suggest the dry palate and bitter sensation in the mouth that result from drinking too much Chinese tea, the kind of feeling one might have after eating the Moon! Again, the rhyme word "toad" forces him to create this far-fetched, though certainly vivid, analogy.

51. Zhu, *Mei*, 1010. "Matching the Rhymes on a Second Visit."

52. Mei implies that Ouyang did get into such a disheveled state.

53. A phrase from a famous Tang poem on tea by Lu Tong, in which he compares the effects of tea drinking to a mystical Daoist vision. See "Written at Speed to Thank Censor Meng for Sending Fresh Tea," in *Quan Tang shi*, 12.4379. Full translation in John Blofeld, *The Chinese Art of Tea* (Boston: Shambhala, 1985), 11–13.

54. For more on this idea, see my "Competing with Creative Transformation," and Ouyang's poem on the moon-shaped ink stone screen in chapter 4.

CONCLUSION

1. *Ouyang ji*, 1037.

2. See the concluding section of chapter 4.

3. A recent Chinese study of poetry societies in the Song and Yuan gives detailed membership figures for fifty-seven societies that are described in surviving written records. Presumably many others thrived without their existence being recorded for posterity. See Ouyang Guang, *Song Yuan shishe yanjiu conggao* (Guangdong: Gaodeng jiaoyu chubanshe, 1996). See also Yoshikawa, 169–72, 182–85; and Yoshikawa Kojiro, *Five Hundred Years of Chinese Poetry*, trans., John Timothy Wixted (Princeton, NJ: Princeton University Press, 1989), 66–70, 76–83, 177–80. The subsequent spread of poetry composition groups to a broader range of classes is also vividly depicted in the classic Qing novel by Wu Jingzi (1701–1754) entitled *The Scholars*, whose plot is set in the Ming dynasty. In the novel, all kinds of people, from butchers to innkeepers, boatmen, and self-taught amateur scholars, compose classical verses and exchange them with each other and with their superiors, often in the hope of getting ahead in life.

4. Ironically, the subsequent enthusiasm for literary games and poetry composition societies during the Southern Song seems to have led to a revival of the shorter, regulated verse forms. See Yoshikawa, 41–42, 169–73, 182–84. One deciding factor, as Yoshikawa notes, may have been that poetic composition in the Southern Song was increasingly attracting less educated writers, who were happy to imitate rather than innovate. Fuelled by this interest, numerous poetic composition manuals appeared, and these drew most of their examples from the shorter regulated forms of famous Tang poets. Nonetheless, scholars like J. D. Schmidt have pointed out that the regulated verses of the best Southern Song poets did incorporate much of the wit, prosaic diction, and incongruous juxtaposition of Northern Song ancient-style poetry. Hence, one could argue that Northern Song ideals of reviving the ancient in poetry were not totally ignored by subsequent generations, but were selectively borrowed to revitalize the shorter verse forms. See Schmidt, *Stone Lake: The Poetry of Fan Chengda, 1126–1193* (Cambridge: Cambridge University Press, 1992), 23–60.

Glossary

Boliangti	柏梁體	*Boliang* form, in which each line rhymes with all others
Canglang shihua	滄浪詩話	Canglang's Remarks on Poetry
Chang'e	嫦娥	Chang'e, goddess of the moon
chui	垂	to droop; be passed down
Chuci	楚辭	Elegies of Chu, also known as Songs of the South
ci	詞	song lyric
ci yun	次韻	matching rhymes
dao	道	the Way
Daoxue	道學	Learning of the Way School
deng	登	to climb; be selected; pass the examinations
Dongpo jushi	東坡居士	Recluse of East Slope
feng	豐	abundant
fugu	復古	to revive/return to the ancient
gong	宮	*gong* mode, first of five traditional Chinese musical modes
gu	古	ancient
guwen	古文	ancient-style prose
Guangyun	廣韻	Universal Rhymer

haofang	豪放	untrammeled; heroic
jingsi	精思	refined in thought
jinshi	進士	presented scholar, national civil service degree
junzi	君子	Superior Person
kan kan	坎坎	onomatopoeic: sound of a drum
lian ju	聯句	linked verse
lingyao	靈藥	spiritual medicine
mei	美	beautiful; tasty; praiseworthy
pantao	蟠桃	peach of immortality
pipa	琵琶	Chinese long-necked lute
pingdan	平淡	even and bland
qi	氣	vital energy; configurational energy
Qianshi sizhi	錢氏私志	Private Records of Master Qian
qin	琴	Chinese zither
Qingli	慶歷	Qingli Reign Period (1041–1048)
qingshan baishou	青衫白首	dark robes and white hair
qingyun baishi	青雲白石	dark clouds and white rocks
Renri	人日	festival held on the seventh day of the first month
shang	商	*shang* mode, second of five Chinese musical modes
shi	詩	poem; poetry
shihua	詩話	remarks on poetry
Shilao	詩老	Poet Elder
Shishuo xinyu	世說新語	A New Account of Tales of the World
shi you	詩友	poetry partner
Song shi xuan zhu	宋詩選注	Selected Anthology of Song Poetry
sui	歲	years

ti zhong bu kang	體中不康	to feel unhealthy
tian ci	填詞	to compose lyrics
wen	文	writing; literature; culture
wuxing	五行	the five phases/elements
xi	兮	pause word between poetic phrases
Xikun chouchang ji	西昆酬唱集	Xikun Collection of Responding Poems
xiaoren	小人	petty person
yang	陽	*yang* force
yi yun	依韻	following the rhymes
yin	陰	*yin* force
Yuanhe	元和	Yuanhe Reign Period (806–821)
zhang	丈	length measurement, equivalent to approx. 3 meters
zhi	志	intent; will
zhi	之	that; it
zishi	自適	self-consolation
Zuiweng	醉翁	Drunken Old Man

Bibliography

WORKS IN CHINESE AND JAPANESE

Chen, Hongtian, and Gao Xiufang, eds. *Su Zhe ji*. Beijing: Zhonghua shuju, 1990.

Chen, Xin, and Du Weimo. *Ouyang Xiu xuanji*. Shanghai: Guji chubanshe, 1986. Reprinted, 1999.

Chongjiao Songben Guangyun. Taipei: Guangwen shuju, 1961.

Di, Huanning. *Qishi lun*. Beijing: Minzu chubanshe, 2002.

Ding, Chuanjing. *Songren yishi huibian*. Taiwan: Shangwu, 1935. Reprinted, 1966.

Fang, Xuanling. *Jinshu*. Beijing: Zhonghua shuju, 1962.

Feng, Yingliu, and Wang Wengao, eds. *Su Shi shi ji*. Taipei: Xuehai chubanshe, 1982.

Fu, Pingxiang, and Hu Wentao, eds. *Su Shunqin ji biannian jiaozhu*. Chengdu: Ba-Shu shushe, 1990.

Fu, Xuancong, Chen Xin, Ni Qixin, Sun Qinshan, Xu Yimin, eds. *Quan Songshi*. Beijing: Beijing daxue chubanshe, 1992.

Gan Bao. *Sou shen ji*. Shanghai: Hanfen lou: Shangwu, 1922.

Gao Buying, ed. *Tang Song shi juyao*. Beijing: Zhonghua shuju, 1959.

Guo, Shaoyu. "Zhongguo wenxue piping shang zhi 'shen' 'qi' shuo." *Xiaoshuo yuebao* 19 (1929): 129.

Guo, Shaoyu. *Zhongguo wenxue piping shi*. Shanghai: Xinwenyi chubanshe, 1957.

Han, Jingtai. "Lun Songshi xiequ." *Zhongguo shehui kexue* 5 (1993): 133–47.

Han-Wei Liuchao baisan mingjia ji. Taipei: Wenjin chubanshe, 1979.

Hong, William, ed. *Du shi yinde.* Reprint of Harvard-Yenching Institute Sinological Index Series: Supplement 14, 1966, Taipei.

Hou, Jian, and Lu Zhimin, eds. *Li Qingzhao shici pingzhu.* Taiyuan: Shanxi jiaoyu chubanshe, 1985, Reprinted, 1991.

Hu Zi. *Tiaoxi yuyin conghua.* Beijing: Renmin wenxue, 1981.

Liu, Tzu-chien [James T. C. Liu]. "Mei Yaochen 'Biyunxia' yu Qingli zhengzheng zhong de shifeng." *Dalu zazhi* 17 no. 11 (1958): 341–46.

Li, Shan, ed. *Zhaoming wenxuan.* Taipei: Wenhua tushu gongsi, 1995.

Lü Liuliang, and Wu Zhizhen. *Song shichao.* Guoxue jiben congshu. Shanghai: Shangwu, 1935.

Mei Yaochen. *Wanling ji.* Sibu beiyao edition. Zhonghua shuju, 1966.

Ouyang, Guang. *Song Yuan shishe yanjiu conggao.* Guangdong: Gaodeng jiaoyu chubanshe, 1996.

Ouyang, Xiu. *Ouyang Xiu quanji.* Taipei: Shijie shuju, 1991.

———. *Ouyang Yongshu ji.* Shanghai: Shangwu yinshuguan, 1936. Reprinted, 1958.

Pei, Puxian. *Ouyang Xiu 'Shi benyi' yanjiu.* Taipei: Dongda tushu youxian gongsi, 1981.

Peng Dingqiu, ed. *Quan Tangshi.* Beijing: Zhonghua shuju, 1960.

Qian, Zhonglian. *Han Changli shi xinian jishi.* Shanghai: Guji chubanshe, 1984.

Qian, Zhongshu. *Song shi xuan zhu.* Beijing: Renmin wenxue, 1958, Reprinted, 1989.

Shen, Songqin. *Bei-Song wenren yu dangzheng.* Beijing: Renmin chubanshe, 1998.

Tang, Guizhang, ed. *Quan Songci.* Beijing: Zhonghua shuju, 1965.

Tang, Jingzhao, and Li Shi'an, eds. *Han Feizi jiaozhu.* Nanjing: Jiangsu renmin chubanshe, 1982.

Wang, Jian. *Wang Jian shi ji.* Shanghai: Zhonghua shuju, 1959.

Wang, Li. *Hanyu shilu xue.* Shanghai: Jiaoyu chubanshe, 1958. Reprinted, 1979.

Wang, Shuizhao. *Wang Shuizhao zixuan ji*. Shanghai: Jiaoyu chubanshe, 2000.

Wang, Xianqian, ed. *Zhuangzi jijie*. Taipei: Sanmin shuju, 1974. Reprinted, 1985.

Wang, Yucheng. *Xiaoxu ji*. Taiwan: Shangwu, Guoxue jiben congshu ed'n, 1968.

Wang, Zhi. *Moji ji qita wu zhong*. Congshu jicheng edition, 1st ser. Beijing: Zhonghua shuju, 1991.

Wei, Qingzhi. *Shiren yuxie*. Shanghai: Guji chubanshe, 1959. Reprinted, 1978.

Xia, Jingguan. *Mei Yaochen shi*. Shangwu, 1940.

Xue, Meiqing, ed. *Song xingtong*. Beijing: Falü chubanshe, 1999.

Yan, Yu. *Canglang shihua*, in *Yushutang shihua ji qita san zhong*. Congshu jicheng edition, 1st ser. Beijing: Zhonghua shuju, 1985.

Yang Yi, ed. *Xikun chouchang ji*. Xikun Collection of Responding Poems. Shanghai: Shangwu, 1935.

Yoshikawa, Kôjirô. *Sô shi gaisetsu*. Chûgoku shijin sen, 2nd series, vol. 1. Tokyo: Iwanami, 1965.

Zhang, Hongsheng. *Song shi: rongtong yu kaituo*. Shanghai: Guji chubanshe, 2001.

Zhang, Jian. *Ouyang Xiu zhi shiwen ji wenxue pinglun*. Taiwan: Shangwu, 1973.

Zhong, Laiyin. *Su Shi yu daojia daojiao*. Taipei: Xuesheng shuju, 1990.

Zhou, Yukai. *Songdai shixue tonglun*. Chengdu: Ba-Shu shushe, 1997.

Zhu, Dongrun. *Mei Yaochen ji biannian jiaozhu*. Shanghai: Guji chubanshe, 1980.

Zhu, Jincheng, and Qu Tuiyuan, eds. *Li Bai shi ji jiaozhu*. Shanghai: Guji chubanshe, 1980.

Zhu Xi. *Zhuzi yulei*. Hong Kong: Zhengzhong shuju, 1962.

WORKS IN WESTERN LANGUAGES

Berthrong, John. *Transformations of the Confucian Way*. Boulder, CO: Westview Press, 1998.

Billeter, Jean Francois. *The Chinese Art of Writing*. Geneva: Editions d'Art Albert Skira, 1990.

Blofeld, John. *The Chinese Art of Tea*. Boston: Shambhala, 1985.

Bol, Peter. *"This Culture of Ours": Intellectual Transitions in T'ang and Sung China*. Stanford, CA: Stanford University Press, 1992.

Carpenter, Francis Ross. *The Classic of Tea*. Boston and Toronto: Little, Brown, 1974.

Chaffee, John W. *The Thorny Gates of Learning in Sung China: A Social History of Examinations*. Cambridge: Cambridge University Press, 1985. Reprinted, 1996.

Chang, Kang-i Sun. *Six Dynasties Poetry*. Princeton, NJ: Princeton University Press, 1986.

Chang, Kang-i Sun, and Haun Saussy, eds. *Women Writers of Traditional China: An Anthology of Poetry and Criticism*. Stanford, CA: Stanford University Press, 1999.

Chaves, Jonathan. *Mei Yao-ch'en and the Development of Early Sung Poetry*. New York: Columbia University Press, 1976.

Cheang, Alice W. "Poetry and Transformation: Su Shih's Mirage." *Harvard Journal of Asiatic Studies* 58 no. 1 (June 1998): 147–82.

Ch'en, Kenneth. *Buddhism in China: A Historical Survey*. Princeton, NJ: Princeton University Press, 1964.

de Bary, William Theodore, and John W. Chaffee, eds. *Neo-Confucian Education: The Formative Stage*. Berkeley: University of California Press, 1989.

Djang, Chu, and Jane C. Djang, trans. *A Compilation of Anecdotes of Sung Personalities*. Taipei: St. John's University Press, 1989.

Egan, Ronald. *The Literary Works of Ou-yang Hsiu*. Cambridge: Cambridge University Press, 1984.

———. "Ou-yang Hsiu and Su Shih on Calligraphy." *Harvard Journal of Asiatic Studies* 49 no. 2 (1989): 365–419.

———. *Word, Image, and Deed in the Life of Su Shi*. Cambridge, MA: Harvard University Press, 1994.

Fang, Achilles. *The Chronicle of the Three Kingdoms (220–265): Chapters 69–78 from the Tzu Chih T'ung Chien of Ssu-ma Kuang*. Cambridge, MA: Harvard University Press, 1952.

Fuller, Michael. *The Road to East Slope: The Development of Su Shi's Poetic Voice*. Stanford, NJ: Stanford University Press, 1990.

Fung, Yu-lan. *A History of Chinese Philosophy*. 2 vols. Translated by Derk Bodde. Princeton, NJ: Princeton University Press, 1953.

Grant, Beata. *Mount Lu Revisited: Buddhism in the Life and Poetry of Su Shi*. Honolulu: University of Hawai'i Press, 1995.

Gregory, Peter N., and Daniel A. Getz, eds. *Buddhism in the Sung*. Honolulu: University of Hawai'i Press, 1999.

Hartman, Charles. "Poetry and Politics in 1079: The Crow Terrace Poetry Case of Su Shih." *Chinese Literature: Essays, Articles, Reviews* 12 (1990): 15–44.

Hawes, Colin. "Fowl and Bestial? A Defense of Ouyang Xiu's Poems on White Creatures." *Journal of Sung-Yuan Studies* 28 (1998): 123–53.

———. "Mundane Transcendence: Dealing with the Everyday in the Poetry of Ouyang Xiu (1007–1072)." *Chinese Literature: Essays, Articles, Reviews* 21 (1999): 99–129.

———. "Competing with Creative Transformation: The Poetry of Ouyang Xiu (1007–1072)." PhD diss., University of British Columbia, 1996.

———. "Plucking Hairs to Save the World? Northern Song Poets on Their Writing Tools." Unpublished paper presented at annual meeting of Association for Asian Studies, San Diego, March 9–12, 2000.

Hay, John. *Kernels of Energy, Bones of Earth: The Rock in Chinese Art*. New York: China Institute in America, 1985.

Hervouet, Yves, ed. *A Sung Bibliography (Bibliographie des Sung)*. Hong Kong: Chinese University Press, 1978.

Hightower, James R., and Florence Chia-ying Yeh. *Studies in Chinese Poetry*. Cambridge, MA: Harvard University Press, 1998.

Kao, Karl S. Y. *Classical Chinese Tales of the Supernatural and the Fantastic*. Bloomington: Indiana University Press, 1985.

Leedy, J. J. ed. *Poetry Therapy*. Philadelphia and Toronto: J. B. Lippincott, 1969.

Leys, Simon, trans. *The Analects of Confucius*. New York: W. W. Norton, 1997.

Liu, James J. Y. *Major Lyricists of the Northern Sung: AD 960–1126*. Princeton, NJ: Princeton University Press, 1974.

———. *Chinese Theories of Literature*. Chicago: University of Chicago Press, 1975.

Liu, James T. C. *Ou-yang Hsiu: An Eleventh Century Neo-Confucianist*. Stanford, CA: Stanford University Press, 1967.

———. *Reform in Sung China: Wang An-shih and His New Policies*. Cambridge, MA: Harvard University Press, 1959.

Loewe, Michael. *A Biographical Dictionary of the Qin, Former Han and Xin Periods (221 BC–AD 24)*. Leiden: Brill, 2000.

Mair, Victor, ed. *The Columbia Anthology of Traditional Chinese Literature*. New York: Columbia University Press, 1994.

Mather, Richard, trans. *Shih-shuo hsin-yu: A New Account of Tales of the World*. Minneapolis: University of Minnesota Press, 1976.

Morrison, Morris R., ed. *Poetry as Therapy*. New York: Human Sciences Press, 1987.

Murck, Alfreda. *Poetry and Painting in Song China: The Subtle Art of Dissent*. Cambridge, MA: Harvard University Press, 2000.

———. "Misty River, Layered Peaks: Decoding Landscape Imagery." *East Asian Library Journal*, 8 no. 2 (Autumn 1998): 17–68.

Needham, Joseph. *Science and Civilisation in China*. Vol. 2: History of Scientific Thought. Cambridge: Cambridge University Press, 1956.

Needham, Joseph, Lu Gwei-Djen, and Huang Hsing-Tsung. *Science and Civilisation in China*. Vol. 6, part 1: Biology and Biological Technology. Cambridge: Cambridge University Press, 1986.

Owen, Stephen. *The Poetry of Meng Chiao and Han Yu*. New Haven, CT: Yale University Press, 1975.

———. *The Great Age of Chinese Poetry*. New Haven, CT: Yale University Press, 1981.

———. *Readings in Chinese Literary Thought*. Cambridge, MA: Harvard University Press, 1992.

———. *An Anthology of Chinese Literature: Beginnings to 1911*. New York: W. W. Norton, 1996.

Pollard, David. "*Ch'i* in Chinese Literary Theory." In *Chinese Approaches to Literature from Confucius to Liang Ch'i-ch'ao*, edited by Adele Rickett. Princeton, NJ: Princeton University Press, 1978, pp. 43–66.

Porkert, Manfred. *The Theoretical Foundations of Chinese Medicine*. Cambridge, MA and London: Massachusetts Institute of Technology Press, 1974. Reprinted, 1980.

Porkert, Manfred, and Christian Ullmann. *Chinese Medicine*. Translated by Mark Howson. New York: William Morrow, 1982.

Rickett, Adele, ed. *Chinese Approaches to Literature from Confucius to Liang Ch'i-ch'ao*. Princeton, NJ: Princeton University Press, 1978.

Sargent, Stuart H. "Huang Tingjian's 'Incense of Awareness': Poems of Exchange, Poems of Enlightenment." *Journal of the American Oriental Society* 121 no. 1 (January–March 2001): 60–71.

Schmidt, J. D. *Stone Lake: The Poetry of Fan Chengda, 1126–1193*. Cambridge: Cambridge University Press, 1992.

——. *Within the Human Realm: The Poetry of Huang Zunxian, 1848–1905*. Cambridge: Cambridge University Press, 1994.

Sivin, Nathan. *Medicine, Philosophy and Religion in Ancient China: Researches and Reflections*. Brookfield, VT: Variorum, 1995.

Spring, Madeleine K. *Animal Allegories in T'ang China*. New Haven, CT: American Oriental Society, 1993.

Stimson, Hugh. *The Jongyuan In Yunn: A Guide to Old Mandarin Pronunciation*. New Haven, CT: Yale University Press, 1966.

Van Zoeren, Steven. *Poetry and Personality: Reading, Exegesis, and Hermeneutics in Traditional China*. Stanford, CA: Stanford University Press, 1991.

Watson, Burton, trans. *The Complete Works of Chuang-Tzu*. New York: Columbia University Press, 1968.

Yao, Xinzhong. *An Introduction to Confucianism*. Cambridge: Cambridge University Press, 2000.

Yoshikawa, Kôjirô. *An Introduction to Sung Poetry*. Translated by Burton Watson. Cambridge, MA: Harvard University Press, 1967.

———. *Five Hundred Years of Chinese Poetry*. Translated by John Timothy Wixted. Princeton, NJ: Princeton University Press, 1989.

Yu, Pauline, ed. *Voices of the Song Lyric in China*. Berkeley: University of California Press, 1994.

Yuasa, Yasuo. *The Body, Self-Cultivation and Ki-Energy*. Translated by Shigenori Nagatomo and Monte S. Hull. Albany: State University of New York Press, 1993.

Index